HV Morton's
BRITAIN

H V MORTON'S
BRITAIN

By H. V. MORTON

Selected by GILBERT CARTER

A GINIGER BOOK
published in association with
DODD, MEAD AND COMPANY
New York

This book includes extracts from the following works of H. V. Morton, published in the British Commonwealth by Methuen & Co. Ltd., London, and in the United States by Dodd, Mead & Company, Inc., New York:

THE CALL OF ENGLAND (Copyright © 1928 by H. V. Morton)

IN SEARCH OF SCOTLAND (Copyright © 1930, 1957 by H. V. Morton)

IN SEARCH OF IRELAND (Copyright © 1931, 1958 by H. V. Morton)

IN SEARCH OF WALES (Copyright © 1932 by Dodd, Mead & Company, Inc., renewal © 1959 by H. V. Morton)

IN SCOTLAND AGAIN (Copyright © 1933 by Dodd, Mead & Company, Inc., renewal © 1961 by H. V. Morton)

. IN SEARCH OF ENGLAND (Copyright © 1935 by Dodd, Mead & Company, Inc., renewal © 1963 by H. V. Morton)

GHOSTS OF LONDON (Copyright © 1940 by Dodd, Mead & Company, Inc., renewal © 1968 by H. V. Morton)

H. V. MORTON'S LONDON (Copyright © 1941 by Dodd, Mead & Company, Inc.)

IN SEARCH OF LONDON (Copyright © 1951 by Dodd, Mead & Company, Inc.)

CONTENTS

PUBLISHERS' FOREWORD

An account of a journey by motor car entitled *In Search of England* was published in 1927. Two years later *In Search of Scotland* appeared, to be succeeded by *In Search of Ireland* in 1930 and *In Search of Wales* in 1932. These books have never been out of print in England or America since they were published, the first more than forty, and the last thirty-seven years ago.

The popularity of H. V. Morton's "Search" books, which has not been matched by that of any similar series, provokes some interesting reflections. Why should these books continue to be widely read? This is due, of course, largely to their readability, and also to the personal character of the writing and the enthusiasm conveyed by the writer to the reader. A more difficult question is why a third generation of readers should find in these books a faithful reflection of countries which have changed in so many ways since the "Search" books were written. The maps of Great Britain have been re-drawn, many of the persons described and quoted are no longer alive, the modern world of atomic power, of speedways and skyscrapers, of radio and television, of miracle drugs and detergents, of moon probes and heart transplants, is, outwardly at any rate, a different place, yet the "Search" books are still full of vitality and new editions continue to appear.

The publishers recently asked the author if he could explain this. He replied:

Perhaps I have been able to put into these books something of the delight of motoring along the often deserted roads and lanes of the 1920s, when the traveller rarely needed to book accommodation but could find a bed ready for him in any hotel or inn. In other words, one could wander about; there was no need to plan anything.

You ask me to define the "technique" of the "Search" books. I am the last person to ask. I did not know that they had a "technique". They were written impulsively, often on the spot or at the end of a day's journey. The time which separates me now from the young man who wrote them is so great that I am able to remember them, and him, with detachment, indeed, I might even say, with something like tenderness and compassion. Some writers have said that the continued existence of their early books has been a source of embarrassment to them in their maturity. This seems to me insincere and pompous. Naturally my pen would now hover doubtfully over many things in the "Search" books, but there is really little that I would change. They reflect a mood and a period, and that is all that I set out to do.

A contemporary of mine, who was a small girl when I was a small boy, recently reminded me of an idiosyncrasy which I had forgotten. "Surely," she said, "you remember how when out walking you would stop on a certain spot and refuse to move and when I asked why, you would say, 'I am wondering who stood here long ago before we were born.'" I was astonished to think that a desire to relate a landscape with its past was already developed in me when I was a child. The belief that one cannot understand a country, a town, or a human being for that matter, unless you know something of their origins and experiences is stronger with me than ever, and I am still always asking myself, "I wonder who stood here long ago." Perhaps my desire, first expressed in the "Search" books, to explain some of the historic events and processes which have shaped the countries of the British Isles may have kept these books alive, since the past does not date.

I must say, however, that it is surprising to receive, as I do so often, a letter from someone who tells me that he has used these long-out-of-date books as his guide, and how grateful he is to me for having pointed out the way. And this in spite of the fact that no airfield, no speedway, no television, are mentioned in these books, for all these were still in the future, while wireless is seen as a new and capricious toy which enabled a West Country farmer to hear a London dance band, if conditions were favourable. Only the other day I received a letter from a schoolgirl in Australia, asking "Dear Mr. Morton, what is a cat's whisker?" I suppose only the oldest radio fans can recall those needles of wire with which the first listeners probed the uneven surface of the crystal until they found that precise spot which induced in the headphones a far-off jumble of sound like dwarfs quarrelling in the depths of a tin mine.

In the 1920s the market places were crowded with old people who had been born in the middle years of the nineteenth century, and the young people of those days are now either middle-aged or old, but it seems that, in spite of all change, the essential characters of the countries which compose the British Isles are still as they always were, and are to be discovered by the searcher of today. This present book, titled and compiled by the publishers, is, I am told, to contain many beautiful pictures of Britain. In the uncertainties of this ill-tempered age I am sure that there cannot be too many beautiful pictures of those ancient and matured islands.

The publishers have pleasure in offering this selection from the "Search" and other H. V. Morton books in the belief that it will be welcomed by many who already know them, and that it will introduce others to the original books, which have been read with pleasure by three generations.

London

[1]

Some cities, such as Durham, which stands on a hill, or Salisbury, which, as I remember it, lies in a snug hollow, lend themselves to apostrophe and appear to have been designed by man and nature to encourage the gentle art of valediction. But London is too big. By the time you reach the fringe of her there is no London to be seen; you cannot waste sentiment on a suburban gasworks.

Of course, no living man has seen London. London has ceased to be visible since Stuart days. It was then possible for the last time in history to stand among the water meadows at Westminster and to see London riding on Ludgate Hill escorted by her church towers and spires. Plantagenet London must have been the best of all the Londons for the purpose of a farewell speech: a city behind its wall, something definite to see and to address. Today, even if you climb to the dome of St. Paul's, you see not London the city-state but London the labyrinth. The nearest approach to a real view of London is that from the tower of Southwark Cathedral or, better still, from a boat on the Thames at night when darkness lends an ancient enchantment to the roof-lines.

[2]

Standing on the steps of the Royal Exchange, I watched the press of omnibuses at the Bank and attempted, as I have so often done, to visualise the beginning of London.

In the days when I was a collector of coins, you could generally pick up at

London auctions a gold coin minted by the Emperor Claudius in A.D. 44 to celebrate the inclusion of Britain within the boundary of the Roman Empire. It bore the head of the Emperor and a triumphal arch with "De Britt" inscribed above it. I always loved this coin. It was like holding the very roots of our history.

Why the Romans decided to invade Britain is obvious. Until that small island, a stronghold of Druidism, had been subdued, the conquest of Gaul was incomplete. Rebels could always seek refuge in Britain and from the groves of Anglesey agitators could always find their way to the Continent. There were also commercial motives and personal ones, for we are told that Claudius desired to stage a military triumph in Rome and to appear before the populace in the unlikely guise of a conqueror.

He selected three Rhenish legions for the expeditionary force: the II Legion, Augusta, from Strasbourg; the XIV Legion, Gemina, from Mainz; the XX Legion, Valeria Victrix, from Cologne; and from the Danubian province of Pannonia he withdrew the IX Legion, Hispana. The whole force with its auxiliaries probably numbered about forty thousand men. When the troops learned that they were to fight in Britain they mutinied, refusing to serve beyond the confines of the known world. But their fears were soothed, and the invasion was planned to take place in the autumn of A.D. 43.

As the Crucifixion is generally placed between A.D. 29 and 33, the Claudian invasion of Britain and the foundation of London occurred some ten years after the events described in the Gospels. It is strange indeed, as you stand at the Bank watching the omnibuses, to think that it is not beyond the bounds of possibility that some of the Roman legionaries who helped to peg out the first boundaries of London might have served with the XII Legion in Jerusalem and may even have been stationed round the Cross.

London's roots go back to the age of St. Paul. He was just starting on his missionary journeys when London was founded, a little Roman frontier post and port on the confines of the Empire. St. Peter was alive. Pilate was probably alive. Although the great Augustan Age of Latin Literature was over, old men were still alive at that time who could remember Virgil and Horace, and men not so old who would remember Ovid, Livy and Strabo. The year of the invasion was the year of Seneca's exile.

The Emperor's parting instructions to his general were that he was to bring the Britons to bay, but not to fight a decisive battle. Instead word was to be sent back to Rome, whereupon Claudius himself would go posthaste to Britain to be present in person and thus qualify for a military triumph in Rome. And the operation worked out as planned. The legions fought two actions, one on the

Medway and the other on the Thames, near some obscure ford called Lyn-din, and then the messengers sped across Europe to summon the Emperor.

Claudius set off with perhaps the most fantastic pageant that ever placed a foot upon English soil. He took with him the Praetorian Guard and a phalanx of war elephants, as well as a brilliant staff of officers and senators. This entourage sailed to Marseilles and then crossed France partly by land and partly by the rivers, arriving in Boulogne three months later. Having landed in Britain, the Emperor moved up through Kent with his astonishing escort and joined his main army near Colchester, which was the capital of Caractacus. Everything was in the bag, as more recent military men might put it, and it only remained for the Emperor to give the order.

The legions went into battle and fought an action so decisive that all the tribes in southeast Britain were subdued, while others in Essex and Sussex paid homage in order to save their territories from fire and pillage. Claudius is said to have spent only sixteen days in Britain before he hurried back with the Praetorian Guard and the elephants to enjoy the triumph he had organized for himself.

How interesting it would be to know what Claudius did during his sixteen days in Britain! It is tempting to imagine him in the unaccustomed gilt breastplate of a Roman general, surveying the site of London, asking the polite questions that royal personages ask on such occasions, while staff officers perhaps unrolled plans and maps of London's first streets, explaining that the Forum was to be on that hill opposite and that the Harbour was going to be down there, where the men were cutting willow trees. It is fascinating to think of the war elephants fording the Thames with their Indian mahouts perched aloft in nests of feathers —the first elephants and castles to be seen in those parts!—and it is surely not unreasonable to suppose that, with so many distinguished staff officers present, the victory was celebrated by a banquet. It is certain that two interesting guests were bidden to the feast, two men who were fated to wear the purple: Vespasian, Commander of the II Legion, and his son, Titus.

What an occasion that must have been! It would be the first time Britain had been linked with the Holy Land, for it was Vespasian and Titus who, nearly thirty years afterwards, fought the Jewish War and fulfilled Christ's prophecy that "Jerusalem shall be trodden down by the Gentiles." It was Titus who conducted the siege and upon its conclusion levelled the walls of the Temple and left Jerusalem a ruin.

We who know their destiny like to picture those two emperors riding through the meadows and woodlands of Britain, listening no doubt to the sound of the first saws, hammers and chisels on the place that was to become London.

London, or Londinium, was a Roman city for nearly four hundred years, a space of time as great as that which separates us from the age of Queen Elizabeth. Generations of Romans and Romanised Britons were born beside the Thames, and family history accumulated.

And all the time the real work of London went on: the loading and the unloading of ships, as the galleys and merchantmen from Gaul and Italy came to the Pool, bringing with them stories from the great and dangerous world beyond the seas.

The unrecorded history of four centuries would be fascinating, could we but know it. Thousands of visitors must have come to Londinium, official reports must have been filed in the local archives, and in the Roman Foreign Office imperial secretaries must have put on record details of royal tours, yet not a single line has survived to preserve for us an eyewitness account of this first London, what it looked like, the layout of its public buildings and how it lived.

Londinium must have been rebuilt more than once. But probably the main features did not change. There is believed to have been a wooden bridge across the Thames, not far from the site of the present London Bridge; there was a massive wall all round the city, built at some unknown period; the harbour was the present Pool of London; and the Forum, the heart of Roman London, lies twenty feet or so beneath Leadenhall Market. There were public baths, arenas, amphitheatres; but where these were, no one knows.

London always has been a commercial city, and there were naturally many inns and hotels. I remember when I was at Herculaneum some years ago, they were digging an hotel out of the volcanic dust. It was a building on the main street, with a balcony. No doubt many of the Roman hotels in London were like that. Guests would have stood on the balconies and looked down upon streets that must at times have been crowded with strange men from the remote confines of the Empire, for the Roman Wall dividing Britain from the Picts and the Scots was manned by every nationality under the sun—except Romans and Britons.

It is believed that before London was converted to Christianity, the prevailing religion was the worship of Diana, the goddess of the chase, and it was once widely held that her temple stood on the site of St. Paul's Cathedral. In support of this, Camden's account has often been quoted of the curious stag ceremony that was held in St. Paul's in ancient times. A stag's head, mounted upon a spear and carried in procession round the church to the sound of horns, was received by the priests, who wore garlands of flowers.

All over London, fifteen to twenty feet below the modern streets, beautiful mosaic pavements have been found constructed above hot-air chambers fired by wood furnaces. The flues of these chambers sent an even current of air through the rooms, so that Londoners in Roman times enjoyed comfort in winter.

The most important monument left to us from four centuries of Roman rule is London Wall, and its significance cannot be exaggerated. It enclosed a square mile of territory. It was a massive construction, with gates, bastions and crenellated battlements, remains of which exist today both above and below ground. So massive are the foundations of London Wall—or the Town Wall of London, to give it its proper title—that special arrangements are made by contractors who need to excavate on the line of it.

The Roman Wall froze, so to speak, the size of London for centuries and also settled forever the frontiers of that square mile known as the City of London.

Although London Wall has been repaired and strengthened, its course has never been altered, and it remains as it was plotted by the Romans. Until the time of Elizabeth every traveller approaching London saw a city surrounded by a wall. The six gates of this wall—Aldgate, Bishopsgate, Moorgate, Cripplegate, Aldersgate and Ludgate—were closed at night. It was not until the reign of George III that, becoming an obstruction to traffic, they were pulled down and sold. Their names, however, exist today and are carried all over the Metropolitan area on the indication boards of omnibuses. Thus the City of London is a square mile of territory enclosed by the Romans nearly two thousand years ago. It is the germ-cell from which the tremendous growth known as the County of London, and an even wider circle, Greater London, have developed. Yet to this day the diminutive little City lives on, surrounded by its now invisible wall, the centre of a stupendous mass of bricks and mortar.

The "Square Mile" is a unique survival. There is nothing else in England so closely resembling a city-state of antiquity. It is ruled by its own chief magistrate, the Lord Mayor of London, the "King of the Square Mile", whose state is modelled on that of a medieval baron. The government of the City is carried out by the Common Council held at Guildhall. The City Police are a separate force, who wear a slightly different-shaped helmet from that worn by the Metropolitan Police, and their armlets are barred in red stripes instead of white. Technically, a Metropolitan policeman has no power of arrest beyond the City boundary and vice versa, but I suppose these matters are nowadays arranged by mutual agreement. Thus in these and many other ways the ancient City of London seeks to preserve its dignity and its independence.

Perhaps the most significant of its traditions, in which may be seen the shadow of London's power in past ages, is the custom, always observed, that the monarch on his or her way to the City, must halt at the boundary and, in theory, request the Lord Mayor's permission to enter his domain.

The unique status of London, well illustrated by this strange and interesting formality, was recognised by William the Conqueror and was confirmed by later kings, with the notable exception of Charles I, many of whose woes sprang from the fact that he never understood the temper of the City. So remarkable is the status of the City that writers such as Sir Laurence Gomme have developed the theory that its municipal privileges and traditions go back to Roman London, and that throughout the Dark Ages that followed the departure of the legions, when England became a prey to Danish and Saxon pirates, a Romanised community lived on within London Wall, carefully preserving its link with the mother city of the Empire. There are many opponents to this view, who believe that from 410, when the legions departed, until 886, when London emerged again as a Saxon town, the city was desolate and deserted, all its links with Rome severed.

But the undoubted fact remains that the shape and size of the City of London is Roman. Though it is no longer possible to see the City standing upon Ludgate Hill behind its town wall, the wall is nevertheless there, a powerful, invisible girdle, and if you would see the remains of it you must go down to the cellars of warehouses or to those few places, such as All Hallows by the Tower, and St. Giles, Cripplegate, where that great relic of the Roman Age may be seen in daylight.

London possesses at least four architectural compositions that are recognised all over the world; one of these is the group composed of the Bank, the Royal Exchange and the Mansion House. The three others, I would say, are Trafalgar Square, the National Gallery and St. Martin-in-the-Fields; Westminster Abbey and the Houses of Parliament; and Tower Bridge, with the Tower of London.

A remarkable transformation of course has taken place at the Bank since Roman and medieval times, and more recently an almost equally drastic transformation occurred when the three great buildings of this group were erected. In the course of this, a market and two churches were swept away.

I imagine that the Bank of England is probably the most imperial and costly of London's great commercial palaces. No expense was spared when Sir Herbert Baker, the architect of many fine buildings all over the world, skilfully and successfully added to the Bank without interfering with the classical windowless lower floor, which was a feature of Sir John Soane's eighteenth-century design. Sir Herbert had ample scope for his love of symbolism, and together with his sculptor exercised a mild touch of humour here and there, such as the electric light reflectors, depicting eagles in pursuit of lions, a reference to the battle then in progress between the dollar and the pound. Deep down in the excavations Sir Herbert Baker discovered two Roman pavements, which he relaid because, as he said, he liked the thought that they should come to life again and bear the tread of Londoners after their buried sleep of fifteen centuries.

There are naturally dozens of stories about the Bank of England, and some are even worth telling. One of the founders of the Bank in 1695, and its first Deputy Chairman, was Michael Godfrey, nephew of Sir Edmund Berry Godfrey, whose body, with money and jewellery intact, was discovered transfixed by his own sword on Primrose Hill one morning in 1678, a mystery that was never solved. Michael Godfrey was sent to Holland, where William III was at war, to open a branch bank to pay the British army. Arriving at Namur, which was besieged, Godfrey was asked to dinner by the King, and after dinner accompanied the monarch on a tour of the trenches. The King suggested that as Godfrey was not a soldier, he ought not to risk his life, to which Godfrey made the courtly reply, "Not being more exposed than your Majesty, should I be excusable if I showed more concern?" The King then said, "I am in my duty and have a more reasonable claim to preservation", which seems to have been instantly proved, because the conversation was terminated by a cannon-ball that killed Godfrey.

The third building of the group, the Mansion House, stands on the site of the old Stocks Market, so named for the stocks that used to stand at the top of Walbrook. At first specialising in meat and fish, the Stocks Market later became vegetarian and floral, at which period, it has been said, it bestowed its name upon the scented stock.

During his year of office the Lord Mayor lives at the Mansion House, which, like the Doge's Palace in Venice, is a house, a court of justice and a prison. In the days when I used to prowl about London at night, I often paused in front of the Mansion House and saw lights burning—the only indication of life in what by day is one of the busiest scenes in the world. The Mansion House is the last great residential house in the City, and although sheriffs and aldermen may sleep in Bromley or Leatherhead, or wherever they like, the Lord Mayor of London must during his year of office sleep in the bosom of his deserted kingdom.

Wandering the City streets at night, pausing to exchange a word with a policeman, a caretaker or a cat, I have often thought how eerie it is that a place that centuries ago was the most densely inhabited square mile in the country should now, after nightfall, be the most desolate.

[3]

Few ancient buildings are able to achieve a greater air of benevolence than the Tower of London upon a fine spring morning or a summer day. At such moments it is difficult to believe in the burden of misery this fortress has carried down the ages. But go there on a wet day or during a fog or, better still, after dark, and you will have a different impression.

As a living survival in a modern city, the Tower is a dinosaur among the institutions of London, something improbable and extinct from the remote past that somehow, in the atmosphere of England, has contrived to adapt itself to modern life. It is staffed by men who wear the dress of five centuries ago, and all kinds of memories, traditions and fictions still persist within its once formidable battlements. Although London has changed from age to age, the Tower remains fundamentally the same. It would be unremarkable were it a ruin; that it is very much alive, that it is still "His Majesty's Tower", that it is still, as it was centuries ago, the royal jewel safe, that it is still garrisoned by armed men and that twice in one generation it should have become a prison again and have visited death upon the King's enemies is more than improbable.*

Whenever I go there, I am struck by the incongruous character of the place. I have often passed through its horrible dungeons, dedicated to old cruelties and hatreds, to emerge in the sunlight before the married quarters where a soldier's wife was rocking an infant to sleep, while a cat licked its paws on a doorstep. How strange it is that normal domestic life should go on, children be born and reared, meals cooked and beds made in that grim spot whose weight of pain and suffering, it might be thought, would have put the Tower of London out of bounds to humanity forever.

But no, the Tower is a pleasant residential spot, and the continuity of its domestic life is one of the most interesting things about it. There has been not a night since Norman times—a matter of something like nine centuries—when men and women have failed to seek their rest within its walls or have ceased to regard the Tower as "home". It is the most ancient inhabited dwelling-place in London, and I doubt whether any other building in the world can boast a longer history of unbroken bed-making.

The rooms in the Tower resemble nothing so much in their rocky massiveness as caves or something hewn out of a mountain. When you glance through a window, you notice that it has been cut in a wall four feet thick. If the windows were blocked up, the room, although high in a tower, would become a dungeon. Electric light, gas stoves and bathrooms have been introduced into rooms that were constructed to defy archers, pikemen and siege engines. The only thing stronger than the Tower of London is the tradition of interior decoration inherited by the wives of some of the warders! You would not think it possible for anyone to take all the drama out of the Tower, to make it entirely everyday and to bring it into line with almost any suburb. But this has been triumphantly achieved, and in this achievement it seems to me the Tower of London has been vanquished for the first time.

*It is now "Her Majesty's Tower" and any enemies are the Queen's.

1 *Belgrave Square, London*

2 *The Bank of England and the Royal Exchange*

3 *The Tower of London and Tower Bridge*

4 *Tower Bridge*

5 *Yeomen of the Guard at the Tower of London*

6 *The tower of Southwark Cathedral, London*

7 *The Lord Mayor's Coach passes St Paul's Cathedral in the Lord Mayor's Show*

8 *St Mary le Strand Church, London*

9 *St Paul's Cathedral*

10 *The River Thames and Cleopatra's Needle*

11 *Westminster Abbey*

12 *The Nave, Westminster Abbey*

13 *The Houses of Parliament and Westminster Abbey*

14 *The River Thames from the Shell Centre*

Whether there was a Roman or a Saxon fort on the site is unknown. All we know for certain of the Tower's origin is that William the Conqueror gave a charter of independence to London with one hand, while with the other he built the Tower to show his "beloved subjects" that, in spite of their liberties, he was their master. He began to build the central keep, which we call the White Tower, eleven years after Hastings. It was only one, but the strongest, of the many royal castles constructed by the Conqueror at strategic points in England. It was the stronghold from which the King, who had confiscated all the land of England, enforced his power; and so it was for centuries the guardian of the feudal system.

While the architect Gundulf, a pious Norman monk, worked year after year at the massive walls, little Saxon London lay round him on the banks of the clear Thames. It was a town of thatched wooden houses lying within the old Roman Wall. Life was rough and uncouth. Swine rooted among the dunghills and the refuse. Wolves descended from the heights of Hampstead in winter. Roman Londinium had been forgotten, and no doubt many a fine marble column was built into a swineherd's hut. The temples of Diana, Mithras and Isis had been overthrown, and instead small wooden churches commemorated Saxon saints: Erkenwalk, Ethelburga, Osyth, Alphege, Swithin and Botolph. And upon Ludgate Hill stood the little wooden Church of St. Paul. We can just see for the first time the faint shadow of the London we know.

The Tower was the portent of a new age: It was the beginning of one of those transformation periods that London has seen throughout her history. The age of Norman stone was about to begin. Just as we today have witnessed the disappearance of Regency stucco and Victorian brick and the arrival of a new style of architecture derived from concrete, steel and glass, so the Saxons saw their humble little town of wood and thatch make way for the solid stone buildings of the Normans.

I passed through the wicket-gate and bought tickets at a little hut near a restaurant that stands on the site of the vanished Lyon Tower. For many centuries this was one of the great sights of London, for in this place, in a semicircular pit, the King kept his "lyons" and other strange beasts.

Henry III began the menagerie in 1235, with three leopards given to him in a fanciful and heraldic moment by the Holy Roman Emperor Frederick II, and in the same year he acquired a polar bear from Norway. This creature is mentioned in the State Archives as the recipient of an allowance of fourpence a day from the Privy Purse. The keeper of "our white bear" was also ordered to provide a long and strong cord to hold the animal when he was fishing in the Thames. What fun the boys of Plantagenet London must have had when "our white bear" was led out to fish.

In the reign of Edward III the menagerie was increased by the gift of an elephant, the first seen in England, it is said, since the war elephants of Claudius in Roman times. A royal order is preserved commanding the erection of a house forty by twenty feet to accommodate "our elephant". It then became the custom to keep lions in the Tower, one of which always bore the name of the reigning king, and was supposed to languish and die after the decease of the monarch whose name it bore. This zoo, added to from reign to reign, was naturally one of the most popular sights of the capital in days when foreign animals were rarely seen in England. The animals remained in the Tower until 1834, when they were moved to Regent's Park, and so the Royal Zoological Society began.

I walked on towards the Byward Tower, and came to a little gate beneath the archway, which is the door to the orderly room of the Beefeaters—and that is the first and last time I shall give this name to the Yeomen Warders. They dislike it and to some extent resent it. It is strange that London has never been able to distinguish the Tower Warders from the Yeomen of the Guard, to whom the name Beefeater might be applied if the derivation is, as some suppose, *buffetier*, for the Yeomen were on duty at the royal buffet, and they even made the royal bed and were generally in personal attendance upon the monarch.

The Tower Warders never left the Tower. They were the porters and guardians of the fortress from Norman times onward, and they regard themselves as the oldest corps of men in the world still engaged in their original duties. In comparison with the Tower Warders, the Pope's Swiss Guard is a creation of yesterday. The confusion between the Tower Warders and the Yeomen of the Guard—a corps created by Henry VII after the Battle of Bosworth—is due to the fact that the Yeomen Warders became incorporated with the Yeomen of the Guard and were given the same uniform. The only difference is that in full dress the Yeomen of the Guard wear a cross-belt, and the Yeomen Warders do not.

The duties of the junior and senior branch of this corps remain distinct. The Yeomen of the Guard, who all wear Vandyke beards, are in attendance only upon the King. They make the periodic search for Guy Fawkes in the vaults of Westminster. The Yeomen Warders leave the Tower only on special State occasions. They have the Crown Jewels in their keeping, and it is their duty to take the Crown and other emblems to Westminster on State occasions—in a taxi, I regret to say.

As I walked on through the Tower I came to Traitors' Gate, which is I think one of the gloomiest places in the fortress. Nothing can make it share the air of benevolence that occasionally shines over many other portions of the Tower.

This spiked water-gate positively drips with melancholy and despair, in spite of the fact that the whole thing is a shocking modern sham. When the Tower was tidied up in Victorian times, a senseless act of vandalism was perpetrated by the Board of Works, which not only removed the old steps, worn thin by the feet of those who had used them for centuries, replacing them by the present neat steps of Bath stone, but also took down the Traitors' Gate and sold it to a Whitechapel shopkeeper for fifteen shillings.

These gates had been pickled by centuries of tides, the Thames water had turned them green, and probably they would have been good for another few centuries. John H. Jesse, writing in 1847 in his *Literary and Historical Memorials of London*, wondered "whether they have been converted into firewood, or turned to some baser purpose". What happened to them was much more exciting than that. Barnum, of Barnum and Bailey's Circus, gave the Whitechapel shopkeeper £50 for them. He shipped them to New York, where they became one of the great sideshows in his circus. But what happened to them after that? Where are they now? Did they return to England, or are they still somewhere in the United States?

The water-gate is, of course, now high and dry, but in the old days the high tide lapped the steps. All the noble and distinguished prisoners of the Tower came there by water and were sent from the Tower by barge to stand their trials in Westminster Hall. On the way back the inhabitants of the Tower gathered at vantage points to learn the verdict, for it was possible to discover it long before the barge and its prisoner came within hail of land. If the verdict were "guilty", the Yeoman Gaoler stood in the barge with the edge of his axe held towards the prisoner; if "innocent", he held it away from him.

Upon the site of the present stairs stepped Anne Boleyn, Catherine Howard, Sir Thomas More, Thomas Cranmer, Edward Seymour, Duke of Somerset, Lady Jane Grey, Sir Thomas Wyatt, Robert Devereux, Earl of Essex, Sir Walter Raleigh and many more. The great Elizabeth, when princess and suspected of plotting against her half-sister Mary, was sent by barge to the Tower and was landed at Traitors' Gate. She sank to her knees on the stairs and protested before God that she had played no part in the Wyatt Conspiracy. It is interesting to reflect that the greatest queen in English history was so sure that she was fated to die in the Tower that she discussed, as her mother, Anne Boleyn, had done, the possibility of being slain by the sword in the French fashion rather than by the cruder axe of the English headsman.

In the White Tower I saw a magnificent collection of arms and armour, beautifully kept and perfectly displayed. It has occurred to many people that as a race we have grown taller during the last few centuries, for the average man today would find most of the armour too small for him. This does not apply, of course, to the armour of the gigantic Henry VIII. His splendid suit of tilting armour gives one a vivid idea of his massive and overpowering appearance.

Under the steps of the White Tower, on the south side, close to the Wakefield Tower, was the burial-place of the murdered princes, Edward V and his little brother, Richard, Duke of York. The only person who knew this was the Governor of the Tower at that time, Sir Robert Brackenbury, who was killed at the Battle of Bosworth, so that the secret was kept for two centuries until, during some alterations to the Tower in the reign of Charles II, the bones of the young Princes were discovered and were, by order of the King, taken up and buried in an urn in Westminster Abbey.

Modern men gazed on the bones of these two Princes when their remains were exhumed in 1933 in the presence of a small gathering of Abbey officials. The bones filled an oblong cavity within the urn. A fairly complete skull and a portion of another lay on top. Many bones were missing, but this was accounted for by the fact that the workmen in the time of Charles II at first threw them away, and they had to be recovered from a rubbish heap. An anatomist who examined the bones found that they were those of two children and was able to date within a few months their ages at death, which were those of the two little Princes; it was said that he also found some evidence that they had been smothered. This exhumation, by dating the age of the Princes, cleared Henry VII from the suspicion of their murder and placed the crime upon the crooked shoulders of the traditional murderer, Richard III. After the bones had been examined, they were wrapped in the finest lawn, and the skull and jawbones of Edward V were wrapped separately. The Dean of Westminster placed the bones back in the urn with a written statement describing the exhumation. He then read part of the Burial Service, and the urn was resealed and reburied.

Ascending and descending stone staircases, I came at length to the finest feature of the White Tower, the beautiful little Norman Chapel of St. John, which has mercifully come unscathed through the hazards of two wars. This stern but exquisite Norman church is the finest of its kind in the world. Although it is nearly nine hundred years old, it looks as though it had been built yesterday. Many an English queen and her ladies have heard Mass in the triforium of this chapel, unobserved by the guards and the courtiers below. It was before the altar that Robert Brackenbury, while at prayers, was tempted to murder the two Princes. It was in this chapel that Mary I was married by proxy to the King of Spain.

In early times the Knights of the Bath held their vigils there. Before they made their vows it was the custom for them to take a bath, symbolic of spiritual purification, and the wooden bathtubs were ranged round a room in the Tower.

When they had been installed in their tubs—there is an engraving showing each tub fitted with a brocade canopy like a little tent—the king, accompanied by his great officers of State, entered the room and walked round solemnly, touching each knight upon his bare back as he sat in the water. After this the knights were put to bed by their esquires. Then, habited as monks, they were conducted to the Chapel of St. John, where they prayed all night beside their armour. The oaths of virtue and excellence, and the ritual of arming, were of an elaborate character.

A delicate situation was created when Mary came to the throne and arose again in the reign of Elizabeth. It was hardly proper for a woman to enter the bathroom of the Order, therefore during these reigns, a deputy was appointed to perform the act of touching in place of the sovereign.

In the Bloody Tower I saw the spot where the Princes were murdered and also, overlooking the river, the turreted walk where Sir Walter Raleigh paced to and fro when he was a prisoner there. Not far away, housed inadequately in a room unable to accommodate the large crowds of visitors, I saw the Crown Jewels.★

In an octagonal steel-and-glass safe, countless diamonds, rubies and emeralds and every kind of precious stone shimmered and sparkled with the strange, fiery vitality that belongs to jewels. I think the most beautiful objects are the king's three crowns. The first is the Crown of St. Edward the Confessor, or the Crown of England. This is placed for a moment upon the head of the monarch during a coronation. The original was a Saxon crown, which vanished during the Commonwealth; the present crown is a copy made for Charles II. In shape it is more beautiful, but in value and historical association much inferior to the Imperial State Crown the monarch wears at the opening of Parliament and on other great occasions of State.

This glittering object is a mass of diamonds and pearls and other precious stones, among them some jewels of romantic interest. In the centre of the cross of diamonds on top of the crown is the large sapphire which was formerly set in the coronation ring of Edward the Confessor. The two pearls, which were once the ear-rings of Queen Elizabeth, are seen pendant where the arches of the crown meet. The enormous uncut ruby belonged to the Black Prince. The clusters of diamonds that run up the arches of the crown are formed to represent oak leaves, with pearls for acorns, an allusion to the oak tree at Boscobel in whose branches Charles II concealed himself when he was fleeing from Cromwell's troopers.

The third crown is the Imperial Crown of India, made for King George V in 1912 when he was crowned Emperor of India at Delhi; it is against the law for the Crown of England, or the Imperial State Crown, to leave the country.

★They have since been rehoused.—H.V.M.

It is extraordinary, considering the casual way the Crown Jewels were kept in former times, that nothing has ever been stolen, if we except the almost successful attempt of Colonel Thomas Blood to steal the Crown in the reign of Charles II. Nowadays such cunning mechanical and scientific devices guard the regalia that a thief would probably be guillotined, and most certainly electrocuted, if he smashed the plate glass that seems to be all that separates him from so much easy wealth.

[4]

I stood at the end of London Bridge shortly after eight o'clock on a silvery-grey morning. The tide was high, the tugs were passing up and down river; on one side the Tower stood as if cut in white steel in the morning mist, and Tower Bridge was a Gothic cobweb drawn across the Thames; on the other side, beyond the black roof of Cannon Street Station, rose the dome of St. Paul's.

There advanced towards me a great army of Londoners, some empty-handed, some with newspapers tucked under their arms, some carrying attaché cases, all marching briskly and purposefully; and all of them going the same way.

There is no better place to study the type of person who works in the City today. At other places London fills with its daily tide of life almost imperceptibly. People arrive from all directions by bus and Underground. They scatter towards their offices like rabbits bolting into a warren. You see them, not as a crowd, but as scurrying individuals. But here on London Bridge in the early morning, thousands cross from the south to the north bank of the river, and you can look at them and study them as if they were an army on the march.

Of all the approaches to London this is the most inspiring and the most romantic. Those who cross the bridge see on their right the old grey Tower, apparently so innocent in the early morning, on their left St. Paul's and, ahead of them, the Monument and the roof-line of the City, with its church towers and spires. Yet how few of those hurrying thousands pause to look at the river.

To me London Bridge in the morning is the very soul of London. It is beautiful, it is romantic and, like all beauty, it is profoundly disturbing. It is the place where countless young people must have dreamed dreams, where, maybe, ambition first touched a young man on the shoulder. I have often whiled away half an hour watching the boys who lean over London Bridge at various times of the day, when they are supposed to be delivering urgent messages. I have wondered what they think about. The majority perhaps think of nothing, but surely there must always be one lad who cannot gaze unmoved upon the Pool of London, who turns away from the ships and swooping gulls and returns to his duty with the resolve to be a Dick Whittington or a Walter Raleigh. Or have modern boys been taught that Dick Whittington was an exploiter and Raleigh a pirate? I suppose so.

In the old days this view from the bridge must have been even more tantalising. The ships were not all corralled far away downriver in the Docks. The Pool held a forest of masts as thick as a fir wood in Surrey, and you could see the merchant-men lying, their sails reefed, back from the Indies, Peru and China, from the Americas and the hot green islands of the Java seas, anchored quietly side by side in the shadow of London Bridge.

Becoming tired of watching the apparently endless flow of men and women to the City, I began to think of old London Bridge—the bridge that spanned the Thames like a street of houses, as if Cheapside were taking a walk into Surrey. They pulled this bridge down at the beginning of the last century and built the present bridge about sixty yards upstream to the west. They sold the stone, the iron and the wood that for so many centuries had resisted the ebb and flow of the Thames. A cutler in the Strand bought fifteen tons of iron that had shod the piers of the old bridge and declared that it made the best steel he had ever seen. No doubt thousands of knives were made around 1835 from the metal of old London Bridge. The stone went to build Ingress Abbey, near Greenhithe, which is, or was when I last saw it, a naval training college. From the ancient elm wood thousands of snuff-boxes and other objects were formed, so that, unknown to those who possess such relics, old London Bridge still lives, although surprisingly transformed.★

Behind the large modern Adelaide House in Lower Thames Street you will find the Church of St. Magnus the Martyr. Old London Bridge came out upon the City bank exactly opposite this church; indeed, the arcaded tower was actually part of the footway.

I have sometimes thought that could I have lived in Tudor or Stuart London, I would rather have had a house on London Bridge than anywhere else, but this may be pure romanticism. Thomas Pennant, who remembered the old bridge, wrote that "nothing but use could preserve the repose of the inmates, who soon grew deaf to the noise of falling waters, the clamours of watermen, or the frequent shrieks of drowning wretches". Still, I think the view westward must have been superb, with its uninterrupted sweep of river curving round towards the Temple

---

★This bridge, officially opened in 1831, probably the fourth span over the Thames at that site, has now been carefully dismantled and shipped to Arizona, where it will be a tourist attraction in a new resort development. A new bridge is being built to replace it.

and Westminster—for there was no other bridge across the Thames until 1749—and in the other direction, the Tower, seen through the rigging of ships, must have been equally lovely. In days when the river was the main highway of London, a house on old London Bridge must have been rather like one on the Grand Canal in Venice. Those who lived on the bridge occupied a watch-tower from which almost everything that happened on the Thames was clearly visible and much of it, no doubt, audible.

Imagine awakening upon a spring morning in Shakespeare's London, in a raftered room on old London Bridge. You would hear the roar of the water rushing through the arches, the clank and wheeze of the water-mills and machines that obstructed the river in so many of the openings and, high in the air above, you would hear a sound long absent from London, the whistle of hovering kites. And, opening the window, what a London you would have seen! The old black-and-white houses that were to be swept away in the Great Fire crowded to the water's edge, their gardens overlooked the river; above their roof tiles rose the towers of the churches and, highest of all, the steeple of old St. Paul's.

The shopkeepers who lived on old London Bridge must have been a community on their own. They were the only landsmen who lived and earned their living on the Thames as if they were anchored there in a great ship. Holbein is said to have lived on old London Bridge. Swift and Pope used to visit an old bookseller, named Crispin Tucker, who had a shop there. Hogarth lived on the bridge when he was engraving for John Bowles of Cornhill, and left a glimpse of it in one of the plates of *Marriage à la Mode*. Another painter who lived there was the marine artist, Peter Monomy. There was a haberdasher called Baldwin who was ordered country air by his doctor, but he returned to London at once because he could not sleep away from the roar and the creak of the water-wheels.

Of course the bridge, which was incredibly ancient even in the times of the Tudors, changed its character from age to age. The houses were sometimes burnt down and had to be rebuilt. The shops became fashionable, or else fashion, in its well-known way, deserted them. At one time, in the reign of Elizabeth, old London Bridge was a great place for booksellers and publishers. Among the bridge imprints to be found on title-pages are "The Three Bibles", "The Angel" and "The Looking Glass". I wonder how often Shakespeare might have been seen turning over the books on old London Bridge, flirting with a copy of Sir Thomas North's *Plutarch* or perhaps wondering how he might justify to himself the possession of an unnecessary volume of Raphael Holinshed, or Reginald Scot's new book, *Discouerie of Witchcraft*, which would come in useful if he went on with a play about Macbeth!

15 *Whitehall*

16 *Royal Horse Guards*

17 *Trafalgar
Square and
Nelson's
Column*

18 *Admiralty Arch*

19 *The Mall*

The only list we have of old London Bridge shopkeepers at one particular period was made in 1633, when a number of houses were destroyed by fire. Among those burned out were eight haberdashers, six hosiers, one shoemaker, five hatters, three silk mercers, one male milliner, two glovers, two mercers, one "distiller of strong waters", one girdler, one linen-draper, two woollen-drapers, one salter, two grocers, one scrivener, one pin-maker, one clerk and the Curate of St. Magnus the Martyr. Later on the pin-makers increased until, Pennant says, in his time "most of the houses were tenanted by pin or needle makers and economical ladies were wont to drive from the St. James's end of the town to make cheap purchases".

The bridge must have been extremely inconvenient. The footpath was not of the same width all the way. At one place it was only twelve feet wide, and at its widest only twenty. There were chains and posts to protect the foot-passengers. The overhanging houses made the bridge dark for most of its length, and frequent arches of timber from rooftop to rooftop kept the rickety old houses from toppling into the water. When coaches became common the traffic blocks must have been appalling. Samuel Pepys described a hold-up that lasted half an hour, when he was trying to get across from Southwark. Becoming tired of waiting, he slipped out of his coach and went into an inn, but when he came out his coach had been swept forward with the traffic, and he was obliged to walk. There was a hole in the roadway, in which his foot became wedged, and he might have broken his leg if someone had not come to his help.

The narrow arches of the bridge offered such obstruction to the flow of the river that the Thames above the bridge was a comparatively placid lake, and that is why there were so many frost fairs in the old days, and why the river no longer froze from bank to bank when old London Bridge disappeared. The obstruction also created rapids that could be highly dangerous to the unskilled oarsman. Many Londoners lost their lives, or were at least flung into the water, during the skilful act known as "shooting the Bridge", which was the act of shipping oars and guiding the boat through the rapids. This perilous act explains the old proverb, "London Bridge was made for wise men to go over and for fools to go under." It was usual for the prudent, on their way downstream, to leave their boats at the Three Cranes in Upper Thames Street and to join them again at Billingsgate, after they had shot the bridge. Pepys, going the other way, described how he got out of the boat and stood on the piers of the bridge while his boatmen hauled their craft up through the rapids.

A sight that impressed old London Bridge upon the minds of all who saw it was the heads of criminals and traitors—and so-called traitors—mounted on pikes upon the central tower. But in an age when skeletons hung in iron cages from gibbets upon lonely heaths all over the country, travellers would probably not lose much sleep when greeted, upon arrival in London, by such a spectacle.

[5]

I walked across London Bridge firmly resolved not to linger there. When I was almost at the Southwark end I saw a great crowd of boys and men leaning over the bridge, gazing downward towards the river in dead silence. Of course I had to edge my way in; and what do you think I saw? I saw a foreign ship leaving London. The captain was on the bridge, the ship was edging its way gingerly into the river, and one or two of the deck-hands, seeing the fringe of heads above on the bridge, cheerily waved to us. I am sure that not one of us did not wish he could sail away with that ship! And it occurred to me that this famous view from London Bridge is essentially anti-domestic. It is unsettling. It appeals to all the vagrant, wandering and no doubt disreputable and regrettable instincts of the male. It makes it more difficult to go home to Streatham. And as the ship moved and left us, we shook ourselves from its spell as best we could and went on our various ways with a vision of foreign towns, blue waters and coral reefs.

On the other side of the bridge a grey church on low ground lifts its tower against the warehouses and the cranes. This is one of the least-known, and one of the most interesting, churches in London. It is Southwark Cathedral. I wonder why so few ever visit it. It is one of the most accessible sights in London.

Southwark today suggests miles of dreary streets and thousands of warehouses, but ancient Southwark recalls Shakespeare, the theatre, bull-baiting, cock-fighting, taverns, murders in dark corners and the notorious Stews. It is natural that Southwark in the old days should have had a bad name, for how easy it was for anyone who had been expelled from London to remove himself from within the walls and just cross the river to the opposite bank.

The traveller coming to London from the south would have had a foretaste of the lawlessness of Southwark when he rode past a clump of trees about half a mile from the bridge. There thieves and cutpurses were executed. One ambassador in the time of Elizabeth mentions having seen twelve corpses swinging from the boughs, a gloomy introduction to London, which old London Bridge itself would do little to dispel, with its distinguished heads rotting in iron cages on the end of pikes.

Throughout the varied centuries the grey church, which is now Southwark Cathedral, has kept watch on the sometimes hectic history of the Borough. Its foundation takes one back to a remote Saxon London when, so it is said, a rich ferryman left his fortune to a maiden daughter called Mary. This pious girl is claimed as the foundress of the church. It was called in the old days St. Mary Overie, which is explained as St. Mary over the Ferry or St. Mary over the Rie (water). In Norman times another church rose upon the site, and parts of it are still preserved in the present building.

What a noble church it is! I entered it again for the first time in many years, and sought out the verger, who knows it stone by stone.

"If this cathedral stood within ten miles of a popular watering-place," he said, "it would be one of the most famous sights in England. Although millions of people pass it every week, they are always in a hurry, either rushing to work or else rushing home after work. It is a great pity that one of the finest churches in London should be known only to students of architecture or to Americans who have been to Harvard University. All Harvard men know it. They all come here because John Harvard, the founder of the University, was born in this parish and was baptised in this church. We sent a bit of the Norman shaft from the left of the altar to America in 1908, and they have preserved it in the porch of Appleton Chapel."

There is no church in the country with a greater interest for writers and dramatists than Southwark Cathedral. The verger took me with pride to the alabaster figure of Shakespeare. The poet lived in Southwark when he was writing his plays, and round him were gathered an immortal company of players and fellow actors, a group that included Christopher Marlowe, Philip Massinger, Francis Beaumont and John Fletcher, Ben Jonson, Philip Henslowe and Edward Alleyn, the founder of Dulwich College. Shakespeare himself must have stood in the church on 31 December 1607, surrounded maybe by this great gathering of Elizabethans, for in the church register for that date is the following entry:

Edmund Shakespeare, a player, buried in ye church with a forenoon knell of the great bell.

This was Shakespeare's youngest brother, who, no doubt encouraged by William's success in London, left his home to join the band of stage players in Southwark. I asked the verger if the site of his grave were known, but all that can be said is that his bones have never been disturbed and must lie somewhere in the church.

Unknown Edmund and his immortal brother lie at the last in much the same atmosphere. There is some resemblance between Southwark Cathedral and Holy Trinity Church, Stratford on Avon; both are beautiful, tall, medieval churches, and both are distinguished by that architectural peculiarity known as a "declination"—a slight difference in the direction of nave and choir—said by some authorities to be a symbolical representation of Christ's head drooping on the Cross.

One of the most charming monuments in the church is a coloured effigy of a man and his wife, John and Mistress Trehearne. He died in 1618, and she survived him for twenty-seven years. The old couple are an example of solid, middle-class Elizabethans, a type not often seen on monuments. They wrote no madrigals or plays and had no interest in navigating the earth, or such-like nonsense! They were interested in living a quiet, peaceful life and in bringing up the two sons and four daughters who are sculptured below in attitudes of prayer. All this is clearly written on the blunt, bearded face of the man and on the careful, stern face of the woman, rather prim and hard, with a tight mouth and hair drawn back under an Elizabethan lace cap.

One of the finest features of Southwark Cathedral is the retrochapel built during the thirteenth century. In Tudor times, when so many churches fell into disrepair, it was leased as a place of business to a baker. It was a workshop for about seventy years, and an attempt to demolish the lovely thing in 1832 was defeated by the Bishop of Winchester and a group of artists and architects.

There are also several beautiful little side chapels that prove Southwark Cathedral is no dead memorial to the past, but that its work and its influence are spread over the world. One chapel is dedicated to missionary work, another to the Good Samaritan and a third to St. Christopher and all the young people of Southwark.

"Let us by our prayers and work," says an inscription, "help to carry the boys and girls safely through the dangers and glories of growing up."

I left Southwark Cathedral thankful that the Great Fire, to say nothing of more recent flames, spared this noble church to gaze out across the Thames as it has gazed for so many centuries.

[6]

The Temple has been loved by generations of Londoners and by others from all countries in the world, because it brings into the heart of a great city the peace of some ancient university town and the dignity of a past age. It is a place of green lawns, of Queen Anne and Georgian houses, of paved courts, of subtle little architectural glimpses, court leading to mulberry-coloured court, a colonnade here, a fountain or a sundial there; and all these things taken together form a complete whole in which nothing is offensive or vulgar. The terrible punishment inflicted upon the Temple during the air raids shattered this unity, and many years passed before the Temple recovered its air of solemn and seasoned tranquillity.

For many centuries Londoners have slipped away from the turmoil of the City, taking with them to this ancient sanctuary the burden of their sorrows and their perplexities. While the Temple belongs officially to the Law, whose minions may be seen hurrying about carrying beneath their arms sheafs of papers tied with red tape, it belongs equally to all the men and women who have taken to it the personal problems of life. I am not thinking of those problems placed upon the desk of "my learned friend", but of the things of which lonely individuals think when they seek the solitude of the Temple in odd moments stolen from a lunch hour, as they sit listening to the shrilling of the sparrows and the sound of feet upon the worn pavements.

No place in London has a more romantic origin than the Temple. The name commemorates the Temple of Solomon in Jerusalem, and came to Thames-side with the crusading Order of the Knights Templars in the twelfth century. It is interesting to sit, as I have done so often in this place, and to try to project the mind back into the distant days when such seeds were sown.

When the Crusaders had captured Jerusalem and had created, so far from the feudal system, an exact copy of a European kingdom, some of them banded together to guard the roads so that pilgrims might in safety visit the Sepulchre of Christ. Those knights were vowed to poverty and chastity. As a symbol of purity they wore a white surcoat with a red cross on the shoulder. They swore to avoid feminine kisses, whether from widow, virgin, mother, sister, aunt or any other woman, and at night they had to keep a light burning, "lest the dark enemy, from whom God preserve us, should find some opportunity".

Those austere knights were accommodated on the large space in Jerusalem that had once held the Temple of Solomon and now holds the Mosque of el-Aksa. They therefore took the name of "the Poor Knights of Jesus Christ and of the Temple of Solomon"; and it was as the Knights Templars that Europe grew to know them. Houses of the Order were soon established in every Christian country. The first London settlement was in Holborn; then the knights, acquiring the strip of riverside land where the Temple still stands, moved there and made it their permanent headquarters in London. They built the Round Church on the model of the Church of the Holy Sepulchre, and it was ready for consecration in 1185, in the reign of Henry II.

This was the time when the Crusaders were being expelled from the Holy Land by Saladin. The completion of the Temple Church coincided with the arrival in England of Heraclius, the Patriarch of Jerusalem, who, hoping that Henry was still smarting for the murder of Thomas à Becket, actually offered the King absolution if he would fit out an army and go to the rescue of the Christians. Henry listened with tears and promised to bring the matter before Parliament at the earliest opportunity—and there the matter rested!

But the Templars took Heraclius to their riverside home and asked him to dedicate their new church. This he did and, perhaps to show there should be no ill-feeling among the soldiers of Christ, also dedicated the church of the rival Order, the Knights of St. John, at Clerkenwell.

As time went on the Knights Templars became so rich and powerful that they roused the envy of their monarchs. Their treasures were plundered, and at length the Order was suppressed. The Temple then came into the possession of the Knights of St. John, who leased it about 1338 to certain professors of the common law; and so the lawyers remained in possession as tenants until the reign of James I, who granted the property to them. Few memories of the crusading knights now remain in the Temple except the title, Master of the Temple, once held by the head of the Order. It might be imagined that he is the head of the two Inns of Court, a kind of "chief bencher", but in reality he is not a lawyer at all, but the clergyman who officiates at the Temple Church.

The Middle and Inner Temples seem always to have been separate societies. The device of the Inner Temple is a wingéd horse and of the Middle Temple a lamb bearing a flag. These law societies are two of the four that by royal grant have the exclusive right to maintain a course of legal instruction, to hold examinations, and to admit persons to practise as barristers. It is the duty of all law students to dine a requisite number of times in Hall, and no one can be called to the Bar unless he has done so.

I am not sure in my own mind whether it is true, as some writers claim, that the extra-territorial status of the Temple is a relic of the independence it enjoyed under the Knights Templars, or whether it is not merely a piece of shrewd legal dealing. But the fact remains that it has not only resisted inclusion under the Union of Parishes Act, but it also assesses its own rates. Although part of it is within the City boundary, it is the one place in the City that the Lord Mayor of London cannot enter in state, because the lawyers have never admitted his jurisdiction. If the Lord Mayor were invited to dine in the Temple, or to attend some ceremony there, and appeared, as he does on official occasions, accompanied by his Sword- and Mace-bearers, he would be refused admission. As recently as 1921 the Benchers declined to admit the City Coroner, who wished to hold an inquest there.

No doubt today such delicate matters would be handled with the utmost politeness, and it is highly improbable that a modern Lord Mayor would behave as Sir William Turner did in 1668, when he was invited to dinner and asked not to come in state. He replied that he would go with his sword and see who could dare to take it down.

When he arrived, a crowd of barristers and students wearing rapiers beneath their gowns met him and told him that unless he lowered the City's sword he would not be admitted to the Hall. As he defied them, there was a rush for the sword, the Sword-bearer was injured, the City Marshal's men were hustled out and the Lord Mayor had to take refuge in friendly chambers. Meanwhile the drums were beaten to call out the trainbands, and messengers were sent to Whitehall to tell Charles II that a first-class riot was about to begin.

His Majesty, wise as usual, advised the Lord Mayor to go home.

If anyone desires a pleasant and interesting walk in London I would like to recommend the walk I have taken so often from Westminster Bridge to Blackfriars along the Embankment, with excursions into the Embankment Gardens on the way. Here you will find a remarkable collection of celebrities commemorated by statues, busts, bronze plaques and medallions, people who have evidently been assembled in a kind of second-class pantheon; for these are the most modest and retiring of all London memorials. Nevertheless, it is a charming spot in which to be tucked away and forgotten; indeed, could a man choose the site of his bust or medallion, surely the Thames Embankment beneath the plane trees, or in the Embankment Gardens within a few yards of the great river, is the most perfect of all places.

The statues begin at Westminster Bridge with Boadicea in her chariot and end at Blackfriars with Queen Victoria. But in between are the oddest assortment of celebrities that could possibly have been brought together. In the first section of the Embankment Gardens at the foot of Villiers Street you will find William Tyndale, who translated the New Testament in 1525; Sir Bartle Frere, the Indian administrator, who later on had a trying time during the Zulu War as Governor at the Cape; and General Sir James Outram, whose gallant conduct during the Indian Mutiny earned him a baronetcy, the thanks of Parliament and the Freedom of the City of London.

Upon the wall of the Embankment, opposite Northumberland Avenue, is a bronze bust of Sir Joseph Bazalgette, the engineer whose great work was the wall on which he is commemorated. A little farther on, also upon the wall of the Embankment, opposite Charing Cross Underground Station, is a bronze medallion of W. S. Gilbert; and if you are looking for Sir Arthur Sullivan you will find him in the next stretch of the Gardens together with Robert Burns, Sir Wilfred Lawson, the temperance advocate, and Henry Fawcett, the remarkable

Liberal statesman who, although blinded when a young man, became Postmaster-General in 1880 and inaugurated the parcels post and carried out schemes that have ripened into post office savings.

Sir Walter Besant, the writer, is commemorated on the Embankment parapet, opposite the end of Savoy Street, and opposite Strand Lane is a memorial to Sir Isambard Brunel, a French refugee who, after becoming a distinguished engineer in New York, made his home in England and built the tunnel beneath the Thames from Wapping to Rotherhithe. In another section of the Gardens, near the Temple Underground Station, are to be found memorials to the Victorian statesman and Quaker, W. E. Forster, John Stuart Mill and the temperance reformer, Lady Henry Somerset, the only woman represented in the whole galaxy of good will, bravery, literary and mechanical talent and political probity. The parade of near greatness is concluded, on the parapet of the Embankment opposite the end of the Gardens, with a memorial to W. T. Stead, the journalist and spiritualist, who lost his life when the *Titanic* went down.

Of course the great sight of the Thames Embankment is Cleopatra's Needle, an absurd name, since the obelisk was in existence fourteen hundred years before Cleopatra was born. It is the only one of the many obelisks removed from Egypt that has not been erected in a great park or square. Rome's finest obelisk stands in front of St. Peter's, the Paris obelisk is in the Place de la Concorde and the New York obelisk in Central Park. What a debt of thanks we owe to those in 1878 who resisted the temptation to erect Cleopatra's Needle in Hyde Park or Kensington Gardens. It is the most ancient monument in London, and it is almost certain that Moses must have seen it, together with its companion now in America, when it stood in front of the Temple of the Sun at Heliopolis.

Both these obelisks were dedicated to the sun god by the Pharaoh Thothmes III about 1500 B.C. They stood in Heliopolis until Roman times when they were removed to Alexandria in 12 B.C. The London obelisk fell down, apparently in the fourteenth century, and became partly buried in the sand. The New York obelisk stood upright as re-erected by Roman engineers, and in this position they remained until they were removed in 1877, one to London, the other across the Atlantic. Both Londoners and New Yorkers call their obelisks Cleopatra's Needle, but few probably know that in doing so they are perpetuating the nickname given to these obelisks, probably in the Middle Ages, by the native Egyptians. "Pharaoh's great needles"—*misallatî Fir'ûn*—was the common name given to obelisks by the fellahin as noted by Arab writers in the twelfth century. But the pair of obelisks at Alexandria were, for some unknown reason, called Cleopatra's Needles.

In order to transport the obelisk to London a special ship was built to carry it. It was a steel shell fitted with a deck and a mast and it was naturally called the

20 *Trooping the Colour: H.M. The Queen on
Horse Guards' Parade*

21 *The Guard changes at Buckingham Palace*

22 *Buckingham Palace*

23 *Hyde Park*

24 *Quebec House, Westerham*

25 *The Wolfe Statue, Westerham, Kent*

26 *All Saints' Church, Maidstone, Kent*

27 *Oast-houses near Maidstone*

Cleopatra. Her steering gear was not good, and she was towed out of Alexandria by a steamship, the *Olga.* In a storm near Cape St. Vincent the *Olga* found the *Cleopatra* too much for her and cut her adrift. Six seamen lost their lives during this operation. Imagining that the *Cleopatra* had gone to the bottom of the sea, the *Olga* continued her voyage. But the *Cleopatra* remained afloat and was later salvaged by a ship called the *Fitzmaurice,* which took her in tow, and put in a claim for £5,000, which the Admiralty Courts reduced to £2,000.

So Cleopatra's Needle arrived safely in the Thames and was towed up to the place near the Embankment where it stands today. The steel shell was cut away, and the obelisk was lifted at low tide by hydraulic jacks. Before the monument was erected someone had the romantic idea that ordinary commonplace objects ought to be buried beneath it, apparently with the idea that if Macaulay's New Zealander ever visited the ruins of London he might like to see the sort of things people used in 1878. Accordingly, sealed jars were buried under the plinth containing a man's suit, a woman's dress and accessories, illustrated newspapers, children's toys, a razor, cigars, photographs of reigning beauties and a complete set of the coinage.

[7]

The Houses of Parliament stand on part of the land once occupied as a royal palace as early as the time of Canute. William the Conqueror added to this palace, Rufus built the magnificent Westminster Hall, which still stands, and for centuries those buildings were the dwelling of English kings.

Parliament naturally gathered near the palace, meeting first in the Chapter House of the Abbey Church, but in 1547 it was moved to St. Stephen's Chapel, within the precincts of the palace. It was enacted by Parliament in the time of Henry VIII that all these premises should be called the King's Palace at Westminster and be so called forever.

When, however, the Palace of Westminster was damaged by fire, Henry VIII —that great estate agent—profiting by Cardinal Wolsey's downfall, seized York Place and rebuilt it as the Palace of Whitehall, which then became the chief seat of the English Court and so remained through Tudor and Stuart times, until a fire destroyed it. St. James's Palace was then brought into prominence as the Court of the Hanoverians.

Through all these changes, Parliament continued to meet in its old place among the relics of the ancient Palace of Westminster. This was burnt down in 1834, and nothing remains of it now except Westminster Hall and the crypt of the Chapel of St. Stephen, called St. Mary Undercroft.

The present Houses of Parliament, built from 1840 to 1867, cover the site of the old royal residences, and the present narrow entrance to the central hall, called St. Stephen's Hall, exactly corresponds to the ground plan of the vanished St. Stephen's Chapel, in which the Commons met for two hundred and eighty-seven years. Brass studs in the floor mark the site of the Speaker's Chair and the site of the table.

A ghost of those old times survives in the name, "St. Stephen's", often used as an equivalent for the House of Commons; in the privilege Members possess of marrying or christening their children in the crypt beneath the hall; and in the habit of Members who bow to the Chair whenever they pass the Speaker, a custom that began, not as a courtesy to the Speaker, but in Catholic days as a genuflection to the altar of the Chapel.

An ancient enactment of Henry VIII's time is still in force and the Houses of Parliament are still technically a royal palace. I have been told, and I can well believe it, that certain pundits in government departments make a point of addressing their letters, when the House is not in session, to "H.M. Palace of Westminster".

The Speaker's position is one that is hedged about with many spectres of tradition. It has been excellently said that while the Premier can do no right, the Speaker can do no wrong. He shares with judges an assumption of infallibility.

It is perhaps, curious that a man who makes no speeches should be called the Speaker. His title, however, refers to his historic position as the spokesman for the Commons: the intermediary between the Commons and the Crown. While the Speaker is an absolute autocrat in the House, he is also its servant. His voice and his eyes are those of the Commons, and this function was memorably defined by Speaker William Lenthall when, in the course of a dramatic and fateful moment in English history, Charles I forced his way into the House of Commons and, striding to the Speaker's Chair, demanded the arrest of five Members. In silence Charles asked where the five men were sitting. Lenthall replied that he did not know because, as his eyes were controlled by the House, he had "neither eyes to see nor tongue to speak but as the House is pleased to direct".

Since 1688 the Speaker has been termed the First Commoner of the Realm, and the House is not properly constituted unless he is present with the mace on the table in front of him. He is, with the exception of the monarch, the only person who can hold a levee, and a symbol of his grandeur was admired by London crowds during the coronation procession of King George VI, when a pair of competent-looking dray horses came along, drawing a heavy old coach evidently constructed before the invention of carriage springs. The Speaker's Coach was built in Holland about 1689 for William of Orange, and I am told on the best authority that its weight is about two tons and fifteen hundredweight, a load much too heavy for ordinary carriage horses. Thus it is that, on those rare occasions when the Speaker goes abroad in state, it is necessary to call in the services of two massive animals who normally spend their lives pulling casks of beer round London.

One of the most powerful symbols in the country is the mace, which is carried before the Speaker by the Sergeant-at-Arms. When it is under the table the House is in Committee; when it is upon the table the House is sitting.

In stormy times in the past, attempts have been made to bring a sitting to a standstill by the forcible removal of the mace, and on one occasion, when the mace was not available, the House had to wait for its arrival before business could be transacted.

Some of the customs of Parliament are persistent ghosts of the old struggle between the Commons and the Crown. Although the Prince of Wales may sit in the House of Commons and listen to debates, that place is the one spot in the royal dominions he may not enter when he becomes king. In her long reign of over sixty-two years, Queen Victoria never once entered the House of Commons.

A relic of the old struggle is the custom, always jealously observed, of shutting the doors of the Commons in the face of a messenger from the sovereign. This always occurs at the opening of Parliament. The Gentleman Usher of the Black Rod is commanded by the monarch to summon the Commons. He makes his way from the House of Lords to the House of Commons, where cries of "Way for Black Rod!" clear a passage for him, for it is an ancient regulation that the journey must not be impeded.

As soon as he approaches, the doors of the Commons are shut and bolted in his face. Black Rod then knocks three times. When the sound of his knocking is heard, a delightful little Parliamentary fiction is observed by the Sergeant-at-Arms and the Speaker.

The Sergeant-at-Arms looks up in surprise. "Who can that possibly be?" he seems to say. He looks for guidance to the Speaker. The Speaker gives a solemn nod of his head, and the Sergeant-at-Arms rises and unbolts the door. Every time this amusing pantomime is acted, one can picture the ghosts of those commoners who fought for the privileges of Parliament chuckling in the shades with approval and delight.

There are other ghosts in Parliament. A Member speaking from the front benches must take care not to advance his foot beyond a certain red line on the carpet. This line represents the limit supposed to keep him beyond sword reach of the benches opposite.

A terrible sin against the tradition of a free Parliament would be committed by a Member who locked a door in the House of Commons. One shudders to imagine such an act! In this custom one can perceive the cloaked and hooded ghosts of plotters like Guy Fawkes.

There is also a certain portion of the House considered to be outside the House, and a Member must be careful not to address the Commons from outside. This barrier is the Bar of the House, to which Sheriffs come with their petitions and to which offending Members of Parliament are brought to receive the reprimand of the assembly.

Another ghost is the cry "Who goes home?" It echoes through the corridors when the House rises. This cry is a ghost of a London full of footpads and thieves and of a time when Members of Parliament banded together to walk through the dark streets for the sake of safety.

These are only a few of the ghosts that haunt an assembly as ancient as the House of Commons.

[8]

One of the remarkable escapes during the air raids of the Second World War was that of the College of Heralds in Queen Victoria Street, a fine Wren building of red brick that magically stands, although everything to the right of it was shorn away as if by a mighty scythe. It is the finest building in the street, and its function as well as its staff the most unusual. Other buildings in Queen Victoria Street may concern themselves with newspapers, bathtubs, typewriters and the salvation of souls, but the College lives in a world where trumpets are still sounding and where emblazoned knights are riding to castle gates.

The staff consists of three kings of arms, Garter, Clarencieux and Norroy; six heralds, Lancaster, Somerset, Richmond, Windsor, York and Chester; and four pursuivants, Rouge Dragon, Bluemantle, Portcullis and Rouge Croix. These appointments are in the gift of the Duke of Norfolk as hereditary Earl Marshal of England.

Whenever the need to consult some document not elsewhere available has drawn me to that red-brick building, I have mounted its steps in a strong *Alice in Wonderland* atmosphere. There is nothing quite so improbable in the whole of London. If one met the King of Hearts, the Queen and the Knave coming out, one would merely raise one's hat and think it all perfectly normal and in order.

"Good morning, sir," said the doorkeeper. "Have you an appointment with anyone?"

Struggling with a powerful feeling of unreality, I asked:

"Is Rouge Dragon in?"

"No, sir, Rouge Dragon is out. Will anyone else do?"

Rouge Dragon is out! How terrible that sounds! Somewhere in London Rouge Dragon, probably rampant, is at large, unknown to the population.

"Is Bluemantle in?" I asked.

"Yes, sir, but he is engaged."

"Well, could I see Portcullis?"

Instead of blowing a silver trumpet, or mounting a horse and galloping upstairs, the attendant picked a telephone from a hook, while I thought that it would not be surprising if Mr. Debrett arrived with a unicorn, or perhaps the editor of *Landed Gentry* might appear, carrying a fine bar sinister he had found in a box room.

"Bluemantle is now disengaged, sir. He will see you," said the attendant, and, glancing round the panelled hall with its banners and its carved throne, in which the Earl Marshal used to sit in judgement upon those who bore false arms, I mounted the stairs into the most fantastic office in London. There have been no serious staff changes since 1480.

One can imagine Don Quixote tiptoeing round the corridors, reading with joy the titles of those inhabiting the various rooms: "Garter King of Arms", I read beneath a blaze of heraldry, "Norroy King of Arms" and "Rouge Dragon", his door slightly ajar in the most sinister manner. What an odd experience it is to knock at one of those doors and to hear a muffled voice say "Come in." Anything might meet one in such a room! Perhaps its occupant will be discovered in a suit of armour, a leopard couchant in front of the fire. But when you go inside you see a man who has the appearance of a barrister sitting at a desk and wearing a black coat and a pair of striped trousers. Can this really be "Portcullis" or "Bluemantle"? Have the trumpets of Agincourt died down to this?

Heralds are always delighted to advise members of the public who wish to place a coat of arms upon their notepaper, their motor cars, their soup-tureens or their perambulators. To such a thin whistle have the drums and trumpets of chivalry dropped! This, of course, costs money. Heralds are still paid on the Tudor scale of something like £16 a year. Therefore, as even a red dragon has to live, they sit like barristers in chambers, waiting to be briefed. And they are almost as expensive. It costs the best part of £100 to take out armorial bearings, and another £50 for a badge that female members of the family may embroider on cushions.

The hunting up of pedigrees is, of course, a great part of the work undertaken by the College, and this is also expensive. The searchers who ransack village registers were, before the war, paid a guinea a day. The most difficult people to trace are the Browns, the Joneses and the Smiths.

"There is a ridiculous belief that a pedigree is often faked for a rich man," a Herald told me. "This is absolute nonsense. A pedigree passed by the College of Heralds is a legal document, and it is passed by a council of experts before it is granted."

Many a searcher has gone to the College, his soul filled with grandeur, only to depart with the depressing knowledge that great-great-grandmother was not properly married.

The library of the College is unique. It began long ago when the heralds rode through every shire at the command of the king to make a complete list of all those who were entitled to bear arms. It contains the roots of every old family in England and Wales. There are two tragic relics in the library: the ring and the sword taken from the dead body of James IV of Scotland after the Battle of Flodden.

The room in which the heralds interview those who desire to "bear arms" is a solemn room built after the Great Fire of London.

"We were burnt out, you know," explains a Herald.

That is how they talk in this building. Time is nothing. If a Herald talks about the Battle of Agincourt, he gives you the impression that he was there. It is a confusing habit.

[9]

Inset in the marble pavement of the nave of St. Peter's in Rome are a number of marks that few visitors ever notice, giving the length of the largest churches in the world in relation to that of St. Peter's. The next longest is St. Paul's Cathedral, followed by the cathedrals of Florence, Rheims and Cologne.

St. Paul's is different from most of the great cathedrals in the world as the work of one man, Sir Christopher Wren, who would appear to have been placed by Providence in the London of Charles II in order to repair the ravages of the Great Fire. That an architect of such extraordinary inventiveness and—even if only half the edifices attributed to him are really his—fertility, should have been waiting and ready to rebuild London is one of the most fortunate accidents in history. No matter from what direction you look at the City, whether from Hungerford Bridge, the Surrey end of Waterloo Bridge, London Bridge or the

Monument—to give only four first-class views—the character of the scene before you was stamped upon it by Christopher Wren.

His grandfather was a London mercer, and Wren was born at East Knoyle, near Tisbury, in Wiltshire, and, like so many great men, was the son of a rector.

He was a genius whose unusual talents were seen when he was a small boy. Under the famous Dr. Busby at Westminster, he became a distinguished Latin scholar, and he gathered round himself, later on at Wadham College, Oxford, some of the keenest intellects of his time. It has been said that had he devoted his life to mathematics and astronomy—and until the age of thirty it seemed probable that he would do so—he might have rivalled Isaac Newton.

Wren was only thirty-four when the Great Fire of London took place, but for several years he had been Surveyor-General to His Majesty's Works, so that the awful scene of devastation had a professional interest for him. The fire had been dead only four days when he appeared with a complete plan for the rebuilding of the City. It has always been considered the best of the plans prepared at the time, and some have said that had it been adopted, London would be a much finer-looking city today. But all kinds of private interests conflicted with the plan, which was shelved.

So Christopher Wren had to be content with the rebuilding of St. Paul's Cathedral, more than fifty London churches, thirty-six company halls, the Custom House, Temple Bar, numerous private and official buildings and the Monument. Such enormous buildings as Greenwich Hospital he apparently built in his spare time. Surely there has never been a more prolific architect nor one who exemplified in his career the old maxim that genius boils down to hard work. He was the least avaricious and self-seeking of men. For the rebuilding of St. Paul's and the parish churches of London the only salary he asked was a paltry £200 a year. He accepted his task in a spirit of piety, not counting the reward in personal gain.

The architect was forty-three years of age when the first stone of the new Cathedral was laid; he was sixty-five when the choir was opened for use; he was an old man of seventy-seven when the last stone was set upon the Cathedral. All his life, from the forties onward into old age, he watched his mighty creation growing higher against the London sky, and they point out upon the Surrey bank of the Thames a narrow house tucked away between warehouses in which it is said he lived and watched.

His inspiration in the designing of St. Paul's was obviously St. Peter's in Rome. He designed surroundings very much after the style of Bernini's magnificent colonnade, but the land was too valuable, and this was never carried out. Wren thought so highly of Bernini that he went to Paris the year before the Great Fire to discuss architecture with him. But every man, no matter how much a genius, and no matter how far in advance of his times, is in reality a child of his own age.

The great genius died quietly of old age. One day his servant entered his room to find him dead in his chair, aged ninety-one. What an astonishing sweep of history was commanded by his long life. When he was born men lived who had spoken to Shakespeare and Queen Elizabeth; when he died infants were living who were fated to see the beginning of the century that saw the invention of steam locomotion. Only thirteen years elapsed between his death and the birth of James Watt, and could Wren have lived so long this old man and the young one just born would have been links, one with the age of Elizabeth, the other with that of Victoria.

As I climbed up to the Whispering Gallery I thought that the fatigue of this ascent is generally much exaggerated. Although there are three hundred and seventy-five steps to the Stone Gallery, and another two hundred and fifty-two to the Ball below the Cross—a region to which few visitors penetrate—the climb is easy because the spiral tunnel is wide and the steps are low.

Arrived in the Whispering Gallery, I was asked by the verger on duty in his patient, automatic voice—for how many times a day must he say it?—to walk round the narrow railed enclosure to a point opposite and then to sit down and listen. In time I heard his voice coming to me a yard or so away—out of the stone, it seemed—telling me practical details of the building of the church, with dates and figures. It is an extraordinary sound freak, and would have been invaluable to the Oracle at Delphi.

The downward view from this gallery into the distant church, where men and women, reduced to the size of ants, moved in a slow noiselessness, is as fine as the view upwards to the Pauline frescoes of James Thornhill. The cleaning of the frescoes some years ago made it possible to see them properly for the first time in our generation. The view of London from the gallery—the gallery at the base of the dome—although magnificent, is not as fine as that from the Golden Gallery, another hundred and seventy-five steps upward. And the climb is worth it. On the way I examined the remarkable cone of brick and the outer dome that Wren designed to support the stone lantern with the Cross and the Ball. The dome visible inside the Cathedral is not the same as that seen from the street.

From the Golden Gallery—a small, narrow space, and often windy—there is an unforgettable view of London. You see how London lies in a broad, shallow valley and how the green heights of Sydenham, on the south, and Hampstead, on the north, enclose it. You see the often narrow, winding streets of the old City, while to the west the towers of the Abbey Church of Westminster rise above the

28 *Walmer Castle, Kent*

29 *Hampton Court Palace*

30 *Hever Castle, Kent*

31 Canterbury Cathedral, Kent

32 The Bishop's Palace and River Medway, Maidstone, Kent

33 The West Gate, Canterbury

white ribbon of the Thames; in the streets below, omnibuses no bigger than flies crawl into the dark cavern of Ludgate Hill.

What a miracle it was that St. Paul's was not burnt down in the Blitz! No building in London was in greater peril, as one can see when glancing down at the ruins of buildings round about, whose destruction ringed the Cathedral with flame. It is a privilege to be able to pay a tribute to the gallantry of the clergy, the vergers and other members of the staff, who for years guarded St. Paul's every night, sleeping there and ready, when the fire bombs were falling, to tackle them with rakes, sand buckets and pumps. Had it not been for their splendid efforts this great church, whose dome is a symbol of London all over the earth, would doubtless have suffered, like its predecessor, in the second Fire of London.

I remember one Christmas during the war—when Ludgate Hill and the little streets leading from it had been turned into hell overnight—walking towards St. Paul's, stepping over fire-hoses and picking my way through piles of broken plate glass. There was a hideous smell of burning in the air, and the great fire of Paternoster Row, in which four million books perished, was still acridly smouldering. At the sight of St. Paul's standing unharmed on Ludgate Hill I lifted up my heart in praise and thankfulness, and tears came to my eyes when I saw framed against the darkness of the façade, at the top of the steps, a Christmas tree full of coloured lights. I went into the Cathedral, where another tree was standing, loaded with gifts for London children and for men of the minesweepers, and far off, isolated in the great space of the church, a few people were kneeling, while a clergyman was praying. I joined them, grateful for the peace of a place that God, it seemed, had not deserted. And while the sound of the prayers echoed round the dome, it was joined by harsh sounds from outside: the urgent note of a fire-bell, the shouts of the weary firemen as they dragged their hoses across the street, the sudden crash of plate glass as a window collapsed. How much longer, I wondered, could this great target remain unharmed? Was it possible, I asked myself, that I was looking at St. Paul's for the last time?

How narrow were its escapes from destruction, perhaps only those who were on duty at the time really know.

As I stood on the Golden Gallery and looked down at the air-raid damage, I marvelled, as I shall always marvel, that St. Paul's came safely through the war.

From the winds that blow round the dome of St. Paul's to the silence and the darkness of the crypt is a sudden transition. To me the crypt has always been the most interesting portion of the church for here, between the massive arches, are the actual graves of those great men whose memorials may be seen above.

"I slept down here for four years," said an elderly verger. "Four years is a long time, sir, isn't it? But it was worth it, for we managed to save St. Paul's. It all seems like a dream. . . ." If future ages continue to gaze upon St. Paul's and Westminster Abbey, let them remember with gratitude the humble and unknown individuals who preserved these great buildings during the Blitz on London.

There are three outstanding tombs in the crypt. The first, and the most simple, is that of the architect, Christopher Wren. Above it may be seen his wonderful epitaph, *Lector, si monumentum requiris, circumspice*—"Reader, if you seek his monument, look around you."

John Flaxman's memorial to Lord Nelson, typical of its period, looks as if it has strayed into St. Paul's from Westminster Abbey. It shows Nelson standing beside an anchor and a coil of rope while Britannia, helmeted but temporarily without her trident, points towards him, and is evidently saying to two extremely young sailors, "Go thou and do likewise." The great sailor lies beneath the dome in a fine sarcophagus of marble that was originally designed to hold the remains of Cardinal Wolsey.

[10]

The mental journey into the remote past expected of visitors to such a shrine as Westminster Abbey is exhausting; I often wonder, as I watch the crowds drinking in the mass of dates and names given to them by guides, how much of it is really absorbed or understood. History can be the most boring or the most exciting of all topics, and, having been so bored by it in childhood, I have had to make it interesting to myself in later life. I wish there were some magic formula to make a place like Westminster Abbey immediately thrilling and exciting to its visitors, most of whom are drawn there by a kind of spell, but there is no such formula.

The history of the Abbey is really a simple one, but it is a long story involving thirteen centuries. It begins before history, in the age of legend, when monks seeking a lonely spot in which to worship God penetrated the brambles of a little island on the banks of the Thames called Thorney. There they built a church, which has grown into Westminster Abbey.

At this time Saxon London was visible to them on its hill, sitting behind its Roman Wall. England was half pagan and half Christian. Shaggy kings were being converted by Roman missionaries beneath oak trees, and baptised in the water of holy wells. Sometimes they remained Christian, sometimes they strayed back into paganism. Mentally they were on the level of childlike tribes everywhere. The first Bishop of London, Mellitus, a Roman missionary, was driven out of London by the sons of a former chieftain: They had reverted to paganism because they wanted the white bread of the Eucharist, yet refused to become converted; they were furious with the Bishop for giving this nice white bread to ordinary common folk and not to them.

The Monastery of Westminster first steps clearly into history with Edward the Confessor about the year 1042.

Before he came to the throne he took a vow to make a pilgrimage to Rome; when he became king he found it impossible to fulfil this vow and sent a deputation to the Pope asking for absolution. The Pope agreed to absolve him if he would rebuild the Monastery. This great task became the main object of his later years.

If we wish to imagine what Edward the Confessor's Abbey looked like we must remember Durham Cathedral, the Chapel of St. John, in the Tower and St. Bartholomew's, Smithfield. It was almost as large as the present Abbey, and was at that time the mightiest building in the country. It took twenty years to build, and was intended to last forever. The Saxons, whose churches were mostly small stone barns with thatched roofs, after the style of the Celtic churches of Scotland and Ireland, must have looked at the new Abbey with amazement and seen in it something colossal and alien.

The great church was to be dedicated at Christmastide in the year 1065. Edward was ill. For some days he lingered, rallied and finally sank, and in the consternation that spread through England when his death was known may we not see the first glimmer of that awe and reverence that was to grow into the cult of St. Edward the Confessor?

From London and from all the villages around crowds packed the new white Abbey Church of St. Peter to see the Confessor lying in a blaze of candlelight before the high altar, his crown upon his head, his royal vestments upon his body, a golden crucifix round his neck and a pilgrim's ring upon his long, transparent hand. While the Confessor lay dead in Westminster, his successor, Harold, was hastily crowned, either at St. Paul's or the Abbey; when Christmas came round again Harold lay dead, and William the Conqueror was crowned in the Abbey on the tomb of its founder.

From that moment every king of England, except Edward V and Edward VIII, who were never crowned at all, has been anointed and crowned in Westminster Abbey. Many lie buried there. Although the Abbey was built to glorify St. Peter, it is Edward the Confessor whom it began to glorify quite early in its history, and his tomb became the heart and centre of the church, as indeed it is to this day. It is also the only miracle-working shrine of the Middle Ages still to be seen in this country.

It has been the object of all kings of England to establish some contact with the far-off Saxon. At the solemn moment of their lives, when they were anointed and sanctified, they assumed for a few ritualistic moments the carefully preserved and treasured relics of his wardrobe. His ancient mantle was placed upon their shoulders. Plantagenet monarchs, standing barefoot in the great church, drew on antique garments said to be the buskins, or trousers, of the Confessor and placed their feet in his shoes. If their hair became ruffled by the anointing, it was with Edward's comb that they smoothed it into place. And the final moment came when upon their brows was placed the gold circle of his ancient crown.

Thus dressed in ancient garments that had come down from Saxon days, the sovereigns of another age and time, completely Byzantine in appearance, went to the Shrine of St. Edward after the ceremony and were solemnly divested of their clothing, which they left upon the altar. Then, wearing new and modern dress and carrying only the sceptres (which had to be returned to the Abbot of Westminster after the coronation feast), they went on their way, having kept a strange appointment with the past.

Edward's body was seen at least three times after his burial, and his bones were disturbed twice. It was seen first in 1098, about thirty years after his funeral, when Henry I, in order to prove the story that the body was uncorrupt, ordered the tomb to be opened. It is said that the Confessor was seen lying, as if in life, and Gundulf, the Bishop, plucked from his colourless beard a long, pale hair. The second time was after Edward's canonisation in 1161, nearly a century after his death. This time the tomb was opened in the presence of Henry II and Thomas à Becket. The ceremony was performed at midnight in October, when, in a blaze of candlelight and torches, the King and the assembled clerics gazed with awe upon the features of the Confessor. He was lying crowned and vested, as he had been buried, and they took the coronation ring from his finger and, removing his vestments, replaced them with others. He was seen for a third time two hundred years after his burial and in vastly different surroundings. The massive Norman Abbey that he had built had vanished. It had been rebuilt by Henry III and was the Abbey we know today. In this different scene, and before the gaze of men as remote from him as we are from the age of Dr. Johnson, the Saxon King was again exposed to the light and was deposited in the place where his bones rest today.

During the Reformation, in the time of Henry VIII, they were again removed, but when Mary ascended the throne she replaced them in the shrine. The last occasion on which the tomb was disturbed was the most extraordinary of all. The story was told by James II to John Evelyn and is to be found in his *Diary*, under 16 September 1685. The King said that when they were taking down the stands after his coronation in the Abbey, a member of the choir saw a hole in the

Confessor's tomb, into which he thrust his arm. He could feel bones there and among them something hard and metallic. He pulled out of the tomb a jewelled gold crucifix attached to a chain.

Realising that he was holding a precious and sacred relic, the man became afraid and put the crucifix back in the tomb. Then, later, when it occurred to him that someone else might go there and steal it, he returned and took it out again, and at the earliest opportunity showed it to the Archbishop of York. The crucifix found its way to James II at Whitehall, and the King kept it.

Henry III, who pulled down the vast Norman Abbey of the Confessor and built the Westminster Abbey of today, was one of the most extravagant of England's spendthrift monarchs. He was ably assisted by an equally extravagant, but charming and elegant queen, Eleanor of Provence, who was almost more accomplished than he in the art of extortion. Henry was also highly intelligent and was the greatest builder, and perhaps the greatest lover of the arts, ever to occupy the English throne.

The age in which he lived was a tremendous one. It was the age of Dante, St. Francis, St. Dominic, Roger Bacon, Buonaventura and Duns Scotus. Architecture, casting aside its solid Norman anchors, had found wings. It was the age of exquisite churches. The greater part of the talent, skill and inventiveness now scattered among a thousand professions and trades was concentrated within the Church. When people look at a church such as Westminster Abbey and say, as they so often do, "How on earth did men do this in those days?" they should reflect that a large part of the total genius of a nation went into these buildings.

It was clearly an age of transition. A new world was being born in which, in England, the Abbey of Westminster was to be a significant landmark. It is curious that Henry III—the son of the evil, excommunicate John—should have been the pious instrument of fate. His greatest sin in contemporary eyes was his excessive fondness for foreigners, yet, so inscrutable are the workings of destiny, he was the king who erected the national shrine of England. Although he did not know it, Henry was the first truly English king.

It is an interesting indication of the state of England from the Norman Conquest to the time of Henry III that when the Norman Abbey of Westminster was pulled down, it did not contain the tomb of one so-called English king, although it had been standing for two hundred years. William the Conqueror was buried at Caen in Normandy, William Rufus at Winchester, Henry I at Reading, Stephen at Faversham, Henry II and Richard I at Fontevrault in France and John at Worcester.

When Henry III began to pull down the Confessor's massive Abbey in 1245 he was thirty-eight years of age, and twenty-four years later he had the satisfaction of seeing his splendid new church complete, except for the western part of the nave. During those twenty-four years the King personally supervised the building. So he created what he intended to be a worthy shrine for the Confessor, whom he closely resembled in so many ways, and also a royal mausoleum for the House of Plantagenet. What would Henry III have said could he have foreseen a day when not only Plantagenets, but Tudors, Stuarts and Hanoverians would be grouped round the Confessor's shrine, when Englishmen of genius and worth, poets, artists, musicians, writers, statesmen and inventors, would be admitted to the shrine; a day when pilgrims would come from all parts of the world to stand for a moment in the one place above all others that enshrines the genius of the British race?

It fell to my lot recently to take a friend from overseas to Westminster Abbey. I soon discovered that this man knew nothing about English history.

It was therefore difficult to know how to show the Abbey to him without confusing him. I thought the best thing was to explain the foundation of the Monastery, first by St. Edward and then by Henry III, which I did as well as I could. When we arrived at the Abbey we looked at the Unknown Soldier's grave and at the new Royal Air Force Memorial Chapel at the west end of the nave; then we stood for a long time admiring the glorious view up the nave to the east end of the church, when he delighted me by saying that it was one of the most beautiful buildings he had ever seen.

I asked him to look at something few people notice. It is that the west end of the nave, in which we were standing, was built two centuries later than the east end of it, yet so perfectly was the earlier style of architecture copied that few people can tell where the work of Henry III leaves off and that of Richard II and Henry V begins. The extraordinary thing is that the later builders did not carry on the work in the style then fashionable, but deliberately copied that of an earlier day.

We then made straight for the tomb of St. Edward. Here I asked my friend to note how the Confessor lies in the centre of his chapel, surrounded by all the Plantagenet kings since the time of Henry III, except two, who are buried elsewhere. Then I asked him to notice the extraordinary design of the tomb. There is nothing like it anywhere else in the Abbey, or in England. It is as foreign in appearance as if it were the tomb of a Byzantine emperor or a Saladin, and the Eastern look is accentuated by the Oriental carpet slung above the tomb to conceal the wooden superstructure. Tombs not unlike that of the Confessor are to be seen in ancient mosques in Turkey.

While we were looking at this, a young man with an over-educated voice came up with two women and, to my amazement, said: "Now do look at the Confessor's tomb, which is too enchanting for words. Don't you think the Anglo-Saxon work . . ."

Yet, I said to myself, how reasonable it is to mistake this piece of medieval Byzantinism for Anglo-Saxon; for the art of the Saxons was Byzantine. How right and at the same time how wrong the young man was.

There is naturally a reason why this Byzantine jewel came to be placed out of its real setting, which is medieval Rome or Constantinople. Abbot Ware, who was in Rome when the church was nearing completion, returned to England with Italian workmen, including Peter of the Cosmati family, a worker in mosaics. Whether Henry III had asked the Abbot to look out for some foreign artist capable of designing the Confessor's tomb, or whether the Abbot, visiting such churches as St. Clemente, St. Prassede and St. Pudenziana, became enthusiastic about mosaics and determined to persuade the King to employ the Italians, we shall never know. But the strange fact remains that, after spending twenty years or so extracting the essence of what was best in contemporary French church architecture, Henry III decided to place the central jewel, for whose glorification the whole edifice was intended, within a casket as striking as a single cry of *Kyrie Eleison* in a Latin service.

The Shrine of the Confessor became one of the great miracle-working shrines of the Middle Ages, as it was in Norman times, because the designers of the tomb, anticipating that it would continue to be visited by pilgrims, provided recesses, three on each side and one at each end, in which might kneel those who had come to be healed by proximity to St. Edward's body.

Having explained this to my friend, and finding him still interested, I was faced by the problem of introducing the Plantagenets, by whom we were surrounded, to one in whose mind their names evoked no answering echo.

"Well," I suggested, "let us take these kings and queens in the order in which they were buried round the Confessor's tomb. First, of course, is Henry III himself. Let us walk over and look at his tomb."

So we stood at the tomb of Henry III, and saw that noble spendthrift lying above us in bronze, two elegant pointed toes protruding from the hem of his bronze coronation robes.

"Those feet," I said, "walked shoeless from St. Paul's to the Abbey Church of St. Peter when the King, habited as a monk, held above his head a crystal phial containing a drop of the Saviour's blood sent to him from Jerusalem. He walked beneath a canopy, while two bishops, one on each side, supported his arms all the way. So he passed through awed and silent crowds, who dropped upon their knees as he went past, noting that 'he kept his eyes ever fixed upon the

Blood of Christ and wept many tears'. Such was the man who built this church."

We then passed to the tomb next to Henry's, where Queen Eleanor of Castile lies, the next royal burial in the Abbey, eighteen years after the funeral of her father-in-law. She was the wife of Henry's eldest son, Edward I. Her effigy shows a grave and lovely lady whose hair falls on each side of her face from beneath a foliated crown. Her left hand, at the level of her breast, grasps the end of a chain that encircles her neck.

"Did you ever hear of a queen who went on a Crusade to the Holy Land with her husband and sucked the poison from an arrow wound?" I asked.

A faint look of recognition lit his face.

"I think I have," he said.

"Well, this is the queen, Eleanor of Castile. She is also the queen for whom Charing Cross was made. When she died in Lincolnshire her sorrowful Edward erected twelve memorial crosses, one on each place where her body rested on its way to London. Charing Cross was the last of them. And note the exquisite iron gate that encloses her, its top a succession of three-pronged spikes that look like flames, or a bed of crocuses. Upon St. Andrew's Eve, the anniversary of her death, two hundred wax tapers impaled upon those spikes burned round her every year for two hundred years."

The next royal burial was that of Edward I, her husband. He lies on the other side of Henry III. Seventeen years passed before he followed her to the grave. He warred against the infidel, the Welsh and the Scots. He drove the Jews out of England, and he carried on the Englishing of the country that had begun under his father. He was so often away at war that, in order to see anything of him at all, Eleanor had to spend much of her life as a camp-follower. Her children were consequently born in all sorts of unlikely places, one of them at Acre, in Palestine. During the war in Wales, when they were at the great Castle of Caernarvon, Edward met the Welsh chieftains, who offered homage if he would give them a prince who could speak neither English nor French, expecting that he would appoint one of themselves. But Eleanor had already provided the answer, and Edward, producing his three-day-old son to them, demanded and received their homage, and so created the first Prince of Wales.

"Now," I said, "we must leave the royal tombs and look at the Coronation Chair. Beneath the seat is the awesome Stone of Scone which Edward brought back from Scotland. The Chair itself is the one that Edward made for the stone."

We examined as much as we could see of the much-battered chunk of sand-stone. It is of the kind which is found on the northwest coast of Scotland, and a less likely sacred relic can hardly be imagined; indeed, dare I say that if anyone

34 *Winchester
Cathedral,
Hampshire*

35 *Winchester
from St Giles' Hill*

36 *Chichester Cathedral, Sussex*

37 *Salisbury Cathedral, Wiltshire*

38 *Stonehenge, Wiltshire*

39 *Another view of Stonehenge*

saw it lying on his rockery he would hardly give it a thought? Yet national sentiment has caused this stone to be one of the most hallowed objects in the world.

After taking a look at the Coronation Chair, we returned to the royal tombs and came on the south side of the place where Philippa of Hainault, the queen of Edward III, is buried. Her effigy, obviously a candid portrait, shows a plump Flemish woman with a round, humorous face and a good-tempered mouth. She is wearing a peculiar head-dress, fashionable in the fourteenth century, called a *crespine*. She was the mother of the Black Prince.

Although her mighty monarch was not always a model of fidelity, Philippa on her deathbed, as recorded by Jean Froissart, asked him to promise "that you will rest by my side in the cloisters of Westminster Abbey".

This was not strictly observed, for Philippa and Edward do not lie side by side —an impossible position in that restricted space—but he is as near to her as he can be.

The effigy of Edward III is extremely interesting, for it is said to have been taken from his death-mask. It shows a sad old man, his face lined with care. There is nothing about it in its pathetic loneliness to suggest the mighty conqueror of Crécy and Poitiers.

One more tomb completes the royal burials grouped round the Confessor. It is that of Anne of Bohemia, who died in 1394, and her husband, Richard II, who followed her five years after. The tragic King and his young wife are seen together in effigy, and before their figures were mutilated during the Commonwealth, they were holding hands. Richard, who adored Anne, was half mad with grief, when, at the age of twenty-eight, she died, probably of the plague. He ordered that her funeral effigy should include his own figure, and this was done during his lifetime, so that he must often have seen this strange tomb in which he appeared lying, as if dead, grasping the hand of his beloved queen.

[11]

The failure of the English people to provide their king with a London palace suitable to his dignity and power has often struck the foreigner as a strange and singular fact, and as recently as 1828 the Duke of Wellington said in the House of Lords that "no sovereign in Europe, I may even add, perhaps, no private gentleman is so ill-lodged as the king of this country".

The kings of England, however, have been repeatedly housed on paper in the most splendid fashion. Any monarch during the last two centuries who, feeling "ill-lodged", wished to console himself with the many fine schemes devised from time to time, has had only to take down a volume in the Royal Library at Windsor Castle, in which plans of at least twenty magnificent palaces are to be seen, any one of which would have altered beyond recognition the part of London in which it was erected.

Why, it might be asked, were none of these palaces built? I suppose lack of money was one reason, and also, more subtly, maybe there was a feeling that a Louvre or a Versailles was not a suitable home for the British monarchy. It is, nevertheless, interesting to glance at some of the unborn British palaces, beginning with the tremendous scheme for a new Whitehall Palace devised by that great architect of the stillborn, Inigo Jones. His stupendous scheme for a sort of regal township extended from Charing Cross almost to the Abbey, taking in all Whitehall and St. James's Park. So vast was this conception that Buckingham Palace (then Buckingham House) was to be merely a "royal lodge, observatory and Chamber of Rarities", and Marlborough House a "greenhouse for Exotick Plants". Both Houses of Parliament, the Law and the whole of the Civil Service were to be housed in this palace, after the ancient pattern, and in the centre, or, more accurately, on the river frontage, the sovereign was to inhabit a gigantic building like a couple of streets in Rome, one on top of the other.

Then came Sir Christopher Wren, who would have dearly liked the chance to transform Whitehall, but was obliged to be content to leave at Greenwich some idea of the magnificence he would have created at Westminster. William Kent, who gave us the Horse Guards, designed a fine Palladian palace for George II, which he desired to erect in Hyde Park; for George III, Sir William Chambers drew plans and made a model of another Whitehall; and in 1766 yet another great castle in Spain was created by George Wright, with an eye on St. James's Park. Sir John Soane and John Nash increased the number of these interesting propositions.

Behind all this bid for splendour one seems to sense the feeling that the kings of France were regally accommodated, while the kings of England were living in ancient, unplanned and makeshift buildings, or in houses smaller and less distinguished than those of many a private person. It was felt by some to be a national disgrace that no architectural composition capable of rivalling the Louvre had been erected on the banks of the Thames. And, considering the large number of amateur architects in the aristocracy at that time, it may appear surprising that sufficient enthusiasm was never generated to carry even the more modest of these plans into reality. The fact is that the continental conception of a royal palace would never take root in English soil.

Instead, we have Buckingham Palace, which, by a process of natural growth, has become, not the Court, which is still officially at St. James's Palace, but the home of the royal family and, by virtue of the personal qualities of George V, George VI, and the present Queen, has become the best-known and best-loved palace in the world. And it is part and parcel of the English reluctance to create a palace in the grand manner that "Buckingham House" should have become a palace in spite of itself.

The ground it occupies appears in history as a mulberry garden planted as food for silkworms by James I, who had an idea that silk manufacture might help to "wean his people from idleness and the enormities thereof". But this scheme died a natural death, and the mulberry plantation became a superior roadhouse where gallants in the time of Charles II took their lady friends to eat mulberry tarts. Diarists John Evelyn and Pepys both visited the place, and so did John Dryden with his favourite actress, Madame Reeve.

Near the mulberry garden three houses were built in succession: Goring House, Arlington House and lastly, on the site of the present palace, Buckingham House. Prints of the time of Queen Anne show a charming square red-brick Dutch country-house, linked to its stables and outbuildings by two semicircular colonnades. There was a wide courtyard in front of it, a fountain, iron railings and fine gates with the Duke of Buckingham's coronet, arms, Garter and George all beautifully worked in wrought iron. When the Duke looked out of his upper windows he saw an avenue of elms and lime trees, which is now the Mall. In the distance rose the dome of St. Paul's, surrounded by the spires of the City churches and, nearer, to the left, across meadows and parkland, were the towers of the Abbey Church. As he looked down the Mall, he could see a long canal and a duck decoy made by Charles II, which is now the lake in St. James's Park. Writing to a friend about his new house, the Duke said that near his windows was a little wilderness full of blackbirds and nightingales.

When he died, he left Buckingham House to his duchess, his third wife, who was said to be the daughter of James II and Catherine Sedley, a mistress whose charms were such that Charles II considered that she must have been bestowed upon his brother by his confessor as a penance.

When the haughty and eccentric daughter of this union died, Buckingham House was bought by George III as a dower house for Queen Charlotte; and so began its association with the royal family. The pleasant red-brick country-house was occupied by King George and Queen Charlotte, who lived a pleasant and fruitful domestic life there while they held levees and courts at the official Court of St. James's. When that great builder, the Prince Regent, came to the throne as George IV, it was natural that he should have called in the architect of Regent Street to rebuild Buckingham House, or the Queen's House, as it was then called.

But John Nash never completed the interior, for both he and his royal patron died within a few years of each other. The new king, William IV, actively disliked Buckingham Palace, as at last it had become. He never lived there, and, indeed, thought so little of it as a residence that he offered it as a temporary shelter for Parliament when the Houses of Parliament were burned down.

It looks uncommonly as though fate had reserved Buckingham Palace for the young Victoria. No sooner was she queen than she moved in, and her first act was to order a royal throne to be installed there. But her Palace looked very different from the Buckingham Palace we know today. It was the Palace designed by George IV. The frontage was set back a considerable distance, and there were two projecting wings. Strangest of all, to modern ideas, the Marble Arch stood in front of it and formed the ceremonial entrance, with the Royal Standard on top.

The Palace was twice altered, once in 1847, and again in 1914, just before the war, when the Queen Victoria Memorial Scheme, with the widening of the Mall and the erection, at one end, of the Admiralty Arch and, at the other, of the Victoria Memorial, made the old palace look extremely old-fashioned. The front of the palace, as we see it today, was refashioned, without even disturbing the glass in the windows, in the short time of three months.

Fortunately, the back of Buckingham Palace was not altered. Many of those who have attended a garden party there will remember that there is a remarkable difference between the appearance of the front and the garden side of the Palace. The back is the practically untouched work of Nash and Edward Blore. It is a beautiful piece of Classical architecture, and looks its best on a sunny afternoon from the edge of the artificial lake. It is at the back of the Palace that the royal family live, overlooking the gardens and one of the largest stretches of turf in the world.

During Queen Victoria's long widowhood Buckingham Palace was remote and withdrawn from the life of the capital, but with the First World War it suddenly became the rallying-point of the nation during the sorrows and triumphs of those days. It was as if by some instinctive movement of a people towards its hereditary head that the first of those great crowds surged down the Mall on a hot August day in 1914 and called for the King. After the war, George V, aided by the radio and a perfect broadcasting voice, became the father of his people.

His son, George VI, and Queen Elizabeth kept the Royal Standard flying on Buckingham Palace throughout the Second World War, although the Palace was hit by bombs and damaged by blast. Buckingham Palace, pinpointed by the Mall and lying in its large gardens, is, from the air, one of the most easily identified landmarks in London. Some extraordinary stories were spread during the war that deep underground shelters, which no bomb could damage, were constructed beneath the Palace, stories that had no foundation. During some of the noisiest nights London has ever known the King and Queen lived in the palace with a fatalistic attitude to danger, which, as many of their subjects learned, was the only attitude to adopt.

Their air-raid shelter was merely a storeroom in the basement, which may have been blastproof, but could not have resisted a near miss, much less a direct hit. It was furnished with a few of those gilded chairs inseparable from Palace life, and a large gilded Regency settee. Facing the door was a circular Victorian mahogany table on which stood oil-lamps, electric torches, a bottle of smelling-salts and a number of monthly magazines carefully laid out by the hand of an experienced footman. Axes were hanging on the walls so that should the exits become blocked the royal prisoners might break their way through the windows into the Palace gardens. I had the opportunity of visiting this shelter once during the war, and thought that, unimpressive as it was, it was historically important and deserved a commemorative tablet.

[12]

To me, Hampton Court is the place above all others where it is easy to imagine Henry VIII and his great daughter living their everyday life, sitting in front of the fire in wintertime, playing tennis, gardening, riding out to hunt the stag, dancing and entertaining their friends. But the emphasis is placed upon the Stuart State apartments, and one comes last of all to the older Tudor rooms and the Great Hall where Henry VIII feasted and revelled and where possibly Shakespeare may have acted.

I wish visitors might see Hampton Court in the right sequence. Instead of entering the Stuart State apartments, I should prefer to enter by way of the Great Hall and go through the few remaining Tudor rooms, which in a perfect world would be sumptuously furnished with tapestries, oak chairs, tables, sideboards and clocks. It would then be possible to see the kind of rooms in which Wolsey and Henry VIII lived four centuries ago.

Cardinal Wolsey chose Hampton as his country home because the doctors told him that it was the healthiest place within twenty miles of London. Like many another large and possibly robust man, Wolsey was terrified of illness, and his country palace was a safe retreat from the crowded streets of London during times of plague. One of his first acts was to bring a good water supply from

Coombe Hill, three miles away, and the lead pipes passed beneath the Thames above Kingston Bridge.

The Cardinal had good taste, a love of pomp and splendour and enormous revenues, so that his palace soon became the most magnificent in the realm. Henry VIII was at first enchanted and then envious. The scale of Wolsey's establishment would have been surprising in any age, and incredible in this servantless age of ours. Presiding over two kitchens, one of them the Cardinal's privy kitchen, was a master cook, who dressed in velvet and wore a chain of office; they show you the little room in which he used to draw up his menus. Under him were eighty assistant cooks, yeomen and scullions. About a hundred servants were at work in the wardrobe, the laundry, the woodyard, to say nothing of the stables where the Master of the Horse controlled a great number of grooms and stable-boys. Apart from the domestic establishment there were sixty priests and officers of the chapel, the choir and a crowd of personal attendants and functionaries. As Lord Chancellor, Wolsey maintained a second establishment that included heralds, sergeants-at-arms, minstrels, clerks, armourers and running footmen.

It is said that upon one occasion Henry VIII asked why a private subject should have created such a regal home, and Wolsey, who was evidently well prepared for the question, answered tactfully, "In order to present it to his sovereign." He may have said this as the Spaniard says "My house is yours", or as the Arab offers a guest anything that he admires; but both Spaniard and Arab would be sadly disconcerted were they to be taken literally! Nevertheless, Henry chose to take Wolsey at his word and eventually became the owner of Hampton Court.

The palace was then the background to Henry's matrimonial adventures. Each of his six queens walked the red-brick courtyards, the galleries, the gardens, the park, each one tasted brief happiness there, one queen bore his only son there and another was taken from Hampton Court to the Tower. It was, of course, the scene of several of his honeymoons. The palace saw him first, in Wolsey's time, as a gay young man of twenty-five married to thirty-one-year-old Catherine of Aragon, the widow of his dead brother, Arthur. They were happy for some years, until Henry's roving eye settled upon Anne Boleyn. He installed her in the same palace with his queen at Hampton Court. After she had become queen, Anne Boleyn detected in a room at Hampton Court her husband's flirtation with her successor, Jane Seymour, and it was at Hampton Court that Jane died of puerperal fever after having given birth to the son who became Edward VI.

After her death Henry awaited apprehensively at Hampton Court the arrival from Dover of his "great Flanders mare", Anne of Cleves. He had been betrayed into marriage, it is said, by an optimistic portrait by Holbein. Unable to bear the anxiety, Henry went off to meet her in disguise and came up with her in a house at Rochester. Anne was looking out of a window at a bull-baiting. Henry, who must have been an advanced sentimentalist, approached incognito and presented her with a token from himself. She thanked him briefly, but was evidently much more interested in the bull-baiting. Henry then retired to another apartment and put on a suit of purple velvet and returned to introduce himself.

The royal sacrifice for England was not, however, of long duration, and at Hampton Court, some few months later Anne waited complacently for the news that she had been divorced and given the title of "royal sister", which suited her quite well. Against the leafy background of Hampton Court, Henry was captivated by the youthful charm of Catherine Howard, and two years later he rode away from the palace broken-hearted by the knowledge that his rose was not without a thorn. The old palace, which must by that time have become rather cynical, was the place of Henry's sixth and last honeymoon. If experience counts in matrimony, Henry and Catherine Parr should have had the recipe for success. They were married in the Queen's Closet at Hampton Court, Henry vast, unwieldy and almost a cripple, she a small, fair-haired woman of thirty-one, who had been twice widowed. She would have been known in the eighteenth century as a bluestocking. She was a Greek and Latin scholar and could argue theology with any doctor of divinity, but she also possessed a fund of feminine sympathy that was spent upon the ailing King and upon his three neglected children.

In Elizabeth's time Hampton Court became a holiday palace in which the Queen sought escape from the affairs of State. Anyone of the time who glanced through the windows overlooking the Privy Gardens on a sharp winter morning might have seen the unusual spectacle of the Virgin Queen taking a brisk walk "to catch her a heate", which she did regularly while at Hampton Court, though when in public she was never guilty of the vulgarity of quick walking, but "went slowly and marched with leisure". She loved the Privy Gardens, whose walls were overhung with rosemary and whose hedges and trees were clipped to resemble men, beasts and birds. In these surroundings she talked with Sir James Melville, the Scots Ambassador, who has left an account of Elizabeth's attempt to make him admit that she was more beautiful and more accomplished than Mary Queen of Scots; Melville, although a highly competent flatterer, escaped from the ordeal only with difficulty and with his loyalty to his mistress barely intact.

Elizabeth's projected marriage, which became England's foreign policy for so many years, was first discussed at Hampton Court when William Cecil produced the Earl of Arran for her inspection, the first of her many suitors. But she did not like him. He had no brains, was nothing to look at and, as she said to the Spanish

Ambassador, "she would never have a husband who would sit all day by the fireside". She would marry only a man who could ride and hunt and fight. Possibly remembering her father's disastrous marriage with Anne of Cleves, whom he had espoused, as the custom was in those days, on the strength of a portrait, Elizabeth would have nothing to do with the miniatures and pictures of princes that were shown to her, but obliged the young men to travel across Europe before she flirted with them and turned them down. I suppose the modern psychologist would trace to her father's many unsuccessful marriages Elizabeth's refusal to take a husband. So Hampton Court was the scene of Henry's many honeymoons, as it was of the beginning of his daughter's long resistance to the state of matrimony.

At Christmas time the Great Hall, where one stands in another world and age, was the centre of the Court's merrymaking. Wires were stretched across it from which hung hundreds of oil-lamps. This early theatre was the scene of masques and plays from Christmas Eve until Twelfth Night. To see the Hall now, beautifully tidy, polished and empty, is to have no idea of the scene it must have presented in Tudor times when the carpenters were putting up the stage and erecting elaborate scenery, introducing trees from the park to represent a forest and painting canvas houses; when the actors were rehearsing in the Great Watching Chamber, and the tailors, dressmakers and seamstresses were busy making and adapting costumes for the players. What would we not give to have a film of those events? If only the cinema camera had been invented four centuries ago and one placed in the hands of Leicester, what a scene would have been preserved of Hampton Court at Christmas time: of the Queen and her ladies watching the play, of the Queen dancing a coranto or a galliard, or possibly even the daring volto, which was banned in many European Courts, but was danced by Elizabeth, as we can see from a picture at Penshurst that shows her being lifted into the air by her partner like a ballet dancer.

The State Apartments, the chief sight of Hampton Court, were built by Christopher Wren for William and Mary, who considered the old royal quarters antique and inconvenient. They form a colossal royal flat through which the visitor wanders, pausing to admire the splendid pictures, the tall State beds, a superb clock by Tompion and a gorgeous barometer by Daniel Quare.

After the reign of Charles II nothing spectacular happened at Hampton Court—except a mole. Into the tunnel made by this mole a horse called Sorrel stumbled one day in the year 1702, and William III, who was in the saddle, was flung to the ground and received injuries from which he died. The Jacobites of that time, rejoicing at the death of Dutch William, raised their glasses to the mole of Hampton Court—"the little gentleman in the black velvet coat".

40 *Chalk downs (with figure of George III on horseback) near Weymouth, Dorset*

41 *New Forest ponies, Hampshire*

42 *A glade in the New Forest*

43 *Beaulieu, Hampshire*

44 *Beaulieu Palace*

45 *Buckler's Hard, Hampshire*

46 *Chesil Beach, Dorset*

47 *Weymouth Harbour, Dorset*

As I explored the State Apartments I thought that, much as I should like to have seen the palace in the time of Henry VIII, it would have been seen best in the time of Charles I, before the art treasures had been put up for auction. Few people realise the enormous number of treasures lost to England, now dispersed throughout Europe and many of them lost forever, when the Commonwealth Parliament sold the contents of the royal palaces after the execution of Charles I.

I sat in the gardens and watched children playing ball, I admired the fountains and the ducks and I saw the Great Vine. I then saw the old Tennis Court, built in 1529 by Henry VIII, where members of the Royal Tennis Court Club still play— surely the oldest athletic association in the country.

Henry, who was a good player, was perhaps the first person in England to wear tennis shorts. Nothing half as spectacular was ever seen at Wimbledon, for they were silk or velvet drawers slashed with "cuttes" and the edges sewn with gold cord. The King began his tennis career without a racket, using a padded glove instead, and a hard ball stuffed with compressed wool. The tennis "net" was merely a fringed cord drawn across the court.

Southern England

[I]

Westerham in Kent wears an air of age and quality. I have no doubt that the people who live there are agreeable, sensible folk. It must be admitted, however, that they have ruined the approach to their town on one side by permitting a rash of villas to be built there, but they must at least be congratulated that this lapse in architectural manners cannot be seen from the dignified and harmonious main street.

On the town green, which slopes gracefully downhill, I saw the statue of a man waving a sword. He wears a long-waisted coat to his knees, a peruke and a tricorn hat. He is not waving his sword defiantly or dramatically, which is remarkable, because, as you will agree, it is difficult not to wave a sword in either one or other of those ways. And if you have studied the stone and bronze swordsmen who are so lavishly scattered about the world, you will perhaps also agree that defiant and dramatic attitudes, especially in·Latin countries, can become monotonous and irritating, so that a mild swordsman is a restful and unusual addition to any town. In Quebec, for instance, which I shall always think of as a city of pre-posterously active statues, every other street has its lunging, panting swordsman, some at the last gasp on their knees, others with mouths open in an ecstasy of leadership, and all of them lunging and pointing with tremendous verve and enthusiasm at the passers by. Could Don Quixote have visited Quebec, he would have been fighting a perpetual chain of duels with the great departed, who lean down as if to attack a man who is about to buy a newspaper, or to threaten the existence of a harmless visitor to the post office. Even politicians in Quebec are charitably depicted in the act of doing something, unlike our own sombre standers and sitters. They are either making speeches or signing treaties, aided by the leaping and flying figures of Faith, Hope and Victory, who gambol in the air round and about them in the best tradition of Gallic Baroque. Thinking of those furiously active immortals in Quebec, I approached the tame, but elegant, swordsman of Westerham, and read with a smile that he was none other than General James Wolfe, the hero of Quebec.

It is a good statue and an excellent likeness. Wolfe's sharp, rather peaky features have been admirably portrayed, and although, as I have said, there is nothing dramatic in the way he lifts his sword, as if to smack a reluctant battery mule upon the hindquarters, there is a dramatic appeal in the isolation of his graceful figure against the sky of his native town. He stands there, it seems, not in the centre of a Kentish market town, but high upon the far-off Plains of Abraham.

Unlike prophets, soldiers are rarely forgotten in their own country towns, partly perhaps because they offer the sculptor some scope for effect. And certainly Wolfe has not been forgotten in Westerham. His figure is the most prominent object in the town. There is a Wolfe Café and a Wolfe Garage. The wall of the George and Dragon proudly announces that Wolfe once stayed there; and any passer by can direct you to Wolfe's House.★

I was shown into a panelled hall and into a panelled room to the right, which was full of relics. It is difficult to say what degree of fame must be achieved by a hero before such objects as "eight table knives, eight table forks and one carving fork, formerly in the possession of the Wolfe family" cease to be ridiculous when placed in a glass case. But hero worship is a profound and deep-seated emotion, and it is undoubtedly true that many people who have no interest in Wolfe and could give you no clear idea of his life and achievements have probably gazed with reverence at those knives and forks.

How extraordinarily alike were Wolfe and Nelson, both frail and delicate children and never robust as men, both of them nervous, quick, emotional and talkative, possessing too that rare quality that caused them to be worshipped by the common soldiers and sailors who served under them, and, at the last, meeting the two most dramatic deaths in British history, expiring in the moment of their triumph as if upon a stage.

Perhaps they were both throwbacks to an earlier England, maybe to the emotional Tudor England when men boasted and bragged and were unashamed to shed a tear. Already in their time the upper-class Englishman was, I suspect, altering. He was already on his way to the public school. And it is interesting to remember that upon two notable occasions both Wolfe and Nelson were considered by certain of their contemporaries to have behaved in a manner not befitting the dignity of gentlemen. Before Wolfe sailed for America he dined

★Winston Churchill's beloved Chartwell, his country home during the last forty years of his life, now shares with Wolfe's House the attention of all visitors to Westerham.—H.V.M.

with William Pitt and Richard Grenville Temple, and it is said that after dinner, worked up by the thought of the great mission that lay before him, he drew his sword and, to the embarrassment of his hosts, burst "into a storm of gasconade and bravado" that shocked them profoundly. But I am willing to wager that neither Shakespeare, Drake nor Raleigh would have been shocked or embarrassed by such behaviour. Nelson had precisely the same effect upon the Duke of Wellington on the only occasion those two great men met.

It would be interesting to know the precise period in history when it became ungentlemanly for Englishmen to cry in public, or to boast or brag and indulge in picturesque rhetoric; in other words, the precise moment when the strong, silent, public-school Englishman became the masculine pattern of English conduct.

We came in time to the most interesting of all the relics, a pale, elegant Flemish dressing-gown in which Wolfe's body was brought home from Canada to be buried at Greenwich. That garment hangs there like a ghost and really has something painful and tragic about it. As I looked at it, I remembered the line of boats that floated down a dark river in a silence unbroken save for the splash of an oar. Our history books all say that, as the troops were carried down the St. Lawrence, the soldier who was soon to die was heard to repeat in a low voice, "The paths of glory lead but to the grave", then, turning to his officers, added, "Gentlemen, I would rather have written that poem than beat the French tomorrow." There is some reason to doubt the truth of that fine story. There is evidence that Wolfe quoted Gray's *Elegy*, not as the troops were moving out to scale the Heights of Abraham, but on the previous afternoon, when he made a reconnaissance from a boat in order to find a way up the steep cliffs. He had a foreboding that he would not survive the action, and the night before he called a friend to him and confessed his fear, entrusting to him a miniature of Katherine Lowther, the girl whom he hoped to marry.

Wolfe was wounded three times. At first he was shot in the wrist, but, wrapping a handkerchief round the wound, he continued to command the action. He was again shot just as he had given an order to charge; again he carried on, believing, as he had once said, that "while a man is able to do his duty, and can stand and hold his arms, it is infamous to retire". But in the heat of the battle he received a shot in the breast and was unable to stand any longer. His first anxiety was to conceal his plight from the troops. "Support me," he whispered to an officer, "let not my brave fellows see me fall. The day is ours—keep it."

When it became known that he lay dead upon the Plains of Abraham the grief of his men was swiftly transformed into fury. They charged the French like madmen. Exactly the opposite occurred to the French when they knew that their leader, Montcalm, was mortally wounded. They lost heart and went to pieces.

[2]

Outside in the sunlight, the cruel and frustrated face of Henry VIII gazes from the inn sign, and a few yards off is a red lodge covered with wisteria, which leads to Hever Castle, once the property of Sir Thomas Boleyn. It was here that Henry courted Anne Boleyn.

In 1903, William Waldorf Astor, the first Lord Astor, fell in love with Hever, which was then a farmhouse. This was a love affair the villagers found more difficult to understand than the earlier one, because Hever Castle, by that time badly in need of repair, hung over its moat heavy with years.

And they marvelled even more as Hever's new lover poured out money on it, set it up again proudly behind its moat and planted the gardens. In Hever they still talk of the fifteen hundred men who worked for five years to move back the River Eden in order to make room for guest houses, because the new lord refused to spoil the old castle by building on to it.

I entered a park where the birds were singing. Pheasants were running across the grass into the woods. As I walked along I began to think of Henry VIII and Anne Boleyn. It was not the world's most perfect love affair maybe, but is perpetually interesting because of the mighty issues at stake, because of the tragedy in which it ended and because of the great queen of England who was the fruit of it.

It is difficult to believe that Anne was ever really in love with Henry, but there can be no doubt that at first he loved her sincerely and devotedly. His tragic search for a wife who would give him a male heir might perhaps never have continued had the infant Elizabeth been a healthy boy.

Such thoughts brought me within sight of the Castle. I saw, lying on slightly lower ground, at the level of the river, a crenellated grey building and a gate-house rising above the moat. At first I was not sure that Hever was real, for it looked like some castle in a poem. It might have fallen out of a chapter of Froissart. Everything that wealth and good taste can do to bring a weary old castle back into the world has been done to Hever.

It was smaller than I expected it to be: more of a medieval manor house than a castle. It is the modest, embattled home of a country knight who might never have been heard of if his daughter had not become the Queen of England. And this is a part of its charm. If it were twice the size, it would not be so lovely to look at.

Before I crossed the drawbridge, I had a good look at Hever: at the skilfully simple flower beds round the moat; at the dark maze; at the formal Elizabethan garden with its fountain, its set of gigantic yew chessmen, the dovecote rising above tall, valeted hedges like little Tudor houses on poles. It is not often that one sees a scene so perfect and so cleverly restrained. It is difficult to believe that art has played so great a part in the creation of this glimpse of Tudor England. And, looking at Hever, it is easy to see why Waldorf Astor fell in love with it, for Hever, unlike many an old castle, is a happy place. At least, that was my impression.

The many lovely rooms at Hever are almost too full of things worth looking at, for the late Lord Astor was a great collector and liked to live with his treasures. I saw in one room a book of devotion believed to be the one Anne Boleyn read while she was waiting for death in the Tower. It is full of marginal notes, and on one page, written presumably by her, are the words:

Remember me when you do pray,
Hope doth lead from day to day.

This, though it may not add to her reputation as a poet, no doubt reflects the state of her mind during the horrible days before her death. Almost to the last she thought that the King was only making her suffer in order to try her, and would not take away her life.

Among the bedrooms at Hever is one that for centuries has been pointed out as the room in which Henry VIII stayed when he was courting Anne. From its window you look into the lovely gardens where he is supposed first to have met her. When he was unable to be with her, he kept in touch by letters beginning "Sweetharte" and "My own darling", and ending sometimes, like any callow youth, with an outline of a heart inside which he drew her initials.

[3]

Maidstone is an ancient county town whose streets, crammed to bursting point with traffic, reflect the prosperity of the "Garden of England". It is not a pleasant town to enter, because every kind of wheeled vehicle contends for mastery in its streets. In the middle of the High Street a youthful version of Queen Victoria, standing beneath a little shrine that looks like as much of the Albert Memorial as the town council of that time could afford, presides with dignity over an age so different from her own.

The town is an expression of the commercial drive of the Men of Kent, as well as the Kentish Men; and having mentioned those terms, I suppose I ought to explain them. The River Medway divides the Men of Kent from the Kentish Men. The Men of Kent live on the east of the Medway; the Kentish Men on the west. This ancient distinction may go back to a time when there were two tribes in Kent, one with its capital at Canterbury, the other with its capital at Rochester. I have also heard it argued—and this topic, for some reason, is a fruitful subject for argument—that the Men of Kent earned their distinction when they went out with green boughs to meet William the Conqueror and, in return for their embassy, obtained a confirmation of their ancient privileges.

I went out to see what I could find and I was not long in finding it. The four finest things in Maidstone are the Library and Museum, housed in a grand old black- and-white manor house, the Parish Church of All Saints, the neighbouring Archbishop's Palace on the banks of the Medway and, a few yards away, in Mill Street, a superb tithe barn.

Maidstone's church is like a small cathedral. It is hung with the ghostly colours of county regiments, and in the quiet building lie many of the great ones of Kent. Twelve columns, six on each side of the nave, symbolise the Twelve Apostles; four in the chancel, two on either side, represent the Evangelists. It is a pity that many of the fine windows are ruined by stained glass of the worst Victorian kind.

One of the most flamboyant, but most interesting, monuments in the church is that of the Astley family. It is a huge architectural mass of alabaster showing, at the top, Sir John Astley, who was Keeper of the Jewel House to Queen Elizabeth and, lower down, his son, Sir John Astley, who was Master of the Revels to James I and Charles I.

I approached the former Palace of the archbishops of Canterbury, which, by one of the chances not uncommon in the career of an ancient building in England, is now Maidstone's Maternity Welfare Centre. The old Palace is as perfect a building of its type and period as it can be. It is a lovely silver-grey colour and stands proudly on the riverbank, wearing an air of quality and experience. Instead of entering by a front door in the centre of the building, you have a choice between two flights of steps running to the left and right. The flight on the right is used by mothers and children, and the left flight by visitors in search of the caretaker.

The bell was answered by an agreeable woman of sensible age, who took me into a number of high, snuff-coloured rooms with imposing chimneypieces and windows that look straight down on the no-longer-limpid Medway. She told me a lot of history and, unlike many a caretaker I have known, had a genuine love and respect for the old place.

It was one of the many country residences of the archbishops of Canterbury until Cranmer, who, as you remember, was always ready to oblige Henry VIII, exchanged it for some other form of revenue; and from that time until Queen Victoria's Jubilee it has passed from hand to hand. It was during the Jubilee rejoicings that Maidstone decided to buy the Palace and give it a municipal purpose.

I walked across the road to the great barn in which the archbishop's tithes were once stored, and from the size of the building, it seems that he took an adequate share of the produce of Kent. It is redolent of a thousand harvests and, as you look at it, it is easy to forget the passing cars and lorries and to see men of another age passing through its many gateways with the riches of the year.

[4]

As I was motoring along the road between Maidstone and Ashford, my eye, in passing, caught sight of a notice that had been placed on a board in the hedge: "Leeds Castle: open today."

Coming to the Castle gates, I drove into a park. In a few moments, lying ahead on slightly lower ground, I saw a castle that might have been created by Tennyson or Walter Scott. It was indeed what writers of the last century were thinking of when they used the phrase "this noble pile". It is enormous. Its tall, turreted walls are pierced by Gothic and Tudor windows. When the sun is shining, the effect of the stone is striking: it is as white as marble. The white walls descend into still water and are mirrored by a reflection interrupted only by thousands of water-lilies.

But to say that Leeds Castle is moated does not convey the right impression at all: A moat suggests a surrounding ditch or trench filled with water. What makes this Castle so beautiful is that it lies in the centre of a lake that is anything from fifteen to twenty acres in extent. Among the lilies swim black and white swans that, against such a background, suggest the enchantments of Merlin.

The name has nothing to do with Leeds in Yorkshire. It takes its name from an Anglo-Saxon thane, called Led or Ledian, who built the first rude fortress on the island in the lake about A.D. 850.

I crossed the drawbridge to the Inner Barbican and then walked over another bridge to the Gatehouse and the Porter's Lodge. The space where a portcullis used to hang and the grooves into which it fell when lowered are plainly seen in these defensive gateways.

Standing there and looking back across the moat, it was obvious that before the invention of gunpowder, which literally blew the medieval baron out of his castle, this stronghold must have been proof against all danger but famine or treachery from within.

Beyond the gatehouse is a wide courtyard, the Inner Bailey, at the far end of which stands the castle and the main entrance. Men- and maidservants were

48 *Clovelly, North Devon*

49 *'Down-a-long', Clovelly*

50 *St Ives Harbour, Cornwall*

51 *King Arthur's Castle, Tintagel, Cornwall*

52 *Glastonbury Abbey, Somerset*

53 *Wells Cathedral, Somerset*

54 *The Bishop's Palace, Wells*

gathered in the hall, evidently enjoying the novelty of showing people round. In charge of a tall and aloof manservant, I made a progress through a series of living-rooms, where long windows provided a glimpse of the waters of the moat below.

The castle is not at all as venerable as it looks from the lakeside. A good deal of the main structure is Victorian Tudor, and this is connected by a bridge over the moat with a smaller, more ancient portion of the building, which stands on its own little island.

My guide was unable to tell me anything that was new to me about the castle, except that it has a ghost, as indeed a castle of its size and age should have: the ghost of a little old lady in grey, who appears with a black dog. No one knows who she is, but she has been seen, I understand, by the present housekeeper. She might be a number of people, for the history of Leeds Castle teems with women, and some of them must have been little, old, grey and addicted to black dogs.

The castle was for many centuries part of the dowry of the queens of England. The first queen who possessed it was Eleanor of Castile, the beloved wife of Edward I. She it was who went with her lord to the Holy Land and is said to have sucked the poison from his wound. She also gave birth to a daughter in Palestine, who became known as Joan of Acre. It was this Eleanor also who became the mother of the first Prince of Wales and held the infant aloft on a shield in Caernarvon Castle. When she died in Lincolnshire, funeral crosses were erected at every stopping-place of her coffin all the way to Westminster Abbey, the last one being the Cross at Charing, or Charing Cross.

A touch of novelty was brought to Leeds by Queen Joan of Navarre, the second wife of Henry IV, and stepmother of the popular Henry V. She arrived there under escort, charged with witchcraft. That a queen dowager of England should have been suspected of witchcraft is interesting, but nobody was able to prove anything. The affair ended tamely enough when Henry sent her some money to buy new clothes and released her.

My guide handed me over to another, who took me to a detached building called The Maidens' Tower. The story now current with the staff at Leeds is that Henry VIII built this tower for his queens, but even Henry was not such a whole-sale Bluebeard. It is more probable that he built the place for the maids-of-honour in attendance on his queen of the moment.

Beyond this tower some old steps descend to a mysterious place, now a boat-house, known as Edward I's bath. The explanation is that when he was in the Holy Land, the monarch acquired a novel taste for bathing and returned to build this forbidding cavern full of icy moat water. If there were any heating arrangements, this story might be plausible, but, so far as I could find out, there is no trace of them. The only baths that would have attracted a visitor to the East in those days were the luxurious Roman baths in the Byzantine cities, of which the modern Turkish bath is the direct descendant.

It was interesting to learn that in ancient times they made wine of English grapes at Leeds, and a portion of the garden is still known as the Vineyard. Wykeham Martin says in his book that several of the cottages in the village are covered with vines that bear peculiar small grapes known as "cluster grapes". He believed that they were the descendants of the grapes from which Queen Eleanor made wine in 1290.

With a farewell glance at the superb castle reflected in its lake, I went back to the main road and within an hour was in Canterbury.

[5]

The Canterbury Pilgrims gave a verb to the English language and a name to an English flower. The name Canterbury Bell was given five hundred years ago to one of our most charming wild flowers because it was thought to resemble in shape the little bells the pilgrims tied to the bridles of their horses. John Gerard, who wrote his *Herbal* in 1597, complained that it was not right to give the name to certain bell flowers that grew round London, because the true Canterbury Bell was a native of Kent and was to be found in great profusion near Canterbury. The habit has grown since Gerard's time, and if you open any seedsman's catalogue today you will find that all kinds of cultivated flowers of the genus *Campanula* are called Canterbury Bells, some of them huge exotic flowers that bear only a distant resemblance to the real bell.

Then the verb "to canter" is, of course, a contraction of a "Canterbury gallop", which was the easy hand gallop into which the pilgrims urged their horses, possibly when they came to level stretches of the South Downs. It has also been claimed that the word "cant", meaning religious jargon, is derived from Canterbury, but I am not at all sure of this. But the phrase "to tell a Canterbury", or lie, was one used by the Puritans, and though it has long since fallen out of use in this country, it was carried across the Atlantic by the Pilgrim Fathers, and may still be heard in the United States.

Soon after the Cathedral was open in the morning, I went there and asked if I might see some of the treasures.

The most beautiful object was a thin, hand-beaten chalice of silver-gilt that was discovered in the grave of a man buried in the year 1205. The man was Hubert Walter, Archbishop of Canterbury in the time of Richard Cœur de Lion. When his grave was opened in 1892, those who were present at the time looked with awe as they saw for one second, before the air caused the body to fall into dust, an archbishop vested, with his crosier beside him, just as he had been buried by the monks of Canterbury six hundred and eighty-seven years previously.

It is believed that Hubert Walter took the chalice with him to the Holy Land, when he went with Richard on the Third Crusade. If so, it was used at Mass long ago, among the palm trees at Acre. It does not often fall to any man's lot to hold a relic such as this.

There is not a place to which this chalice travelled in Palestine that I do not know. I have wandered through the ruins of Acre, Ascalon, Tyre and Sidon, watching the Mediterranean rollers come swinging in from the sea, to break in foam against the piles of masonry that were fortresses in the days when Hubert Walter said Mass with the English army. He was the outstanding man of his time, and the strong man of England. He was a good man and, like many an early churchman, stood between the people and the tyranny of king and noble. It was said of him that "he was so bountiful in providing for the poor and the wayfarer that his income seemed common property".

It was Hubert Walter who, when Richard foolishly got himself into prison on the Continent, went round England with the hat and raised the fabulous ransom (in those days) of £100,000. I have always felt that he might have spent it to better purpose, for Richard, our dear hero, could not speak English, knew nothing of England and, out of a reign of ten years, spent only nine months in this country!

Walter ruled England when the King was away. Among his constitutional innovations was the appointment of coroners. Few J.P.s know perhaps that they owe their office to him, for he appointed knights whose duty it was to enforce an oath to "keep the peace", and such knights developed into our Justices of the Peace. When Richard died, Hubert Walter crowned John. He was the only person in England who could stand up to this King, and when he died John remarked: "Now, for the first time am I truly King of England."

Such was the great man whose chalice, after lying for six hundred and eighty-seven years in the darkness of the tomb, is sometimes used in Canterbury Cathedral today. There are more ornate and more costly chalices in the world, but not one, I think, of greater interest.

We ascended spiral staircases to the triforium, then up again into the dark passages above the nave and transepts. It was like walking under the timbers of an old ship, dark and dusty, with only an occasional handrail to guide one over the narrow planks that stretch across the vaulting. This is the exquisite roof visitors admire from the floor of the church, but from this position it looks like a crop of enormous stone mushrooms growing in the darkness.

Perhaps few of those who admire the glory of Canterbury, or any other cathedral, know that between vaulting and roofing is this vast V-shaped no-man's-land where the wind whistles through slit windows, where pigeons nest and bats hang from rafters cut from oaks that were probably giants at the time of the Norman Conquest.

There was no beauty in this dim and unvisited region, but we explored it eagerly, discussing the marvels of thrust and counter-thrust and admiring the workmen who built this stupendous church centuries ago.

We ascended the steps of the central tower, known as the Bell Harry Tower, but before we had gone very far we saw what must be one of the few medieval cranes in existence. It is a gigantic wheel that was used by the masons of the Middle Ages to lift heavy stones from ground-level to the summit of towers. It was worked by manpower. Several workmen stationed inside the wheel would walk, as if on a treadmill, which caused the wheel to revolve and wind up a rope to which stones were attached.

It is still in perfect order, although I don't suppose it has been used for five centuries. Standing inside it, I discovered that the balance is so delicate than when I placed one foot only a few inches in advance of the other, the huge wheel began to turn.

We climbed still higher—much higher—and came out on the summit of Bell Harry Tower, where the stone, now in process of restoration, is eaten away by wind and rain. Below us lay Canterbury in the calmness of a spring morning. The trees so far below hardly moved in the breeze, though a sharp wind was blowing across the tower. From this height the huge cruciform building looks like a giant aeroplane, the transepts its wings, the body of the church its fuselage.

The bells, dismantled during the reconstructions, lay mouths up, the heavy clappers resting against the rim, where a spot of bright bronze marked the striking point.

We descended those exhausting steps to the ground and looked at the Cathedral from the outside. The Archbishop of Canterbury's Palace is joined to the Cathedral by the Great Cloister, and, although it is a modern building, it stands on the ground occupied by the Palace of the early primates.

It was from that Palace that Thomas à Becket took sanctuary in the Cathedral on the night of the murder, and there are three stairs left in the Palace on which he must have walked that night. . . .

I had no idea that the Archbishop of Canterbury lived in such a modest house. The word "palace" is purely a formal title, for many a penurious vicar would be grateful for so small a vicarage.

On the upper floor we found the fragmentary remains of an old stone staircase, with three of the original treads remaining. It was the same kind of narrow stone tube in which we had spent so much time that morning when we climbed to the roof. In this house it is clearly seen how, when the murderers had armed and were ready to do their work, Becket left this building unseen by them, using a small, private door that once opened into the cloisters.

Civilised adult human beings are rarely in the habit of falling into ungovernable rages, of biting the carpet in fury and exhibiting other signs well known in badly conducted nurseries. But in early times our kings and nobles were not ashamed to give such violent exhibitions.

On a night towards the end of December, in the year 1170, King Henry II of England, who was then at the Castle of Bur, near Bayeux, fell into one of these royal rages. The cause of his anger was the action of Becket, who for eighteen years had been fighting the State's attempt to dominate the Church. The King loathed Becket as only an autocrat can loathe an equally strong rival, and what perhaps made their relationship even worse was that, before Becket had entered the Church, he had been a gay man of the world and the King's favourite. No people can fight more bitterly than old companions.

Henry had forced Becket to be Archbishop against his will, because he wished to have a complacent friend at the head of the Church he wished to subdue. But he had chosen the wrong man. No sooner was Becket consecrated than he ceased to be the King's man and became God's man; from that moment, and for eighteen years, the story of England is the fight between the Church and State, between Becket and Henry.

On that night in December Henry worked himself into a frightful paroxysm. He called Becket "a fellow that came to Court on a lame horse with a cloak for a saddle". He said that a man he had "loaded with benefits" was insulting him. Then, turning to the assembled courtiers, he shouted:

"What sluggard wretches, what cowards have I brought up in my Court, who care nothing for their allegiance to their master! Not one will deliver me from this lowborn priest!" He rushed from the hall.

That same night four men crossed the Channel, Reginald Fitzurse, William de Tracy, Richard le Breton and Hugh de Moreville. They crossed by different routes, two arriving at Dover and two at Winchelsea. They rode to Saltwood Castle, near Canterbury, which was held by one of Becket's enemies, Dan

Randolph of Broc, and there, in a darkened room, they discussed a plan of action. It was the twenty-eighth of December.

The murder of the Archbishop is one of the best-documented events in medieval history. He was slain in the Fleet Street of his time—if I may be forgiven the comparison—surrounded by the only reporters of that age, the monks and priests of the Church. Some who stood beside him, some who ran away and hid, others who vested his corpse for burial, have left descriptions from which it is possible to paint a true picture of that night seven hundred and sixty-nine years ago.

In addition to many contemporary narratives, there are no fewer than five eyewitness accounts of Becket's death: the account of William of Canterbury, a monk: William Fitzstephen, a clerk in attendance on Becket; Benedict, another monk who was there; John of Salisbury; and Edward Grim, a clerk of Cambridge, who was on a visit to Becket at the time. From these five accounts it is possible to reconstruct the murder in every detail—and this is what happened:

On the twenty-ninth of December, the day after the four knights had crossed the Channel, at three in the afternoon Becket sat down to dinner in the hall of the Archbishop's Palace, which was separated from the Cathedral by the Great Cloister. He sat at the high table with his household and the monks, while at the long table sat the poor people and beggars whom he entertained every day. The floor was covered with fresh hay; the smoke of burning logs ascended through the hall, and the grey light of a December afternoon shone beyond the narrow windows.

At the end of dinner, after a thanksgiving had been sung, Becket went to his retiring-room, and the servants flung themselves on the broken meats. The sound was heard of horses clattering into the courtyard. In a few moments four knights in ordinary dress strode into the hall through the crowds of departing beggars.

The servants asked if the visitors would like something to eat, but they refused and went to Becket's room. The Archbishop, seated on a couch, was leaning on the shoulder of a monk, while monks reclined on the floor near him. He was over six feet tall, handsome and with a keen and piercing eye. He was fifty-two years of age and, though his figure was really spare, he felt the cold so acutely that he wore an incredible number of garments in order to keep warm; these gave him a padded, corpulent appearance.

As the knights entered, he continued to talk with the monk next to him. They came in silently, without a greeting and sat on the floor at his feet. Then Becket looked at them and spoke to Tracy by name. The knights began to talk violently.

They charged Becket with undermining the royal authority and with causing disturbances, and they demanded that he should lift the ban of excommunication from the Bishops of London and Salisbury. Becket, who was a man of quick temper, also raised his voice, and soon knights and Archbishop were quarrelling violently.

The knights flew into one of their Norman passions and stamped about the room, twisting their long gauntlets, advancing close to Becket, gnashing their teeth and waving their arms. They screamed that he had threatened to excommunicate them; he shouted back that they could not frighten him.

"Were all the swords in England hanging over my head," he shouted, "you could not terrify me from my obedience to God, and my lord the Pope."

Crowds of monks and servants ran into the room and gathered round Becket. The knights roared at them to stand back if they were loyal to the King. They refused to move. The room was soon a pandemonium, and through it the knights ran to the door shouting, "To arms, to arms!"

It was now nearly five o'clock. The winter's darkness had fallen. Beneath a sycamore tree in the courtyard the knights put on their armour. The monks bolted the doors and Becket sat down again on his couch.

"It is wonderful, my lord," said John of Salisbury, "that you never take anyone's advice."

"I am prepared to die," replied Becket stubbornly.

Some of the monks, discussing the scene together, believed there was nothing to fear, as William Fitzstephen noted, "the men had come drunk" and "would not have spoken like that before dinner". Others were not so sanguine. At this moment a frightened monk rushed in to say the knights were arming. All save a few companions fled into the Cathedral. "All monks are cowards," said Becket. His attendants, believing that the knights would not dare to shed blood on consecrated ground, forced Becket against his will to leave the Palace. Half pushed, half lifted, he was taken through the cloisters and into the dark church, where vespers had just begun. As they gained what some of them hoped was sanctuary, they heard behind them the crash of woodwork as the knights broke into the Palace.

What then happened took place almost in darkness, a gloom lit only by tapers burning before the shrines. A hammering echoed through the church. Becket ordered the doors to be opened, and when no one would do it he strode forward and himself flung back the bars. A terrified crowd of monks fought to enter. Becket helped them, saying, "Come in, come in, faster, faster!"

By this time the church was full of flying and hiding men. Only three remained with the Archbishop: Robert of Merton, William Fitzstephen, his chaplain and

Edward Grim, the clerk. They tried to get Becket to hide in the crypt or in the triforium, where he would never have been discovered, but he declined to do so. At last they persuaded him to mount the steps from the north transept, in which they were standing, to the choir, but, as they did so, the knights, covered to the eyes in chain mail, broke into the church. Fitzurse came first, with a sword in one hand and a carpenter's axe, which he had picked up in the Palace, in the other. He could see nothing in the darkness, and stood calling for the "traitor Becket". There was silence. He called again, and then Becket came down the steps.

"Reginald, why do you come into my church armed?" he asked.

Fitzurse placed the carpenter's axe against Becket's chest and said:

"You shall die. I will tear out your heart!"

"I am ready to die," replied Becket, "for God and the Church, but I warn you, I curse you in the name of God Almighty, if you do not let my men escape."

The knights, fearing to commit sacrilege, then tried to hustle Becket out of the church. "I will not fly, you detestable fellow!" he shouted, pushing Fitzurse away. Then they tried to place him on Tracy's shoulders, but Becket seized Tracy and flung him to the floor. At that moment Fitzurse came up with lifted sword, and Becket, now furious, cried out, "You profligate wretch, you are my man—you have done me fealty—you ought not to touch me!"

Fitzurse shouted back: "I owe you no fealty or homage contrary to my fealty to the King", and made a blow at Becket's head. It did not touch him, but knocked back his skull-cap.

Tracy then came up and aimed a blow that the clerk, Grim, who had his arm round Becket, tried to parry. The blow cut Grim's arm, grazed the crown of Becket's head and also cut into his shoulder.

"For the name of Jesus, and the defence of the Church, I am ready to die," whispered Becket and, with those words, fell flat on his face. Richard le Breton stood over him and delivered a tremendous blow that severed the top of the skull; so violent a blow that the sword snapped as it met the marble floor.

Hugh of Horsea, a subdeacon who had joined the murderers, was then taunted with having taken no part in the murder. He came up and thrust his sword into the wound, scattering Becket's brains over the pavement.

So, with Becket newly slain on the pavement of his church, the murderers, beside themselves with rage and triumph, ran through the cloisters, shouting "The King's men, the King's men!" as if they had been in battle, for that was the war-cry of the English; as they rode away, a thunderstorm of great violence broke over Canterbury, striking terror into the hearts of the people.

That night a strange scene took place before the high altar. The monks undressed the body of Becket for burial. They took off the incredible assortment of

55 *The Roman Baths at Bath, Somerset*

56 *The River Avon, Bath*

57 *Gloucester Cathedral*

58 *Clopton Bridge and the River Avon, Stratford-on-Avon, Warwickshire*

59 *Holy Trinity Church and the River Avon, Stratford-on-Avon*

60 *Harvard House, Stratford-on-Avon*

garments covering him. First a brown mantle, then a white surplice, then a long coat of lamb's wool, then two woollen pelisses, then—to their utter astonishment —the black robe of a Benedictine monk. At the sight of it their grief and emotion knew no bounds. It astounded them to think that the Archbishop, whom they regarded as a great noble, fond of purple and fine linen, should have secretly assumed a monk's habit.

"See what a true monk he was, and we knew it not!" they sobbed.

A greater surprise awaited them. When they stripped the body, they saw that Becket wore a hair shirt next to his skin, and that beneath it his body was marked with the weals of scourging. So he was a more austere monk than any of them!

Then they saw a thing that is nauseating to our minds today, but in those days proved beyond doubt that this man had subdued the flesh and humiliated the body in order that his soul might shine; they saw that Becket's hair shirt crawled with vermin. Their joy and amazement at this revolting sight were boundless, and they cried, as indeed I can imagine a Coptic monk of Egypt crying today: "He was one of God's saints!"

So on the very night he died, within a few hours of his martyrdom, Thomas à Becket was hailed as St. Thomas of Canterbury.

The townspeople who had filled the Cathedral during the murder fought for pieces of his attire and, washing the bloodstains, took them away as sacred relics. Miracles were reported almost at once. No one can say that they were invented by the monks, because the Cathedral, having been desecrated, was closed for a year; the altars were stripped; the crucifixes were veiled; the bells were silenced; and the offices were conducted in the Chapter House without chanting. Indeed, there was every reason why the monks were desperately anxious to hush up the growing cult of St. Thomas, for fear of the King and the terrible Randolph of Broc, who had seized the Archbishop's Palace and was their next-door neighbour. The measures taken to hush up these miracles from motives of fear and policy, and the failure to do so, is one of the most curious stories in the history of medieval pilgrimage. Despite every discouragement, crowds of people began to visit Canterbury to pray at Becket's tomb, to touch his garments or to apply to afflicted portions of the body water in which the Archbishop's blood had been mixed. The wave of horror that had swept over Christendom was succeeded by a feeling of amazement and wonder when stories of the cures and miracles began to get about. The Pope was obliged to send a legation to England to inquire into them. They took back with them part of a tunic stained with Becket's blood, a fragment of his brain and some portions of the pavement on which he died, relics that are still preserved in the Church of Santa Maria Maggiore in Rome. The result of the inquiry was the canonisation of Becket three years after his murder and the appointment of 29 December as the Feast of St. Thomas of Canterbury. There was now no further need for concealment. Canterbury became one of the great pilgrimage shrines in Europe. Churches dedicated to St. Thomas sprang up in Christian countries all over the world. And four years after the murder a wonder-stricken, but approving world, heard that Henry II, barefoot and in sackcloth, had gone on foot to Canterbury to be scourged at Becket's tomb.

[6]

When I arrived at Walmer I found it to be the one day in the week, a Thursday, on which the Castle, the residence of the Lord Warden of the Cinque Ports, is open to the public.

I bought a ticket and was admitted to a garden that I thought was almost perfect. It was simple and full of colour and scent, and its peculiarity is that it lies on the edge of the moat that runs round the Castle.

I should have been willing to while away my sixpenny ticket in the garden, enjoying the scent of the flowers and the hum of the bees, but I felt that I ought to know something about the rooms in which the Iron Duke lay down his eighty-three years.

An official took me through a fearsome-looking gateway into a house that has been made almost hysterically cheerful in contrast to the grim bastions of its exterior. The problem of making a home out of a rugged mass of masonry, constructed with the sole object of repelling first the Spaniards and then the French cannot have been easy. Lord and Lady Willingdon, who were in residence, suffer the public to tramp through their drawing-room once a week, on the way to the room where the Duke of Wellington died in 1852.

As soon as I entered this room, I was completely captured. Its sternness, its simplicity, its touch of almost priggish discomfort and its lonely pathos, seemed to reflect the life that had been lived there. It has been kept, whether by accident or design I do not know, almost exactly as it was the day he died. Nothing has been altered. You almost expect the door to open and to see the old Duke, hook-nosed and silver-haired, glide in with a frosty gleam of blue eyes.

Wellington made no concessions to old age. With the whole of Walmer Castle to live in, he preferred one small bed-sitting room modelled on the tent of a subaltern—and a frugal subaltern at that. His bed was an iron camp-bed three feet wide. He allowed himself no luxurious blankets, but only a German quilt. The one sybaritic touch is a horsehair pillow covered with chamois leather, and this he used to take about with him whenever he spent a night away.

A mahogany desk, a few books, a few engravings, a reading-desk at which he wrote his letters standing and one or two chairs complete the furniture. An ivory statuette of Napoleon sitting astride a chair once stood on the mantelpiece.

"That was how he commanded at the Battle of Wagram," Wellington once told a certain Mr. Tucker as he pointed to the statue. Such was the simple room in which the hero of Waterloo spent much of his life from the age of sixty until his death.

"He was always called at six of a morning," said the guide in an appropriately military voice. "He went for an early morning walk, ate very little breakfast, came up here and read, or wrote letters standing at that desk by the window. He answered all his letters himself, and people used to write to him about all sorts of silly things, just to get a reply. Sometimes they got ticked off good and proper. At eleven-thirty at night he used to light a candle and come up here to bed."

This grand old Tory, who resisted every reform with the stern formality of his native century, the eighteenth, remained a national hero all his later life, with one brief exception. When he opposed the Reform Bill, he rode slowly through London, high-nosed and bleak, to the jeers of a mob and to a hail of brickbats and mud. As he reached Apsley House in Piccadilly, he turned and said to the police constable by his side: "An odd day for them to choose." He had remembered that it was the anniversary of Waterloo.

As he grew older, his role merged naturally from that of Achilles into that of Nestor. They consulted him about everything. When the Crystal Palace was first erected in Hyde Park, the London sparrows failed to show proper respect for the assembled works of art, and with so much glass about it was impossible to shoot them. So the Queen sent for the Duke: The dear Duke would know what to do.

"Try sparrow-hawks, Ma'am," he said instantly.

"It was Wellington's last victory," commented Philip Guedalla, in *The Duke*.

Perhaps his last victory was really the conquest of age. At eighty he was as bright and sprightly as a robin. To the public, he was always a tight-buttoned, reserved figure, aloof from the warmer passions of life, and great would have been the astonishment could the public have seen the Duke now and then behind the ramparts of Walmer.

He loved children to stay with him. Before dinner he would dress, always in the uniform of Lord Warden, a blue coat with red facings and tight, white overalls strapped under the boot and would sit reading the newspaper. The children then played a game they called "the Battle of Waterloo". This began when one of them threw a cushion at the Duke's paper.

He died in the little bastion room after only a few hours' illness. "I feel very ill," he said to his valet. "Send for the apothecary." Those were his last words. He had a fit in the night and died the next day, aged eighty-three. He was buried to the sound of a nation's grief, and when the guns boomed across London, as his funeral car swayed through the hushed streets to St. Paul's, England said farewell to the eighteenth century.

The guide took me downstairs to a room fitted up as a museum. I saw the last coat worn by Wellington and the telescope he used at Waterloo.

There were two gruesome relics: his death mask and the silk handkerchief that was used to tie up his jaw. A certificate attached to the handkerchief, signed by James Kendle, the valet, stated that the handkerchief slipped from the jaw but the knot never became untied, and so remains today the knot that was made on 14 September 1852.

While I was looking at these things, a huge man, almost as wide as he was tall, came into the room. He was bubbling over with vitality and high spirits. Buried in the flesh of his huge face was the mischievous countenance of a boy of ten.

He swept up the guide and myself in his terrific enthusiasm, and soon we were listening to a lecture about the Iron Duke. It was a good lecture. We tried to interrupt it once or twice, but without success.

"Wellington was a grand old boy," he said. "Although I don't agree with any of his politics, he was a grand old boy. I'm writing a book to be called *Pattern of English Life*, in which I have a lot to say about the old man. You heard some of my book inside, didn't you?"

"I was interested to hear you call Wellington the first modern English gentleman."

"I think the modern idea of the Englishman as a quiet, silent, stoical bloke, who considers it bad form to show his feelings, dates from Wellington. His influence on English life was so terrific that the public-school Englishman copies his un-emotionalism. 'Behaving like a gentleman' was Wellington's contribution to English manners.

"As a nation we are by nature emotional to a degree. We're sloppy and senti-mental, and it's only within the last century that crying in public has gone out of fashion. Think of the Elizabethans! They were always in tears. The whole House of Commons used to burst out crying! Think of Nelson, an Englishman of the old type, emotional, sentimental, bombastic. How different were Nelson and Wellington; what worlds apart they were! On the only occasion they ever met, in a waiting-room in Whitehall, Wellington thought Nelson was no gentle-man. Why? Simply because Nelson talked too much. It wasn't done! 'Kiss me, Hardy!' Can you imagine Wellington saying that? Of course you can't. It was the voice of good old dramatic, tearful, Elizabethan England. Nelson was the last Elizabethan. Wellington was the first modern English gentleman."

[7]

I set off to cross the high chalk downs into Hampshire late in the afternoon with the vague idea of reaching Winchester by bedtime. Several side roads got in the way, so that in no time I found myself lost in a tangle of up-and-down lanes that connect village to village. When taking my bearings I saw on the summit of the highest down an object that I took to be a flagstaff. But why a flagstaff on the bald head of a great hill? I took out binoculars and saw a gallows standing up there, a mark for several counties, firm and unmistakable, as if ready for a hanging.

A gibbet!

Before climbing the steep road I thought I would ask a few questions. I stopped a labourer on a bicycle.

"What is that on the hill?"

"Gallows," he said suspiciously.

"Who was hanged there?"

"Dunno."

"When was it last used?"

"Dunno."

"Have you ever heard any story about it?"

"No."

I discovered that he had been born and bred in the shadow of Inkpen Beacon, which is the name of this hill. The next man was just as negative; so was a third. Dusk was falling. I decided to waste no more time. The road climbed round and round: To the right lay a misty panorama of distant green fields, dark clumps of trees, tiny white roads like threads intersecting them, the whole view shut in by low-sailing, dark clouds. I left the car at the end of the road and struck off over grassland.

Soon the top of the gallows showed itself, outlined against the pale sky as I advanced, and in a few moments I was standing on a high mound, with before me a great dip in which, a thousand feet below, lay Hampshire, like a green table.

No gallows I have ever read of has been complete without wind whistling through it. Combe Gallows lives up to the tradition. The wind tore through it, screamed past it, so that I had to hold on to it; it vibrated slightly in the wind. It was eerie standing up there so near the slow-moving clouds, with dark coming and no one near, only the low bushes bent forward in the wind, and a few drops of rain falling.

What grim crime was commemorated by this old cross? I noticed that the wood was not of one date. The gallows had been repaired in fairly recent times. That struck me as curious. A white paper fluttered in the wind from four nails. Suppose this told the history of the crime! I read with difficulty—for it was almost dark —the following words: "Teas can be obtained at Combe."

That sent the skeleton back to the bushes! I laughed and went back along the grass to the car.

This is the story of Combe Gallows, unravelled later in Winchester Library. On 7 March 1676, a man and a woman were hanged on this gibbet, and their bodies exposed as a warning to all sinners. Their names were George Browman and Dorothy Newman, and they were hanged for the brutal murder of two children the woman had had by a former husband. The children's bodies were discovered in the little hill pond near the gallows.

The strange part of the story is this: The gallows owes its existence to a clause in the lease of Eastwich Farm, at the foot of the hill. The tenants of this farm have for two hundred and fifty years been obliged to keep the gallows in repair. The present gibbet is the third erected on the site. I am told that a charity in Combe owes its existence to the upkeep of the gallows. If the gallows disappears, so does the charity.

[8]

I must tell you that as I dipped into Winchester at eight o'clock they were ringing the curfew from the Guildhall—a bell that has been ringing for eight hundred and sixty years. Such a snug, friendly old town—a town full of bells, for it was practice night at the Cathedral.

By bedtime a hush had fallen over Winchester, and I put my head out of the window in the hope of seeing King Alfred's ghost riding down the street, but it was raining, and the street was empty.

The rain ceased in the night and, awakening early as one does in a strange room, I saw a brightness behind the blind that told me the sun was shining. Winchester was not yet awake. It was that lovely hour in early spring when the world, it seems, is swept and furbished for a festival. As I walked through the empty streets I wondered when the citizens of Winchester, now snuggling down into that last self-indulgent half-hour of bed, would soon realise their folly and, opening their doors, come tumbling out to go a-Maying. A thrush was singing in the Cathedral limes, and the sun, still low in the east, played early morning tricks in the streets, gilding unexpected places, casting improbable shadows. It was mellow over that old school that has sent so many men into the world labelled. You can generally tell them at a glance, especially in the law courts when they rise for the prosecution and, with a kind of cold pleasure, stab the rhetoric of the defence with an intellectual instrument forged at Winchester—*aut disce, aut discede, manet sors tertia caedi,*★ someone who knew Winchester (it may have been Wren) carved that on the wall of "School" in 1683!

I went on, thinking that if one were looking for the germ of the British Empire it is to be found in this quiet little city of Winchester. The princes of this city emerged from their long war with the Danes as the kings of Wessex, who later became the kings of England; and it was the royal city of Winchester that was truly the very heart of England until Westminster Hall and the Abbey gathered round them the royal city of a new England.

Sitting on a sunny wall, I tried to look back into a time when many a poor swineherd raked the embers of his fire over a Roman pavement. The fern and the elder tree were pushing asunder the walls of London, and I wondered how many strange tales were whispered beyond the walls at night of ghosts in the old dead city on the hill. Did any man prowling those empty streets by day rest awhile upon the statue of a fallen Caesar holding in either hand a statue of Christ and Isis and wondering who they were? What a mist it is into which a man looks from a wall in Winchester! "The era of Celt, Saxon and Dane is like Macbeth's battle on the blasted heath," says G. M. Trevelyan in his *History of England*. "Prophecy hovers around. Horns are heard blowing in the mist, and a confused uproar of savage tumult and outrage. We catch glimpses of giant figures—mostly warriors at strife. But there are ploughmen, too, it seems, breaking the primeval clod, and we hear the sound of forests crashing to the axe. Around all is the lap of the waves and the cry of seamen beaching their ships."

Surely there was also, as the prophetic mist blows aside a little, a glimpse of men walking the old Roman roads of England bearing a cross, the legions returning with shaven heads? Surely the most important sound in that mist was the sound of chanting; surely the most gigantic figure, greater than Guthrum with his shield and sword, was the holy man under an oak tree talking to a bearded king about something strange and wonderful that happened long ago in Bethlehem? I think so. For Rome conquered England twice, once with a sword and once with a story, and as horns blew in the mist, and the warriors roared together at the palisades, the monasteries locked their doors on all that was left of civilisation or fled with their relics, still along the roads of Rome, conscious that they guarded the little flame of a new world. And it seems, as we look into this mist, that these

★"learn, leave, or be licked".

men from Rome, from Wales, from Ireland, ran through England, over the wild heathland, through the dark forests, crying their good news in the half-light as boys run through the streets of a city in the first hour of the New Year.

The Cathedral bell began to ring, and the birds were singing in the lime trees.

[9]

I went to see the Great Hall of the Castle of Winchester, all now left of the royal palace that stood on the traditional Castle of King Arthur. How the prestige of Winchester endured! When Henry VII wished to strengthen his hereditary claim to the throne in 1486 he could think of nothing better to his purpose than to bring his queen to Winchester in order that the heir to the throne might be born in the Castle there.

I expected to see more Norman work, but it is Early English, aisles, dormer windows and high, slim pillars of Purbeck marble. In Winchester Great Hall, and in how many other halls, castles, abbeys, earthworks and monasteries throughout England, the imagination halts before the richness of their associations!

The Round Table of King Arthur has hung for over five hundred years on the walls of Winchester Hall. It was first mentioned by John Hardyng in 1378:

> *The rounde Table of Wynchester beganne*
> *And there it ended and there it hangeth yet.*

Henry VIII brought the Emperor Charles V, when he was visiting England in 1522, to see this table, which he exhibited as one of the most interesting sights in the kingdom. It cannot, of course, be the Round Table of legend, but it is a fascinating piece of carpentry. It was repainted in Tudor times and shows King Arthur sitting crowned in Tudor robes. A point in favour of the legend is that it is large enough to seat a king and his twenty-four knights.

[10]

He was standing in the choir of Winchester Cathedral surrounded by the first tourists of the year. He was a clean-shaven man with the mobile face of an actor, shrewd, humorous eyes and white hair brushed straight back over his head. I learnt afterwards that he is well known in America.

Vergers as a class are not likeable. The profession of verging appears to induce

61 *Magdalen Tower and the River Cherwell, Oxford*

62 *Plas Newydd, Llangollen, Denbighshire*

63 *The Dee Bridge, Llangollen, North Wales*

64 *St David's Cathedral, Pembrokeshire*

65 *Whitesand Bay, St David's, South Wales*

66 *The Conway*
    Estuary, North
    Wales

67 *Conway Castle, Caernarvonshire*

mousy manners and complete ignorance of history. When I saw the verger of the Cathedral of the kings of Wessex, I edged up to the group miserably, thinking:

"I might write something about the balderdash these fellows hand out like cold muffins. . . ."

In two minutes I had discovered that the man was alive. He had imagination, magnetism; he had a real sense of history and a good technique; he threw out ground-bait and then began from the beginning and built up. A fat, middle-aged motorist who, I judged, had been too busy making money all his life to be more than eight years old in other things, stood gaping on the edge of the crowd; he seemed to be struggling reluctantly with a new point of view:

"This chap's good," he whispered, "isn't he? I expect he's pulling our legs a bit. He talks about the old days as if he was there. . . ."

As the man with the white hair talked in the silent choir of Winchester— before him the long sweep of that marvellous nave, on either side those lovely Norman transepts soaked in a pale gold light—he moved his hands in time to his words, and his eyes went over the group to each listener. There was not a shuffle. He had gripped them! They had come prepared to be bored; they stayed strangely thrilled by this man's enthusiasm and by the pictures he called up. That was it: He humanised the history book. . . .

We saw as he talked, down a long tunnel of time, the kings of Wessex riding through a country that was not yet England; we saw the longboats of the pirates pointed to our shores; we saw the Roman cities desolate on their hills. Darkness and fighting. We saw the monk from Rome come walking over English meadows; St. Augustine, preaching beside the pagan wells, bringing the Cross from Rome again, telling the world's greatest story to king, to noble, to common man. So the seed of all cathedrals was sown. The speaker then rebuilt Winchester stone by stone.

The old story, like all old stories told properly, took on new importance, became dramatic and somehow near at hand. The crowd had heard it before at school; but they had never *seen* it before.

"Who's coming up to the roof with me?" said the verger. "Come on, and you'll have the treat of your lives, and on the way I'll let you walk where the monks walked who day and night guarded the golden shrine of St. Swithin, which once stood where you are standing."

Up spiral staircases we went, holding on to ropes, feeling the smooth face of the stone in the dark, till we came to a dim, dusty tunnel crossed by a narrow wooden platform. We were walking above that lovely vaulted nave of Winchester, overhead was the roof, and crossways stretched vast oak beams that uphold the structure.

"Just look at them!" he said. "Eight hundred years old, and as good as new. The architect who was here the other day says that all they need is a little lead treatment. And those giant oaks were felled by the Normans! Come on, mind your heads!"

We came to that eerie spot where the great bells of Winchester tick off time so patiently, and here this amusing verger lined us up—solemn elderly women, fat men, thin men and little children—gave each one of us a bell, delivered a lecture on bell-ringing, numbered us off from the right and, pointing to each one in turn as he wished him to ring, drew forth from the unpromising assembly "Abide with me".

We were delighted with ourselves.

Up we went again, and round and round, till we bent under a little stone doorway and came out on the roof of the Cathedral; below us London's old rival—Winchester!

We looked down on the tops of feathery lime trees, on the river and the distant hills, the little town lying pleasantly in a blue haze of smoke from its chimneys: Winchester!

"I love it," said the verger. "You ought to come up here on a moonlit night and look down. You can imagine things: You can see ghosts. . . ."

"You must," I said, "have devoted your life to this."

"When I was appointed verger, the spirit of Winchester gripped me, and I knew that I had found my right job. I love every stone of this Cathedral."

"Who are your most intelligent listeners?" I asked him.

"American women over forty!" he replied instantly.

Down we all trooped over those sheer corkscrew stairs and out into the lime avenue. We found that we all knew each other. We all shook hands before we parted. Such is the power of one man's enthusiasm!

[11]

I was walking between Compton and Winchester in the morning when I came upon a tattered old man sitting by the side of the road. He was, he told me, "looking for odd jobs", but there was something about him that implied that if an odd job showed itself he would look keenly enough, but in the opposite direction.

When we came to the outskirts of Winchester, he caught sight of another shabby figure ahead and began to hurry.

"I don't wanter miss my beer," he mumbled.

"Your beer?" I said. "You can't get beer now; it's not yet ten o'clock."

"I can get beer all right," he told me, "as long as those blinkin' —— [he was a nasty-mouthed old man] don't swill it all down first!"

We came to a lane that led to the River Itchen, and at the end of the lane was a lovely grey gatehouse leading to a courtyard, beyond which stood a second gateway framing a gracious picture of green trees and old grey stone buildings —rather like the Charterhouse.

Round the porter's hatchway at this second gate were two or three seedy-looking men, drinking out of horn mugs and eating dry white bread. My unpleasant old friend hurried up, pushed through the group, rapped on the door, which was opened by an aged porter, and said:

"Gimme the wayfarer's dole!"

Immediately the porter handed out a horn full of ale and a big slice of white bread.

"Won't you offer me the wayfarer's dole?" I asked.

The porter put his head out.

"We never offer the wayfarer's dole," he replied. "You have to ask for it."

"Well, please give me the wayfarer's dole!"

Promptly appeared his hand, holding a horn of ale and a slice of bread.

I went in through the gateway to the Hospital of St. Cross.

In the year 1136 Henry de Blois founded the Hospital of St. Cross to shelter "thirteen poor men, feeble and so reduced in strength that they can hardly or with difficulty support themselves without another's aid". They were to be provided "with garments and beds suitable to their infirmities, good wheaten bread daily of the weight of 5 marks, and three dishes at dinner and one at supper suitable to the day, and drink of good stuff". The Hospital was also to give food and drink to poor wanderers who came to its gates.

This has been going on for seven hundred and ninety years. The Hospital still retains its ancient charter and its buildings. The poor Brethren of St. Cross are still sheltered by the ancient walls; the poor men still come from the king's highway and are not refused.

St. Cross is the oldest almshouse in England.

Such places are so steeped in the peace of unhurried years that they seem out of the world: You feel that the worries of life have ceased at the gates. On the west side of the lawns stand the houses of the Brethren distinguished by tall chimneys, each house containing, like those of the Carthusians, two rooms, a pantry and a garden. Over the smooth grass, in the shadow of the gracious grey stones, walk the ancient Brethren of St. Cross, each one in a long gown, with a silver cross worn on his breast. When a Brother dies his silver cross is cut from his gown and placed on a red velvet cushion, which is placed over his heart in the coffin. Then it is removed, and the Master of St. Cross fastens it on the gown of the next Brother, thus admitting him into the Hospital.

"There's a waiting list as long as your arm," said a smiling old Brother. "We are very lucky to end our days here. Would you care to see the church?"

We went into one of the finest Transition-Norman churches I have ever seen: a calm, majestic, splendidly proportioned church, with great stone columns down the nave, vast as giant oak trunks. When the church was restored recently, traces of colour were found on the stones, and this colour has been renewed. The church is a mass of geometric patterns in red and blue and yellow. It was painted in 1866 and the colours used reproduce those discovered beneath the lime-wash that then covered the church. Few people, so the Brother told me, like this colouring, but I do: It has brought the church to life in an amazing way; there is nothing cold and unclothed about it.

The Brethren's Hall where, for centuries, old men have eaten their "mortrell" of "was-tell" and milk, or herring-pie and, sometimes, "plum broth", not forgetting, of course, their "galiones" of small beer, is a building that dignifies the word charity. A study of charity through the ages is a good subject for a man with the taste to write it, and in this hall we are in touch with an age that gave nobly and gladly. Side by side with hideous cruelty and callousness existed this pious love for "the poor of Christ". There is a raised hearth in the centre of the Hall round which the Brethren gathered at a charcoal fire. At one end of the room is a delicious gallery in which the minstrels played on great occasions.

When passing through the gateway I stopped to talk to the porter about the wayfarer's dole.

"Every day," he said, "we give away two gallons of beer and two loaves of bread, divided into thirty-two portions. It's just a snack, but a very old one, for it goes back over seven hundred years."

About thirty wayfarers—mostly tramps who appreciate the horn of ale—receive the dole each day.

In the lane I met a tramp hurrying along with an anxious face.

"It's all right," I shouted. "You're in time!"

And I thought what a strange sight it would be could one assemble all the men, and women, too, who have hurried down that lane with empty stomachs in the course of nearly eight centuries of wayfaring.

[12]

Here, in Beaulieu—they pronounce it Bewley—nothing happens or, it seems, could happen except the coming and going of the tide in the river, the budding and the falling of the leaves, the rising and the setting of the sun and the moon. . . .

This is a strange, lonely place in the middle of the last of England's great forests. I am inclined to think that it is one of the strangest places I know. The people are slow Saxons, well-mannered, deferential people, with their wits about them and their tongues padlocked. Their ancestors most wisely took to cover when William Rufus came crashing through the bracken in search of the stag that—as you remember—led to a grave. They are still good at taking cover behind the barriers of their reticence. The place, like the people, encourages a delicious slowness. You feel that London with all its fret is not quite so important in the ultimate scheme of things as Mr. Smith's new litter of pigs; and it seems to you as you lean against a fence in a portentous silence that those things men break their hearts upon are not worth so much in the long run as the sight of the moon tangled up in the boughs of a young birch wood. Heresy, of course!

It would be fatal to stay too long in Beaulieu; you would wish for nothing better than to lean over Mr. Smith's pigsty or to stand by the mill stream and watch the stars grow bright in the evening.

This tiny hamlet with its magnificent Abbey ruin was from 1204 till 1539 one of the chief places in England to which the murderer, the thief, the plotter and the general fugitive from justice flew literally for his life. Once within the wall no one could touch him: "The peace of the Church" was over him like a shield, and the Sheriff might bang on the great gates as loud as Judgement Day and the knights might ride round the wall for as long as they liked with their swords drawn, but the fox had gone to holy earth; he was as safe as though he had never sinned!

Through the Middle Ages Beaulieu must have entertained one of the world's record assemblies of rogues and vagabonds: men who dared not take one step outside the walls. The white monks farmed the land and fished the river, saying Mass every day in the lovely Abbey Church; and I suppose no one was startled or excited at so usual a sight as that of a man on a winded horse riding full tilt at the gate to join the brotherhood of the hunted. I imagine that the Abbot of Beaulieu owned a visitors' book rather like Scotland Yard's file of wanted faces!

All that remains of this old storm is a tall ruin in the light of that same moon on the banks of that same river. The evil seems to have gone from Beaulieu, but the feeling of sanctuary remains; the feeling—it may seem a strange thing to say—

that "the Peace of the Church" is still over the fields, making something more than solitude.

I thought in this way one evening when the tide was going out, and the sun was setting. It was low in the west behind trees, lost in a blaze of sudden, unexpected splendour.

There were two layers of cloud, one low and moving, the other high and stationary. The low clouds were indigo-blue and stormy; the high a soft, apricot-pink colour. The west was burning with gold light, and the edges of the dark clouds were etched with thin lines of fire. The pageant moved, changed . . . the river against the sun was a sheet of dull silver on which a jet-black duck moved noiselessly; a swan, silhouetted as if cut out of black paper, swam with his neck beneath the water; a wind came fretting the river, blowing a handful of pale blossoms into the grass. The hush of evening deepened. I could hear a dog barking far away, and the words of two men talking over a lichened wall were clear as bells.

Yes, said one, his garden could do with a week of sun, that it could. . . .

Click! went his spade against a pebble.

The water shivered in the fretful wind, the gold in the sky deepened and dulled; above it extended a pearly greyness, not so much the death of light as the birth of a new, unearthly light. . . .

There is one moment at sunset in the country when the whole visible world seems to gather itself in prayer, and it seems to you strange that men should move on unconscious of this with spades over their shoulders, instead of falling on their knees in the grass; for in that hush, in that benediction of seconds before the first star shines, the universe seems waiting for a revelation, as if the clouds might part and Man know something of his destiny. . . .

Lights shine in windows, there is the sound of steps on the road, someone laughs loudly, night falls and—the dream is gone.

The port of the little kingdom of Beaulieu is some three miles south along Beaulieu River; it is called Buckler's Hard.

Buckler is the name of a man who lived there centuries ago, and Hard refers to the character of the riverbank in this locality. Now when you enter Buckler's Hard you feel at once the queer atmosphere that clings to a place in which men have expended great energy; the village seems to be resting after effort. The street, as wide as Regent Street, is only a hundred yards long! It ends, as if cut off suddenly, in green hummocks and mounds on which cattle graze.

Below this single street standing among fields the ground falls gently to the banks of the Beaulieu River. The stream is wide at full tide and at low exposes a great tract of shallow, reedy bank. Beyond the river, wood lies piled on wood to the skyline.

When you walk beside the river you notice once again that evidence of a dead village buried under grass. Here are more green hummocks and mounds. Great timbers go down into the water, rotting and covered with weed. In the field are gigantic dips and hollows full of lush grass and flowers.

In those dips and on those rotting slipways once rested the stout oak-built ships that helped found the British Empire. This unknown, forgotten village in Hampshire was once loud with the sound of forge hammers, here thousands of great oak trees were formed into ships of the line; into the water of Beaulieu River was launched in 1781 the *Agamemnon*, a 64-gun ship of 1,384 tons burden, in which Nelson lost his right eye at the siege of Calvi.

The history of Buckler's Hard is, apart from its interest as a dead village that played its part in Empire, well worth telling; for it shows how swiftly time and fate can alter a place.

One hundred and fifty years ago, John, Duke of Montagu, then lord of the manor, owned the sugar-producing island of St. Vincent in the West Indies. His manor was stocked with fine oak trees, and his little port of Buckler's Hard was a free harbour—a legacy inherited from the old abbots of Beaulieu. What prevented his land from becoming a great centre of West Indian trade?

John Montagu, being a keen businessman, thought it would be a fine thing if he could steal a little of the shipbuilding trade from Southampton and transplant it to Buckler's Hard. He already had oak there and ironworks at Sowley Pond. All he required were shipbuilders. He got them. He offered quay frontages on a ninety-nine years' lease, at a yearly rent of six and eightpence! For every house erected he gave three loads of timber. The noble Duke used to stride the hill and rejoice in the sound of the builders' men; for the dream of his life was to create a great seaport in this sheltered wilderness, and he rechristened the village Montagu Town.

Henry Adams, the veteran shipbuilder, settled here, and soon the country was loud with hammers knocking against the wooden walls of England.

Between 1745 and 1808 about forty-four men-of-war were built and launched at Buckler's Hard. Here were built, in addition to *Agamemnon*, *Swiftsure* and *Euryalus*, whose guns thundered at Trafalgar.

This now desolate little village was the scene of great excitement when a ship was launched. Sometimes as many as ten thousand came from far and near to see the launching. Many came in tumbrels and farm wagons. Scaffolds were erected, and the great crowd waited—the ship on the slipway—watching for the tide to become full. It must have been an amazing sight: one bank of the little river buzzing with life and colour, the other peaceful and green, the woods stretching to the horizon. Then there would be shouting, "Off she goes—off she goes!" and a big 74-gun man-of-war would move slowly to the water with a band playing "God Save the King".

The wooden children of Buckler's Hard found their way about the world and discovered in their travels plenty of fighting. They carried the Union Jack into every quarrel that was going, their great keels cut foreign waters and met the French on every sea.

John, Duke of Montagu, who died at his house in Privy Gardens in 1749, five years after the hammers came to Buckler's Hard, went to Heaven with the belief, perhaps, that in Montagu Town he had founded another Portsmouth.

Time stepped in.

The wooden hulls gave place to the iron; the sail to the funnel. Gradually fewer and fewer ships were launched in Beaulieu River. Swift as had been the rise of the village, as swift was its fall. Its old name came back; and now the grass has come back; the wildfowl cries where once the caulking hammer sounded, and the heron perches on the great oak pathways from which ships of the line stepped majestically into our naval history. . . .

A ghostly place! When the last slipway cracks and falls into the water I would like to think that some old native will see, faint as if spun in mist on Beaulieu River, a gallant ship, her sails glimmering, her colours shot to shreds, come creeping home to Buckler's Hard to fade like a night fog into the English grass that gave her birth.

[13]

The four main streets of Chichester are called North, South, East and West Streets, and you will not find a better example in England of a city that was planned eighteen centuries ago by the legions of Rome.

The American gridiron cities, which we think so modern and sensible, were, of course, the rule in the Ancient World. No Greek or Roman would have been surprised by New York. Alexander the Great built Alexandria three hundred years before Christ just as a modern American architect would do: All the Hellenistic cities of the period were designed on the rectangular principle.

When, therefore, did the winding street and the narrow alley begin? I have an idea that goats and sheep are the architects of the medieval lane! When the Romans left this country, the defenceless inhabitants of the cities fled or were massacred by Saxon war bands. As the marauders were pastoral people, they

68 *Caernarvon Castle*

69 *Denbigh Castle, North Wales*

70 *Snowdon and Llyn Padarn, North Wales*

71 *The summit of Snowdon, Caernarvon-shire*

72 *Beddgelert*

73 *Fishguard,*
Pembrokeshire

74 *Fishguard Bay*

feared and disliked cities and preferred to see them fall into ruin rather than face the claustrophobia of life within walls. They built their villages round about in the fields, but nevertheless adventurous herdsmen must have wandered curiously about the cities with their animals, as they do today in Ephesus.

Is it not possible that, when the cities were reoccupied, the new streets were not the Roman streets, but the winding paths and short cuts made by the sheep and goats?

If there is anything in this theory, cities like Chichester can never have been entirely ruined or deserted, because their Roman street plan is too perfect.

Let us hope that nothing will ever persuade Chichester to remove its wonderful Market Cross, the best in England, planted in the very heart of the city, where the four points of the compass meet.

It stands in what was once the middle of Roman Regnum, the beginning of that North Street, which, as soon as it left the gate of Regnum, became the famous Stane Street that flew to London over down and across weald, as the crow flies. It reached London Bridge, a little over fifty-five miles away, with a divergence of only about a mile and a half. What a marvellous engineering feat this was!

The dignity and pride of Chichester resides in its Cathedral, a huge mass of worn, elephant-coloured stone lifting itself from grass on the side of West Street. Where, I wonder, did I gain the impression that Chichester was small and uninteresting compared with other cathedrals? I was surprised to learn that it has a greater total length than Exeter, Hereford, Worcester, Lichfield, Chester, Ripon or Southwark.

It has one unique feature: the only detached cathedral belfry in England, a tall fifteenth-century tower in the northwest corner of the churchyard, which visitors may enter and ascend. Suspended in the darkness there you see Big Walter, the hour bell, which weighs seventy-four hundredweight, and a peal of bells of various ages, the oldest bearing the date 1583.

How exquisite is the calm dignity of the architecture, chiefly Norman, of this church, and how fortunate it is that no one has blocked the view with a hideous organ; you can see straight down the church from the west door to the east window.

Behind the high altar I saw the place where the Shrine of St. Richard of Chichester used to stand, at one time a great place of pilgrimage, as famous, almost, as the Shrine of Thomas of Canterbury. An inscription in the retrochoir says that St. Richard's body was moved there from the nave on 16 June 1276, in the presence of King Edward I and the chief people of the realm.

Richard's life is proof that violence and murder print a name on the future more securely than goodness and sanctity. Most people can tell you something about Thomas à Becket, but few could describe the life of Chichester's Bishop, who was the most saintly character of his time. Unlike so many early churchmen, he was not a statesman; he was just a good and pure man who, though he was a bishop in a materialistic world, lived like one of the Apostles. Perhaps he is the only Englishman who might be compared with St. Francis.

[14]

I imagine that Salisbury is the only example in England of a town, established upon a hill, that suddenly packed up, lock, stock and barrel and marched into the plain to begin again. When the Romans came they fortified the hill known as Old Sarum and called it Sorbiodunum. The Britons seemed to have shortened it into something like Sarum. The Saxons, conquering it, gave it the name of Searesburh (as if it were the burgh founded by Sear), and the Normans corrupted it to Searesbyrig from which is a short step to Salisbury. What adventures words can encounter in a few centuries of invasion!

I wandered about the ruins of this first Salisbury, prodding the earth with a stick in the hope of finding a piece of that shining Samian pottery that on the most unlikely looking dunghills all over the world proclaims the presence of Rome. But there was nothing. Why did the people of Old Sarum march into the plain? History says there was a difference between the soldiers and the Church that reached a climax one cold windy night when the monks, returning from a Rogationtide procession, discovered themselves locked out of their Church. "Let us," said one of the canons, "in God's name descend into the level. There are rich champaigns and fertile valleys abounding in the fruits of the earth, and profusely watered by living streams. There is a seat for the Virgin patroness of our Church to whom the whole world cannot afford a parallel."

I like the old story that says Bishop Poore, who led the descent into the plain in 1219, ordered an arrow to be shot from the heights of Old Sarum into the valley below, and where it fell he built the Salisbury Cathedral of today.

You cannot help thinking as you explore the mounds of the ruined city of Sarum that overcrowding and lack of a good water supply must have entered into the question. The hill was probably adequate for a camp and a small Saxon stronghold, but when the first Cathedral and its outbuildings rose up, what room could there have been for anything else?

Salisbury is surely the most peaceful cathedral city in England. It seems that all its tragedy was packed into the history of Old Sarum, and with its removal into the valley came a delicious uneventfulness. I like to go out some few miles and look down on Salisbury, its thin spire, the finest in all England, rising from the plain, the smoke of its chimneys throwing a faint blue mist over the city. It is one of the coziest English views. It is interesting, too, to note that Bishop Poore anticipated American town planning. The streets of Salisbury do not wind like a number of glorified village lanes as do the streets of most medieval towns. Was the Bishop original in this or did some memory of the Roman camp linger on in Old Sarum?

I had two great moments on my first visit to Salisbury. It was market day. The cattle market was loud with mooing and bleating. Country gigs stood in the square, and over the pens leaned the burly, red-faced Wiltshire farmers. Many a Tess went off with a basket over her arm to buy—lisle-thread stockings, I suppose! I looked at the crowd and heard their bargaining, I met them in Ox Row and Blue Boar Row and Oatmeal Row, I watched them come from taprooms wiping their mouths with the back of their big hands and—the railway might never have invaded Salisbury! (Today there are fewer farmer's gigs, and nylon has been invented.)

The other moment? It was evening and the sun was setting behind the Cathedral. In that walled close nothing, it seemed, could ever hurt: the soft green grass, the mighty church pointing its slim finger to the sky and the old grey cloistered buildings dedicated to centuries of peace. I went inside. It is not, to my mind, one of the loveliest of our cathedrals, but it is one of the most chastely dignified; it sings on the same note. St. Paul's in London, Truro and Salisbury Cathedral stand alone, I think, as the work of one generation. . . .

[15]

In the chill morning before sunrise I took the road out of Salisbury and made for Stonehenge. Inexpressibly remote those great stones seemed, standing up there in the faint light that was not the light of moon or sun, but the spectral half-light that comes before day. I was reminded of Egypt. There is in this prehistoric circle the same carelessness for human labour that underlies the gigantic works of Egypt. It is not, I think, known how these early men built Stonehenge or whether the stones were carried from Wales or Brittany; but that does not lessen the grandeur of their effort, for they worked with their naked hands.

But Stonehenge, unlike Egypt, is dead. I would sleep on the high altar without a tremor, but there is not one temple in Thebes in which a man would not be haunted. How impossible it is to feel any sympathy or understanding for the distant builders of Stonehenge. It is a gloomy temple. One fancies that horrible rites were performed there, even more terrible, perhaps, than the burning of pretty Berkeley Square ladies in wicker-work cages as depicted by the Victorians. Stonehenge is like a symbol of all the dark beliefs at the root of ancient theology. Here is a fitting sanctuary for the Golden Bough.

Even so, it is lifeless. The ghost of the priest-king has been laid long ago. The wind whistles mournfully between the monoliths, and the sheep crop the grass on the ancient barrows that lie in the shadow of the dead temple.

The sun rose. A thin streamer of pink light lay across the east. The stones were jet-black against the sky. The grey clouds that had so recently moved across the stars now caught fire and became golden arrows in the heavens. The light grew second by second, the pink turned to a dull red, then to mauve, a veritable furnace of light blazed up above it, and in the midst of this the sun came up over Salisbury Plain.

[16]

There is something about Weymouth that suggests a big travelling carriage swinging along between the sand-hills near the sea, the postilions with dust on their eyebrows, their wigs awry, the horses in a lather; and inside, against the cushions, His Majesty King George III, ill and tired, trying to forget the word Whig, hoping there will be Dorset dumpling for dinner.

Weymouth has not yet recovered from the surprise that George III discovered it as a health resort. It looks patchily Georgian, as if trying to live up to the ugly statue of that monarch on the "front". You cannot be here for more than ten minutes without hearing something about George III, and I rather like this about Weymouth in a world of short memories. The hotel lounge, which has a loud-speaker and many naval officers dotted about it, was once the reception room of Gloucester House, the royal residence, and I am told that many important Cabinet meetings have been held there. There is something in the garden that looks like a stone coffin. They tell me that it is the bath of George III. Weymouth has no museum, so they have put the King's bath in the garden where the sparrows can enjoy it.

Fanny Burney, whose *Diary* I have been rereading in bed, was one of Queen Charlotte's maids-of-honour when the King went to Weymouth in search of rest. Precious little rest the poor man found. All George III wanted to do, I take it, was to potter around quietly, throw a few stones in the sea, take walks with his humdrum family and find out the recipe for Dorset puddings.

That loyalty, however, which blinded England to the comedy of the Hanoverians' succession, went right to the heads of the natives. It must be terrible to be a king. Every time he broke cover they gave tongue, and he could seldom escape from the National Anthem. It followed him even into the sea. Fanny Burney describes His Majesty's first bathe:

"They have," she says, "dressed out every street with labels, 'God save the King'. The bathing-machines make it their motto over all their windows, and those bathers that belong to the royal dippers wear it in bandeaus on their bonnets, to go into the sea; and have it again in large letters round their waists, to encounter the waves. Think of the surprise of his Majesty when, the first time of his bathing, he had no sooner popped his royal head under water than a band of music concealed in a neighbouring machine struck up 'God Save Great George our King'!"

One of the most impressive seascapes in England is, I imagine, that of the Chesil Bank from the high western end of Portland. The Chesil Bank is an extraordinary thing. It is, with the exception perhaps of a beach on the Baltic, the longest pebble beach in Europe. For seventeen miles the sea has flung up a great barrier of pebbles that varies in height from fifty to sixty feet. As the beach goes west, so the pebbles, owing to the action of the currents, become smaller and rounder. Fishermen tell me that if they land on the Chesil Bank in a fog they know exactly what part they have struck when they examine the shape and size of the stones. In storms ships have been lifted right over the Bank.

Quite near Weymouth is a wishing well at a place called Upwey. It lies behind a farm gate tucked away at the edge of a wood. The well bubbles up, ice-cold, within ancient moss-covered masonry, and I imagine that the Georgians, those great spa-finders, believed that it had healing properties. A girl who seemed to be in charge of the magic waters dipped a cup for me and said all in one breath:

"Turn your back on the wishing well, wish and take a drink and throw what's left back into the well over your left shoulder, and then your wish'll come true!"

"Are you sure?" I asked.

She looked alarmed, as though she might be asked to sign a guarantee.

"George III used to drink it," she replied sturdily.

"And did his wishes come true?"

"I don't know," she said, very confused and pink.

So I wished and drank and threw what was left into the well.

The West Country

[1]

I have always wished to see Clovelly because for years I have been travelling in railway carriages that picture the charm of its curious High Street, the only high street in England too steep for wheels. The first thing I saw when I arrived was a grocer's boy delivering goods on a toboggan that banged loudly from terrace to terrace.

Clovelly is difficult to write about because it is the old, established beauty queen of England—and knows it! It cannot be left out of any tour because it is unique: an English Amalfi rising sheer from the bay. Beneath its apparent simplicity is a deal of artifice; it is a beauty spot that has been sternly told to keep beautiful. Its washing is displayed discreetly on a certain day. No signs disfigure its bowers; no motorcar may approach within half a mile of its sacrosanct charms, and when an old cottage dies it rises phoenix-like from its ashes exactly as it was, looking at least five hundred years old.

Its steep irregular High Street, with its little gabled houses bowered in flowers rising from the cobbles, their balconies nodding to each other across the narrow way, is a charming sight. The donkeys, with panniers on each side, that clip-clop up the cobbles with hooks on their hind shoes are "quaint", and even the usual band of fishermen in blue jerseys who stand forever gazing out to sea seem instinctively to adopt "quaint" poses as they sweep the horizon.

When you get tired of buying postcards, or "quaint" brass spoons with a Clovelly donkey as a handle, you can sail with the fishermen from the "quaint" little harbour, or you can go fishing in the bay. If you do either of these you will realise why Clovelly was built. The cliffs around the bay are all of soft, red sandstone, with the exception of that cliff on which Clovelly stands. This is an unexpected spur of solid rock. Evidently in the old smuggling days this rock appealed to the first Clovellians as an admirable retreat, and, undeterred by the difficulty of constructing a village on an almost perpendicular slope, they set to work to make a harbour and a main street.

The view of Clovelly from the sea is one of the finest views in north Devon. The village looks like a bunch of white blossom in a green hedge. A row of white-balconied old houses stands at the water-level, and in the foreground rise the masts of fishing boats.

"What do you do here in the winter?" I asked a fisherman.

"We prepare for the herring fishing. The Clovelly herring is the best in the world."

"And in the summer you fish for visitors?"

"Yes."

"Is it true that the next village, Bucks Cross, is inhabited by descendants of shipwrecked Spaniards from the Armada?"

"I don't know, but they're a different kind of people from we!"

Early morning and late evening, when the High Street is not congested, are the best times in Clovelly.

In the morning you are awakened by a terrible clatter beneath the window. A herd of donkeys, you think, must have gone mad? You run to the curtains and see below one sedate animal walking down the street arm in arm, so to speak, with the village postman. On the donkey's back are the mailbags.

In the evening the air becomes full of the scent of flowers, the white houses gleam sharply in the fading light, windows are lit, and you receive the strange impression that you are living on a stage. Clovelly seems too good to be true! From the little bastion overlooking the bay you can look out where, on the left, lonely Lundy Island lies like a whale out to sea. Girls with sunburned legs and sandals stand meditatively in the hush, drinking their evening draught of beauty; men suspiciously like artists prowl through the dusk; up the hill walk an affectionate couple—Clovelly is a great place for honeymoons—and the scene grows darker, more flower-scented and more beautiful every minute. . . .

You fight with yourself! You struggle with the devil in you! You grit your teeth! You will be strong! You will not give way! No matter how beautiful it becomes you will not say . . . Resist, resist, keep a tight hold on yourself! You will not. . . .

"Oh, isn't it *too* quaint?" says a voice.

Did you say it or—thank goodness! It was the girl with freckles who blushed when she signed the hotel register.

"That's the word I've been looking for," whispers her husband sentimentally. "You always say just the right thing, my darling!"

Somewhere a donkey brays; and you walk slowly up the hill.

[2]

I have blundered into a Garden of Eden that cannot be described in pen or paint. There is a degree of beauty that flies so high that no net of words or no snare of colour can hope to capture it, and of this order is the beauty of St. Just in Roseland, the companion village of St. Anthony.

There are a few cottages lost in trees, a vicarage with two old cannon-balls propping open the garden gate and a church. The church is grey and small and, as a church, not worth notice; but it stands in a churchyard that is one of the little-known glories of Cornwall. I would like to know if there is in the whole of England a churchyard more beautiful than this. There is hardly a level yard in it. You stand at the lich-gate and look down into a green cup filled with flowers and arched by great trees. In the dip is the little church, its tower level with you as you stand above. The white gravestones rise up from ferns and flowers.

Beyond the church a screen of trees forms a tracery of leaves through which, shining white in the sun, you see the ground sloping steeply towards the creek beyond which is that strong arm of the sea, Carrick Roads. Over the roof of the church blue water gleams; above it rise the distant fields of the opposite bank. This churchyard is drowsy with the bee and rich with a leafy pungency. There is also a tropic smell in it, a smell of palms and foreign trees.

An elderly clergyman was training a plant over a wall. He looked up and smiled.

"Yes, I am the vicar. Which do you prefer—those wine-dark rhododendrons or the pink? And do you notice that rather subtle shade in between? I like that, don't you?"

"Who was St. Just, sir?" I asked.

"St. Just was," he replied, taking off his broad black hat and smoothing his silver hair, "St. Just was—I want you to admire those pansies! Now look at this. Isn't it beautiful?"

He bent down and, taking a deep velvet flower between two fingers, turned its head gently towards me.

"You were saying that St. Just was——"

"Ah, yes, forgive me! St. Just—oh, the trouble I've had with those japonicas." He shook his head.

"St. Just?" I murmured hopefully.

"That tall tree over there came from Australia," he remarked proudly. "By the way, I have a tropical garden behind the church that you must see."

I abandoned the saint.

"You have made this garden?"

75 *Harlech Castle, Merionethshire*

76 *Cardiff Castle, Glamorgan*

77 *The City Hall, Cardiff*

78 Colchester Castle, Essex

79 Norwich Castle, Norfolk

80 *Norwich Cathedral, Norfolk*

81 *The medieval font in Norwich Cathedral*

"With my own hands I have made it," he replied lovingly. "It took a long time." Here he straightened his spare figure and cast a look round over the indescribable tangle of loveliness. "But it was worth it."

He smiled at me and quoted Isaiah:

" 'Instead of the thorn shall come up the fig tree, and instead of the briar shall come up the myrtle tree; and it shall be to the Lord for a name, for an everlasting sign that shall not be cut off.' "

I could say nothing. I watched the sunlight soaking through the leaves from above, moving in shadows over the tombstones; I listened to the song of the birds in the trees and the drone of the bees' wings. I looked into my companion's calm eyes and at his brown gardener's hands, and my first sense of irritation vanished; I understood that there was religion in this gardening; that to him every new touch of beauty he brought to birth out of this rich earth was like a psalm of praise; that year after year he had added beauty to beauty around the House of God.

"The origin of Roseland—look at those briar roses—is a moot point. The legend is that it got its name when King Henry VIII spent his honeymoon here with Anne Boleyn. They are supposed to have stayed in the Castle at St. Mawes. The story is—smell this leaf; it comes from New Zealand. I wonder if I did right to put that clump of rock plants so high. What do you think? Oh, the story? They say that when Anne Boleyn got here she asked the name of the place, and, receiving no answer, turned to the roses and said, ''Tis Roseland, forsooth!' Now foxgloves in a shady spot . . ."

I tried desperately to hold him a moment, but he was off after some snapdragons. I managed to drag him back.

"Yes, it's a pretty story, but it probably isn't true! The antiquaries derive the word from Rosinis, meaning 'the Moorland Isle'. Do you hear that thrush? He's in a wood at the back of my house."

We parted the trees and looked out on the peaceful beauty of the creek; the tide coming up; the high, still woods; and, beyond, the deep waters of Carrick Roads.

"Incredible, unspoilt beauty!"

We walked on until we came to a grave in a lovely corner of the garden.

"My eldest boy," he whispered, and we went on among the flowers.

"Wasn't I telling you about St. Just? Well, he, you know, was Jestyn, son of Geraint."

I drew a deep breath.

"Geraint of the Round Table, who married Enid and 'crowned a happy life with a fair death'?" I asked.

He nodded his head and smiled:

"And the legend is that when he died he was borne across the bay at Gerrans, just at the back there, in a golden boat with silver oars and buried beneath Carne Beacon. Just before you go, do come and look at the fuchsias, won't you?"

[3]

I came to Tintagel as a man should, tired, fearful and at evening. . . .

I have thought of Tintagel all my life as one of those places that no man should see. For eight hundred years the story of that king who rides down history on a harpstring has soaked itself into the imagination of the English people. Charlemagne for France; Arthur for England. The story grew here. On this grey rock above the sea, Uther Pendragon took that lovely queen, Igerne; and so began the story that ran through medieval Europe challenging the imagination of poet and writer, gathering strength and beauty, to break at last in the splendid climax of the "Grail" music. . . .

Tin-tagel!

To thousands of English people those syllables go clothed in grandeur because there are two Tintagels: one is in Cornwall, the other in cloudland. One on the map; the other spun out of verse and music; and this is the real Tintagel, no dead rock in a grey sea, but a country of dream more real than reality, where there are still music, the breaking of lances and the pain of love.

The sun was sinking seaward as I climbed a rocky gorge and came to the most desolate little valley, I think, in all the wild West Country. The sides of the cliffs were scarred with grey splintered slate; half-way the rocks approach each other to form a kind of gate; at the end of the valley is a little bay, the sea foaming over a grey pebble beach and running through a cavern called Merlin's Cave.

It seems as though a great sword has split this valley in two; on one side, perched high, is the tiny village of Tintagel; on the other, covered in grass, wrecked by a landslide, are fragments of an ancient wall known to legend as King Arthur's Castle of Tintagel. The key is kept in a cottage among lemonade bottles.

"No, please, sir," said a little old woman who uses the word "please" unexpectedly. "Please, it's too late for you to go up to the Castle tonight, please. But if you promise not to be long, please, I'll give you the key. . . ."

I began to climb steep, winding steps cut in the face of the rock. The waves boomed below in Merlin's Cave, the seagulls flew below crying, and in my hand was the key of Tintagel.

Think of that! What a moment! In my hand was the key of Tintagel!

As a ruin Tintagel is the most disappointing Castle in England. A wall that is several centuries later than King Arthur runs its crazy course on the cliff edge. It is indescribably remote, thrust up out of a grey sea towards the sky, with the jagged peaks of lesser rocks lifted like spears below it, and all round it the hiss and whisper of the sea. Birds rose from the grass before me as I walked; rabbits scuttled away to dive into burrows in which—who knows?—may lie some fragment of a sword.

A disappointing ruin, but a great experience. As I climbed the rocks and looked over the gaunt cliffs I seemed to come nearer, not to the gentlemanly knights of Tennyson or the paladins of Malory, but to the rough chieftains of history from whom the epic sprang. I saw Arthur stripped of the spell, with no Excalibur, but only a common spear and the sun of Rome sinking into a sea of trouble on which the fortunes of England were to set their sails. How difficult it is to visualise King Arthur as a half-Roman kinglet. . . .

It grew dusk, and I saw the other picture. Do boys still read Malory? Do they lie on their stomachs in orchards with that book propped up before them in the grass? Do they forget to go home for food and lie on till the harvest-bugs set about them and the dusk falls, reading that wild gallantry? Do they still go back through darkening woods, shamefully late, peopling the hush with the splintering crash of steel point on jesseraunts of double mail, seeing in the waving of the trees the fluttering of banneroles and in the starkness of pines on a hill lances against the sky? I wonder. . . .

Tintagel is haunted. It is haunted not by Arthur and the Knights of the Round Table but by that moment in our lives when imagination caught fire and blazed. The ghosts on this rock are the great army of Englishmen and Englishwomen who in their youth believed in Excalibur and wept in sorrow beside that mere as the three hooded queens came in their barge with a crying that "shivered to the tingling stars" to bear the dying king to Avilion.

When the wind blows from the sea at Tintagel a sudden grey veil is flung over this high ruin: a veil of damp mist that blots out the distant earth; it runs on into the valley like a cloud and is gone. No wonder men believed strange things of this place and of the king who would come again.

At night, with the moon falling over the tumbled walls, Tintagel seems more dead than ever: the ruins of Egypt leap to life in moonlight, so do many of our castles and abbeys; but Tintagel is to be found only within the covers of a book.

And I thought, as I looked down on it from the other side of the valley, saw the thin line of light run along the walls picking out a gateway here and a crumbled corner there, that most of us have belonged to that Round Table—so many of us, in fact, that if Arthur came back to give us youth again and called us out to joyous adventures he would have an army great enough to ride from Camelot to the conquest of the earth.

[4]

The most conspicuous object in the Vale of Avalon is a high, rounded hill, crowned with a lonely tower, rising beyond the ruins of Glastonbury. This hill is known as Glastonbury Tor, and the building is all that remains of the old pilgrimage Chapel of St. Michael.

In the early morning before the sun is strong, a man standing on this hill looks down, not upon the neat, flat pasturelands of the Vale of Avalon, but upon Avalon, an island again, rising from a steaming sea of mist. In summer the mist rises from the fields, as if it were the ghost of that sea that covered the valley in the age of legend.

It was over this sea to Avalon there moved that "dusky barge, dark as a funeral scarf from stem to stern," in which the hooded queens bore the dying Arthur, his scabbard empty of Excalibur. As the low mists move, curling upwards from the land, the lowing of cattle in the fields below rises starkly in the silence as though it might be the wailing that died upon this mere so long ago; as though in the first hour of a summer's day the Isle of Avalon remembers Arthur.

The sun shines, the mists go, and the green fields are smiling to the skyline.

I am writing in the ruins of Glastonbury Abbey.

A hot afternoon is almost over. There is in the air that summer stillness like the peace of a cloister, in which—so they say in Glastonbury—the scent of mysterious incense sometimes drifts over walls to astonish men working in their gardens. I can, however, smell only the incense of new-cut grass.

An hour ago I stood on the summit of the Tor above Glastonbury in the shadow of the tower of the pilgrims' Chapel of St. Michael, now a patched ruin. When I looked east I gazed down at the Isle of Avalon; when I looked west I saw the Isle of Athelney lying in a heat haze. These "islands" are now hills rising from flat fields over which in the age of myth ran wide lagoons; and I thought that if a man were looking for the roots of England, this is the place to which he would come; in Avalon the roots of the Church; in Athelney the roots of the State.

Rising sheer from the grass, appalling in its appealing starkness, is the great arch of the central tower of Glastonbury Abbey, the two piers rising into the air, but not to meet; there is blue sky between, and on the high, cleft towers grass is growing. This with a few tumbled walls and the beautiful St. Mary's Chapel represent all that remains of the once mighty Abbey, the elder brother of Westminster and the birthplace of Christianity in England.

It is, perhaps, not strange that all places that have meant much to Man are filled with an uncanny atmosphere, as if something were still happening there secretly; as if filled with a hidden life. Glastonbury is like that. A band of tourists, who came in laughing and joking, move among the ruins, puzzled and ill at ease. Glastonbury has stilled their laughter. I seem to see the faces of anchorites, saints, priests and kings; and in this pregnant dust of Avalon are drawn two of the greatest epics that have come from the English mind: One is of the Holy Grail and the other of a wounded king.

This quiet field is the only spot in England linked by legend with a man who knew Jesus Christ. For centuries men believed that in A.D. 61 St. Philip sent Joseph of Arimathaea, whose hands had laid Christ in the tomb, to preach the Gospel in England. He is said, according to the later legend, to have come with a band of missionaries bearing the Chalice of the Last Supper, which he had begged of Pilate. This Chalice had held the Sacred Blood from the Cross. Here in this English meadow Joseph of Arimathaea is said to have built England's first church of plaited osiers.

When the missionaries crossed Weary-all Hill ("weary-all" with the journey), Joseph, so the famous old story goes, planted his staff in the earth. It took root and grew into the famous Glastonbury Thorn.

That belief founded the international fame of Glastonbury; for centuries it was an English Jerusalem, one of the holiest places on earth. Men came from the ends of the world to pluck a sprig of the Holy Thorn in order that it might be buried with them. Saints were gathered to Glastonbury to lie in its earth. The bones of Arthur and Guinevere are said to have been buried beneath the high altar. Behind the Abbey at the foot of the Tor still springs the mineral spring that was one of the wonders of the world. Its waters, heavily impregnated with iron, colour the earth and everything they touch a rusty red; and this is the place to which the medieval pilgrim knelt trembling and crying—as I have seen pilgrims tremble and cry in Jerusalem—believing that here was buried the Holy Grail.

As I was walking over the grass of the choir I came to a railed-off plot of turf that marks the high altar of Glastonbury. A man was walking over it behind a motor lawnmower!

He took a turn over the high altar and came back.

"See that bush? That's the Holy Thorn! The original one was hacked down by a Puritan who got a splinter in his eye from it and died. There are several offshoots round Glastonbury, and you'd be surprised at the number of slips we send away. One is going to a big church they are building in New York. We sent one to America not long ago for the tomb of President Wilson."

The grass has come back to the altar of Glastonbury, but the Holy Thorn still lives!

"I have been to Glastonbury!"

Six hundred years ago a man writing this would remember the greatest experience of his life. He would remember the greatest church outside Rome, the sound of its bells, the smoke of its incense, the sound of perpetual prayer, the gilded shrines, the horde of pilgrims at the doors—saints in ecstasy, sinners in tears; and in every man's mind faith in the marvellous story that had grown up round a reed hut in the Isle of Avalon.

"I have been to Glastonbury!"

[5]

I entered Wells Cathedral just before noon. The cream-coloured church seemed empty. When I came to the north transept I saw a crowd whispering, standing about, sitting on stone seats, leaning against pillars and tombs, each member of it looking up anxiously at the west wall.

"What are they doing?" I asked the verger.

"Waiting to see the clock strike twelve!" he replied.

Then I remembered that in Wells Cathedral is one of the most exciting clocks in England; in fact, with the exception of the clock in Strasbourg Cathedral, probably one of the most exciting clocks in the world. It is six hundred years old, and it was invented by a monk of Glastonbury called Peter Lightfoot. The dial, which is six feet six inches in diameter, is a mass of lines and numbers. A large outer circle is divided into the twenty-four hours of the day; an inner circle shows the minutes. Round the hour circle moves a big slow star; round the inner circle a quick smaller star.

A rustle goes round the crowd. The minute star slides on to noon.

To the left of the clock dial, high up on the west wall, sits a smug little wooden man in the costume of Charles I's time. His name is, I believe, Jack Blandiver. He sits with his heels against two bells. . . .

Noon!

Jack Blandiver kicks out his wooden leg and brings his heel back against a bell; then the other one. He does this eight times. The clock dial, however, claims the attention of the crowd! From it comes a whirring sound. Out of the black cave above the dial appear four mounted knights; two gallop round to the left, two to the right; and at every revolution one of them is knocked back on his horse's crupper by the sword of an adversary. The tournament spins round to a standstill: the hourly fight in Wells Cathedral is over. The crowd is smiling with childish delight—the same smile that has gone round the north transept for something like six hundred years.

Wells is perfect. It is genuinely medieval, with no self-consciousness, and no abasement to the tourist. Behind the stout wall that runs round the Cathedral is something you will see nowhere else in England: an inhabited medieval castle, complete with fortifications and moat. In this marvellous place lives the Bishop of Wells.

I sat on the grass beside the moat watching His Lordship's ducks and swans. They have hatched the most delightful fluffy families. I saw a swan swim up and ring the bell of the gatehouse. I rubbed my eyes. Was this a fairy tale? I looked at the white bird, half expecting he might turn into a prince in white satin breeches. He did it again! He took up a string that lay in the water and pulled it! A bell beneath the window of the gatehouse tinkled, the window opened, a crust of bread flew through the air and hit him on the head; he worried it under water, summoned his family to him, rang the bell again, and more food arrived!

I walked over the drawbridge and took the brass knocker in my hand. A small postern opened.

"Whenever the swans are hungry they ring the bell!" explained a girl. "We never disappoint them. We keep a tray of food always ready to throw out when they ask for it. They teach the cygnets to ring, too! The ducks do it sometimes, but not so often as the swans. . . ."

I returned to the grass of the moat, watching the birds ring for their food. The Cathedral bells chimed a quarter. The sun was mellow over old walls. I could see the fortifications of the Bishop's Palace bending round to bastions fitted with sentry walks and slits for bowmen. What a place to live in!

[6]

I have decided that when I grow old, with or without gout, sciatica, rheumatism or lumbago, I will retire to Bath with an ebony cane and a monocle. I like Bath: it has quality. I like Bath buns, Bath Olivers, Bath chaps, Bath brick and Bath stone.

I once heard a bright young man say at a party that living in Bath was rather like sitting in the lap of a dear old lady. Nobody laughed, because it is true! Bath is the dear old lady of Somerset: grey-haired, mittened, smelling faintly of lavender; one of those old ladies who have outlived a much-discussed past and are now as obviously respectable as only old ladies with crowded pasts can be. She nurses you with a shrewd twinkle in which you detect experience mellowed by age. You look at her lovingly, wondering how she could ever have been wicked; wishing that she could grow young again for one wild evening and show you! That might wake you up!

The crowds in Bath move slowly. Bath was made for chairs. Sedan and the other kind. Anything else on wheels is a rude invasion. One of the most soothing sights in England is the vista through the black Georgian pillars in Stall Street—the Pump Room to the right, the lovely Abbey in the background.

O gracious Old Lady of Somerset, how I love to be nursed at your once naughty knee. . . .

I just half-close my eyes and . . . those two old men talking above the pale green water of the great Roman bath! One is a general, the other a judge. Why are they wearing togas: Why are their feet in white-laced boots? It is, of course, because I have half-closed my eyes; and when you do this in Bath you see ghosts. Look how the tumbled pillars of the Roman bath build themselves up, how the dusty tesserae shine again with colour and form a pattern! The Roman bath is alive: Old General X and Sir Archibald Y are standing on a polished pavement on which Diana runs with her hounds in leash! Do they know that they are wearing togas? Ought I to tell them?

But is it General X? No, he is General Caius Sciaticus of the Valens Victrix. Is it Sir Archibald Y? No, he is Marcus Rheumaticus of Londinium. (Funny nightmare place, Bath!)

"What a climate," says General Sciaticus. "By jove, sir, what a damnable climate. It gets me in the knees. . . . By the way, is it true that Boadicea's great-grandson has gone Red?"

"He's a firebrand. It runs in the family, you know. I had to crucify his uncle at Camulodunum last year. Perhaps you heard about it?"

"A terrible country, but we're civilising them by degrees. How's your rheumatism this year? Has it ever struck you that this hot water was placed here by Providence to hold the Empire together? If there was no place in Britain in which one could feel warm, what would one do? By jove, that's a pretty woman, the one with the yellow hair!"

"Yes, the wife of Dion Neurasthenes, the Greek financier. Just travelling. Have you heard her speak? A pretty accent. Listen. . . ."

"Say, now, don't tell me that all this hot water comes right up out of the earth like this! Well, you certainly do surprise me. It's the only centrally heated spot I've struck in this little cold island. . . . Oh, I'd love to; I haven't been warm since I

82 *The Chester 'Rows'*

83 *Bridge Gate, Chester*

84 *East Gate, Chester*

85 *The River Mersey at Liverpool*

86 *Mesnes Park, Wigan, Lancashire*

87 *York Minster*

88 *The City Walls, York*

left Athens. And the draughts! Aquae Sulis is sure the draughtiest spot on earth. . . ."

I open my eyes and see that General X and Sir Archibald Y are properly dressed again, and Mrs. Boston certainly has yellow hair.

In the evening you can walk through the splendid streets of Bath—magnificent streets lined with Georgian houses standing stiff as lackeys behind pillared porticoes; elegant, formal homes. There is the Circus, the Crescent; there is Pulteney Bridge—England's Ponte Vecchio—there are lovely Georgian gateways and little queer streets round whose corners it seems you just miss the flash of a red-heeled shoe, the twinkle of feet beneath brocade, the sound of a rather naughty little laugh. It is very difficult, if you walk in Bath at night, not to find yourself under the rather contemptuous scrutiny of a man with a double chin and a heavy nose, whose three-cornered hat shades eyes that lie in fleshy bags—Beau Nash!

"Sir," says this ghost, "I would inform you that a gentleman of fashion carries a cane. I am glad to observe that you are not wearing a sword. Your hat is, sir, like a scullion's, and your legs are encased in two inelegant tubes of cloth for which, sir, I can find no name. You are, perhaps, a foreigner?"

"No, Beau, I come from London."

Whereupon the ghost of Beau Nash, uttering an incredulous cry, vanishes; the two eyes go last, still fixed in a look of horror on your trousers.

Early in the morning, wrapped in a dressing-gown, I gained the lift and was carried down to the baths to begin a day's treatment, just to see what is in store for most of us. I had decided against a mud pack, because I did not like the picture in the handbook, which shows a nurse building up a big black mud pie on a patient's foot. I considered the whirling bath, the hydroelectric bath, the heat bath, the hot-air bath, the vapour bath, the aeration bath, and came to the conclusion that probably the best bath for a man with no real honest symptoms is the deep bath; the characteristic bath of Bath; the bath with historic and literary associations, because it is simply the scientific version of the treatment as practised by the Romans and by our eighteenth-century forefathers.

A man in a white coat took me into a tiled room. Sunk in the floor was a huge bath with six steps leading down to swirling green water. The water gushed in from the spring steaming hot at a temperature of 120 degrees as it comes up from the nether regions. Cold water was added till the temperature was 100 degrees.

I walked down the steps, was buffeted by the hot stream of radium, and the man in the white coat told me to sit down, which I did trustfully: I could see no seat in the green water, but I met it just as my chin touched the flood. So I sat there, feeling hot and apprehensive. He told me to exercise myself gently: I could tell that he considered me a genuine patient, which made me feel quite ill.

In ten minutes the cure was over.

The attendant stood at the top of the steps and received me into a hot towel. It was then that I felt my first real symptom—a sharp pain in the knee.

I went up and had a melancholy breakfast.

Now with us invalids the next event is the Pump Room.

At about eleven o'clock we drag our weary limbs to the stately Georgian building that, since 1796, has been the ever-open door to the gouty, the rheumaticky and the sciaticky. This classic apartment is built above the three hot springs—the only natural hot springs in Britain—that shoot up half a million gallons of water a day into Bath.

Everybody drinks the Bath water. We invalids do it seriously; the casual tripper does it flippantly. We limp up and put our finger half-way up the glass and whisper: "Only eight ounces this morning!" The tripper strides up heartily and says: "A pint of the best, please, miss!" and the maiden of the healing spring gazes over the top of his head towards the sky, where, no doubt, she sees the great God Neuritis saving up his thunderbolts!

If our joints are equal to it we can walk gently downstairs to see the "source", the very heart of Bath.

An attendant in the nether regions unlocks a bronze door and we walk into a wall of white steam. Our eyes become accustomed to the gloom. It is hot. The steam condenses on our hands and on our face in a clammy sweat. We see a Roman arch and Roman steps leading down to the springs. They are stained rust-red with minerals. Beneath the arch, just out of sight, bubble the hot springs that, as long as there is any record, have been pumping up their daily half-million gallons of water.

Midlands

[1]

Most cathedral cities visited by me in the course of my search have been true to type: Winchester, Exeter, Wells—all sheltering beneath their historic cathedrals like dear old ladies under an umbrella. Gloucester is more difficult to discover. Unlike so many English towns through whose streets history has been flowing for centuries, Gloucester has not sought refuge on the retired list. This city, owing to geographical and other reasons outside the scope of this story, has not lacked the vitality of human endeavour since its right-angled streets were laid out by the II Legion of the Roman Expeditionary Force in the forty-second year of Our Lord. Here is something more than a great cathedral dreaming among elms: here is a Roman-Saxon-medieval city that has thrust its way into the industrial era without quite losing touch with an older time.

What I, and all other casual visitors, love about Gloucester is the unusual experience of living in a medieval inn. When Edward II was murdered in 1327, and his shrine in the Cathedral became a famous place of pilgrimage, the fortunes of many inns were founded; and of these some still remain to shelter the traveller.

The inn in which I am writing is entered through a huge archway constructed to admit a cavalcade, a pious lady in a horse litter or a coach. The inn is built round a paved courtyard. A flight of stone steps in this courtyard leads up to an oak gallery running the four sides of the yard off which are the bedrooms, so that I can open my bedroom door, lean over the gallery and keep in touch with everything happening down below. It is all so interesting and intimate.

I see, as I lean outside my bedroom door, the new arrivals drive into the courtyard and book their rooms. I see the chambermaids busy round the gallery;

I see the waiters crossing the yard bearing trays of food, because six hundred years have not been able to bring the kitchen, which is at one end of the yard, any nearer to the dining-room, which is at the other! In the depth of winter every egg and every breakfast rasher has to be carried through the snow to the table! Hail conservatism! I suppose travellers have been leaning over this balcony for six hundred years watching much the same scene—arrivals, departures, dusting, cleaning, food.

The thrill of Gloucester Cathedral is one that can never be forgotten. I stood dumb with admiration beneath the great drums of the nave built by men who knew how to design fortresses; the height, the proportion, the simple strength of these great columns is beyond description.

In the choir of Gloucester sleeps Edward II under a rich canopy. It was to this tomb that the pilgrims of the Middle Ages came with such profitable results that the monks rebuilt church and abbey from the proceeds of their piety. Then the cloisters of Gloucester! They stand alone among the cathedral cloisters of England. Their delicate fan vaulting is a sheer miracle in stone. Behind the choir I saw the tomb of Robert Curthose (or perhaps "Shorty" might be a modern version of the contemptuous nickname that William the Conqueror gave to his disappointing eldest son). Robert should have been king of England on the hereditary principle, but, instead, he fought bravely in the First Crusade while younger brothers seized the crown. I have an idea that Robert was one of those likeable and attractive misfits who are capable of sudden gallantry and generosity but at the same time are incapable of ruling themselves or anybody else. He died in 1134 at the age of eighty, having spent the last twenty-eight years of his life in prison, the captive of his brother, Henry I. His tomb of coloured bog-oak, believed to have been the tribute of some unknown hero of the Third Crusade to a hero of the First, is, I think, among the most touching in England.

As I was walking at night in Gloucester, admiring the Roman layout of the city, at one moment lost in Glevum, at the next in medieval Gloucester, I heard, from beneath the ground it seemed, the sound of music. I went into an inn yard and came to a flight of old stone steps leading downwards. Above them was the sign: The Monks' Retreat. I descended and entered a cool, dusty cellar that would make the fortune of any man in Montmartre.

At first sight it appeared that the crypt of a church had been turned into a saloon bar. In a long, dim, vaulted cavern men sat drinking beside beer barrels. A bar ran the length of the vault, and a tireless electric organ occupied a remote corner. It was a weird, oddly sacrilegious sight.

As I sat down beside a barrel and cast a curious glance round the dusty vault

I noticed in one corner a confessional box and in another a stone stoup for holy water! I imagine this to be the most remarkable bar in England.

"Some think this place was an underground passage built in the old days, so that the pilgrims could get from their inn to the Cathedral," said the barman, "but others think that centuries ago it was on the street level. . . ."

"Half a pint," said an inhabitant.

The old inn courtyard was dark. A light shone in the gallery, casting shadows over the flagstones, flinging the shape of a great beam over the stone steps. I climbed up and leaned over the balustrade, to stand a moment looking down into the yard that has seen six hundred years of wayfaring.

Modern Gloucester was hushed and in this place seemed a memory of old things. Over the city passed a peal of bells, and in the square of sky above the little courtyard shone a few faint stars.

[2]

These Warwickshire lanes, deep and banked; these mighty trees; these small, arched bridges over small streams—how well I knew them when I was a boy! There were little villages in which men still spoke Elizabethan English, such as Welford on Avon, where there was a Maypole, where they grew the most delicious raspberries and took the sweetest honey from straw skips. Here it was years ago that I saw a man in a smock. There was Bidford—"drunken Bidford" —where an old woman, with a face like a withered apple under a mauve sunbonnet, used to point out the crab tree beneath whose shade Shakespeare, so the legend went, slept off a carouse at the Falcon Inn there.

It is an amusing error to revisit a place which thrilled us when we were young. I seem to remember Stratford on Avon as a quiet little heaven where it was always May, with the nightingales shaking silver in the dark trees at night and the Avon mooning under Hugh of Clopton's grand old bridge. And I was terribly young. I used to rise with the sun and walk over dripping meadows with their wrong-way-round shadows, the kingcups shaking dew over my boots and would read Shakespeare aloud to the astonishment of the cows, pausing transfixed in wonder (on an empty stomach) by such lines as—well, never mind. Only Youth knows; only Youth can achieve that passionate intensity.

I drove into Stratford between those well-loved Warwick hedges.

They gave me a bedroom called Love's Labour's Lost—all the rooms in this hotel are Shakespeareanised—and, as it overlooked the street, I sat a while watching more Americans arrive and thinking how amused Shakespeare would have been. Stratford's fame rests on Shakespeare: This town is the very core of the heart of the American's England.

Stratford on Avon is one of the towns of England that can be compared with the ancient pilgrimage towns; it is, in its way, a kind of lay Glastonbury. (I suppose the old religious shrines also received thousands of sheeplike pilgrims who had no idea why they were pilgrims beyond the fact that it was the right thing to be!)

I went into Harvard House, which belongs to the American university and is used as a rest-room. (It has Yale-blue curtains!) In this house lived Katherine Rogers, who married Robert Harvard and became the mother of the founder of Harvard University. I went to New Place, which is becoming an excellent museum. I went, of course, to the Birthplace, where, because Stratford seems to arouse all the instincts of the souvenir-hunter, they keep a guardian in every room. I must have exhausted my Shakespeare worship years ago, for I found myself more interested in the moonlike faces of the pilgrims bent above the glass cases than in the fact that here, they say, was born the greatest poetic genius of the English race.

Overlooking the garden of Shakespeare's Birthplace, is, if association and surroundings mean anything to a writer, the most perfect workroom in the world. From his desk in the window the curator overlooks the garden in which Shakespeare was hushed to sleep, blew bubbles and tried to catch the clouds.

I found two things unchanged in Stratford. One was a mossy seat on the high wall of Holy Trinity churchyard overlooking the Avon. This is, to my mind, one of the supremely English views. It seems as you sit there with the willows dipping to the river, beyond, on the opposite bank, great freckled meadows, and in the air the sound of the water rushing past the old mill, that all the beauty and peace of the Warwickshire countryside have been packed into one riverscape. Between the tombstones grow vast yew trees. It is so right that Shakespeare's bones should lie in this quiet church . . . now and again from the thin spire a bell tells the time lazily; the tall avenue of lime trees moves in the wind.

And the woods by the river, too, are unchanged. Here in the spring you can hear the nightingale all night long; here the wild roses light up the hedges; and the tiny blossom of the blackthorn lies on the grass like snow. And this is the place where you will meet Shakespeare, if you want to meet him, in this wood, which I swear is that magic wood "near Athens".

It was evening when I went there on a real pilgrimage, and it seemed that Oberon and Titania had just hidden behind the great trees; that Mustard-Seed and Pease-Blossom had withdrawn to their acorn cups at the sound of footsteps. In the middle of the wood that clings to the high Avon bank I met an old man going home to Shottery with a sack over his back and an untrimmed ash stick in his hand. We just said "Good evening" and passed on. But I recognised him! He was one of those homespun Warwickshire yokels whom Shakespeare took to Athens on that magic midsummer night.

[3]

Oxford is one of those places that encourage the art of valediction. How natural it is that a young man, or a young woman, having spent some years in its shelter, should address a few polite words of farewell before turning towards the bleaker regions of reality.

Strangely enough, this custom of saying good-bye to Oxford seems to have been inaugurated by Queen Elizabeth. When Her Majesty was leaving Oxford in 1592, she stopped her coach before it went down the hill to Wheatley, and, turning to the dreaming spires, she addressed them:

"Farewell, farewell, dear Oxford," she said. "God bless thee and increase thy sons in number, holiness and virtue."

It would be impertinent for a stranger to presume to judge the holiness or virtue of Oxford, but he is at liberty to say that Her Majesty's other command has been obeyed: Oxford's sons have increased in such numbers, and each one possesses either a motorcar or a bicycle, that it is now difficult to cross the road except at a hunted run. Few other towns in England leave upon the mind such an impression of congestion.

Wales

[1]

The Welsh are our oldest allies. Five thousand Welsh archers and spearmen fought with us at Crécy. They drew their bows at Agincourt. The Welsh longbow, which became the national weapon of England, gave us victories in France and Scotland. No small nation has ever stood up to the might of England as Wales resisted conquest until, her honour satisfied, she saw a Welshman, the first Tudor, on the throne.

Thoughts of this kind took me from the Midlands, and I was soon passing between green hedges on my way to Wales.

I came to Llangollen, which is a small town, or a large village, lying in the shadow of mountains. A salmon river sings to it day and night. It is the sacred Dee. I now had the feeling that I had crossed a frontier. I was in a foreign country. To come straight out of England into Llangollen is as surprising as if you were suddenly projected in a flash from England to Ballater in the Balmoral Highlands. And Llangollen, although it is softer, is the Welsh sister of Ballater: They are both little stone-built towns among mountains with a salmon river running straight through them. Each of these rivers is called the Dee.

I went into a shop. The shopman was talking to a customer in Welsh. He broke off and said in that precise English that you hear also in the Hebrides:

"And what can I get for you, please?"

He then resumed his Welsh in a pretty sing-song voice, talking as swiftly as an excited Frenchman.

"How have you managed to keep your language on the very borders of England?" I asked him.

89 *Walmgate, York*

90 *Bootham Bar and the Minster, York*

91 *The Shambles, York*

92 *Durham Cathedral*

93 *Hadrian's Wall at Housesteads, Northumberland*

"We had to fight to keep it," he said. "The chapels saved Welsh for us years ago."

"You prefer to speak in Welsh?"

"I can say more in my own language. The words come quickly and are better."

"How many people speak Welsh?"

"I do not know. It varies in districts. Everyone speaks it in Caernarvonshire. . . ."

I went out into the streets of Llangollen that seemed more than ever foreign streets lying in the shadow of their mountains. It was even strange to realise that letters collected by the postman that night in Llangollen would be in London the next day.

I walked beside the Dee all the afternoon, reading what John Rhys and David Brynmor Jones say about the Welsh language. The survival of this language—the ancient speech of the Britons—is a remarkable thing. It is the most marvellous survival in Great Britain. When the Romans conquered Britain under Claudius Caesar in A.D. 43, Latin became the official language for nearly four hundred years. Wales, unlike Ireland and Scotland, was Romanised. Roman castles were dotted about the country; the legions drove their roads through Wales; they based their legions at Deva on the north and Caerleon on the south. Still the speech of the Britons endured.

It is surprising that the British, or Welsh, tongue should have lived on for four centuries with the Latin language that conquered Gaul and Spain, but it is something of a miracle that in after years it should have stubbornly refused to be vanquished by French and, later, by English. No doubt a continuous struggle against invaders, bent on breaking down the barriers of nationalism, causes a people to cling with greater strength to the speech of their fathers. It is still surely a great romance that thousands of men, women and children use today words that would probably be understood by Boadicea and King Arthur.

In the morning I looked out at a pocket paradise. Llangollen in one stride takes you right into Wales. There is nothing of the Border Marches about it. It is definitely a foreign country.

To anyone with an eye for landscape its charm is in compression. Here is a little masterpiece in mountains; an exercise in the blending of hill against hill, woodland against moorland. The Vale of Llangollen looks as though Nature had made a scale model for a section of the milder Scottish Highlands, and, liking it very well, had also gained a few ideas for Switzerland and the German Rhine. It is a neat and well-groomed country. Every meadow, it seems, has its valet and every tree its lady's maid.

One of the glories of Llangollen that could never grow stale, though a man spent all his days there, is the early fifteenth-century bridge over the Dee. Its four pointed arches are set at a part of the river designed, so it seems, to give them full battle with the swift current. I have a passion for looking from bridges into swift mountain streams, especially when, as with this bridge, it spans a river scooped out of a rocky bed. I could lean for hours over Bishop Trevor's bridge admiring the dark pools, the sudden eddies, the quick shallow channels of the nut-brown Dee. It is a great thing for a town to have a salmon river whispering at its walls day and night just as the other Dee whispers to Ballater.

[2]

About a mile out of Corwen is the village of Bryn-Eglwys. This is, I suppose, one of the places in Wales that every American visits. The name means the Hill of the Church. All round about is property that once belonged to the Yale family.

"The Yale family owned it till the other day," writes A. G. Bradley in his delightful book, *In Praise of North Wales*, "and it was from one of them, who did so much towards founding the famous university in New England two hundred years ago, that it derived its name. He lies buried not in the Yale Chapel attached to this Church of Bryn-Eglwys, but at Wrexham, ten miles away, under an inscribed monument on which his career is briefly but quaintly epitomised:

> *Born in America: in Europe bred,*
> *In Africa travelled and in India wed,*
> *Where long he lived and strived: at London dead.*

"Many Americans, I believe, do pay their respects to Elihu Yale's dust in the beautiful church at Wrexham. But I never heard of one coming up to Yale and Bryn-Eglwys, though I came here myself a good deal in old days. The Yale Chapel where Elihu should by rights have been buried, like the rest of his family, forms the south transept of the little Church of Bryn-Eglwys. The name itself has some interest as being one of the very few territorial surnames surviving in Wales. Indeed, I can only recall three or four more, outside English Pembrokeshire, at any period, though the Border counties had many. . . .

"I venture to think that should any alumnus of that famous university find his way up here some Sunday and take his seat in the Yale Chapel of the old Church of Bryn-Eglwys, among a few hill farmers and shepherds, and hear the old Church of England service read and sung through in the ancient Cymric tongue, he will feel that the cradle, or at least the god-parent, of his Alma Mater is a strange and primitive and romantic spot."

About two miles from the church is Plas-yn-Yale, the family seat, whence the father of Elihu Yale left for America, in the days of the Pilgrim Fathers.

"Do many Americans visit this place?" I asked a man who was working in a field.

"Yes, indeed," he replied. "We had two young men from America who were going round Wales on bicycles. Their grandfathers came from these parts, and they could speak the Welsh, too, but not very well. And they could drink beer. They were fine young men. . . ."

I gathered that these ambassadors had paved the way for other pilgrims in the pretty village beneath the mountain of Llantysilio.

[3]

In the evening I stood on the windy height where the Castle of Denbigh gazes over the wild hills. This is one of the finest sights in the Vale of the Clwyd.

The castle rises five hundred feet above the plain on a crag as harsh and definite as Edinburgh Rock. Its high grey walls are lifted to every wind that blows. This was the Castle Queen Elizabeth gave to the Earl of Leicester, who drained the surrounding country of its resources and lined his pockets so well that the Queen had to interfere.

Into this grim keep rode Charles I after the Battle of Rowton Moor, and it was Denbigh Castle that defied the Parliamentarians for eleven months before it surrendered.

"And if you look down there, please," said the guide, "you'll see a little cottage. It stands on the site of a much older cottage where Stanley, the explorer who found Livingstone, was born. He was a poor boy, and his real name was John Rowlands. . . . It's a pity they pulled down the old place, for he was a great man."

[4]

Conway is like an illustration to a history of Wales. These great castles that rise up on hills all over this country are a lasting tribute to the fighting qualities of the Welsh.

Conway, with its fifteen-feet-thick curtain walls and its fortified town, must have filled Welsh patriots with despair when they looked down on it from the distant hills. I walk round the walls gazing down into courtyards and roofless halls. I look down into the battered shell of this Castle and note how the architect employed every cunning dodge of his time to protect the defender and place the attacker at a disadvantage: the arrow-slits, from the outside so narrow, but from the inside commanding so wide an angle of fire; the cleverly designed doorways so impossible to rush; the spiral stairways that assisted the sword arm of the man above; the narrow entrances that would make it easy for ten men to hold a portion of the castle against a hundred.

All the energy and brains that we today put into a thousand trades and professions were poured, in old times, into the building of castles and churches.

There was nothing else in the world but War and Faith, and, of course, the travelling merchant.

[5]

Now Caernarvon Castle is the most magnificent thing of its kind in the British Isles. Here is a great medieval castle that is outwardly intact but inwardly a ruin. Approach it from the sea, stand under its great walls, and it looks exactly as it did to the Welsh of the Middle Ages. It is only when you pass under the great gateway that you see close-cut lawns and battered arches, walls that begin nowhere and end in midair. It is one of the corner-stones of Wales . . . "that most magnificent badge of our subjection", as Pennant, who was a Welshman, called it.

This Castle was built to subdue the Welsh, who were getting a bit tired of hiding in the mountains. The stern King Edward I was determined to put down the armies of Wales. He spent much of his time travelling round that chain of castles that was once the sorrow but is now the pride of Wales—Conway, Criccieth, Harlech, Bere and Beaumaris. But the biggest of them all was Caernarvon.

The guide swept his walking-stick round the courtyards and rebuilt the Castle for us in words. He showed us the place teeming with life. We saw the cooks carrying steaming dishes from the kitchens, the men-at-arms lounging round the gatehouses, the sentries pacing the walls.

"And here," said one guide, indicating a lawn that had been newly mown, "was the royal dining-hall. There the king sat while archers stood on duty, ready for trouble. Notice that the entrance to the hall was so narrow that only one man could enter at a time.

"Why? Because if the castle were rushed the archers could pick off men one by one as they entered. The entrance would be jammed with dead bodies. In the confusion the king could escape down that stairway over there—it's now blocked up—which leads to a little tunnel in the rock where a boat was always waiting. . . . Now, come along, if you please."

He took us up winding stairs to that little room in the Eagle Tower, associated with one of the most famous stories in Anglo-Welsh history. Whether it is true is another matter.

We were told how Edward's queen, Eleanor of Castile, was sent to Caernarvon to bear on Welsh soil an heir to the throne.

In this little dark den of stone, twelve feet long by eight feet wide, the Queen is said to have given birth to the unlucky child who became Edward II. He was born towards the end of April. The King was at Rhuddlan Castle. He was so overjoyed to hear of his son's birth that he knighted the messenger on the spot and gave him wide acres.

Edward hurried to Caernarvon to see Eleanor and his heir. Three days later all the chiefs of North Wales assembled at the Castle to pay their final homage to the conqueror. Then took place the historic episode, mentioned earlier, that created an English Prince of Wales.

The Welsh chieftains begged Edward to appoint a Prince of Wales to rule over them in his name, a man who could speak neither French nor English.

Edward agreed to this. They swore to obey this prince if his blood was royal and if his character was above reproach. Then the King presented his infant son Edward. He was born in Wales, said the King, his character was fine, he knew no French nor English, and his first words should be in the Welsh language!

The mountaineers, conscious that they had been tricked, knelt and kissed the child's hand. In a few moments the small boy was carried on a shield to the Castle gates and proclaimed "Edward Prince of Wales."

[6]

Snowdon is haunted by both Merlin and Arthur.

The magician, Merlin, appears first on the dome-shaped hill of Dinas Emrys, between Beddgelert and Capel Curig, when Vortigern was building a great castle. But in the night the stones that had been erected during the day were cast down. Vortigern demanded that his wise men should explain this. The chief was told to search for a lad without a father and to sprinkle his blood among the foundations of the building. Sometime after, in the streets of Carmarthen, a boy, who was being taunted by his playfellows because he was fatherless, was captured and taken to Dinas Emrys. This lad was the great and fearsome Merlin of the Arthurian legends.

When he was questioned he displayed so great a knowledge that not only was his life spared but the inferior magicians were put to death. Merlin then gave to Vortigern his version of the phenomenon.

"Two dragons," he said, "one red and one white, live in a subterranean cave beneath the hill. They sleep by day and fight by night, and the fury of their quarrel causes the half-built walls to fall down."

The Red Dragon symbolised the Britons; the White Dragon the Saxons. As long as the struggle continued the Castle would never be completed. And this was true.

The White and the Red Dragons fought for centuries. The White often seemed to win, but the Red Dragon was never beaten to the earth.

And to the solitude of Snowdon comes the mysterious hero, King Arthur. Perhaps nothing will ever be known about this hero of romance. His fame has spread over Europe. Countless poems have been made, and continue to be made about him. Two of his contemporaries, Gildas and Aneurin, do not mention him. Bede had never heard of him. Taliesin and Llywarch Hen mention him casually. Then, centuries after his lifetime, he gradually dawns on history as the exterminator of the heathen Saxon, the gallant King who symbolised the heroic resistance of the Welsh, or Britons, to the invader from over the sea.

Some historians even doubt his existence; others see him as a Roman soldier, or as a Romanised Briton, who, when the legions left this island, remembered enough of organised warfare to be a tower of strength in the bloody days that followed.

[7]

I took the road that skirts the vast shoulder of Cader Idris to Machynlleth. On this road is a still, dark tarn called Tal-y-llyn lying cupped between the hills. It is my idea of the lake from whose surface rose the white hand that drew Excalibur beneath the water.

Some miles onward towards Aberystwyth is a little village called Talybont. I can never resist a water mill. I heard one thrashing and groaning like a sty full of pigs, and went to look at it. It was a big old one, green with weed. The stream that was turning it ran over clear stones and was the sort of stream a fisherman dreams about in a bad season.

No one ever buys trout in Talybont, and sometimes an eighteen-pound salmon is grassed within sound of the wheel.

In this place I discovered the most idyllic factory in Wales. About ten people work a tweed factory as if the Industrial Revolution had never happened. The trout stream gives them power and electric light, and about a century ago someone bought machinery that still works!

And there they are!

"The factory began in 1809," I was told, "when the farmers brought in their wool, which the cottagers used to make into flannels and blankets for them. It was a cottage industry. The women used to spin the wool at home, and the men used to weave the cloth at home. Then the industry became prosperous and soon four mills were going. . . ."

The word "mill" in Talybont means a rustic kind of barn with trees all round it, flowers up to the very door and the music of the trout stream competing with the loom.

[8]

When you look at Fishguard Bay you must remember the last hostile invasion of British soil. There is a strong flavour of musical comedy about it, although it caused a deal of excitement at the time.

It was on 22 February 1797 at ten o'clock in the morning that three men-of-war and a lugger were seen coming towards the bay from the direction of St. David's Head. The people of St. David's, considering them to be British ships because they flew the British flag, cheered them heartily until a retired seaman recognised them as French warships. A panic spread through Pembrokeshire. Men and women fled inland with their valuables.

The ships dropped anchor and landed a force of six hundred French infantry and eight hundred French convicts in a little cove at Carreg Gwastad Point, about two and a half miles west of Fishguard. The troops were under the command of an Irish-American, General Tate. We can imagine the alarm in Pembrokeshire, which had known no fighting since the Civil War, with the enemy on its doorstep and no local troops within many miles of Fishguard! Messengers rode north and south. Lord Cawdor, who was the acting Lieutenant of the county, lived thirty-five miles away. He was awakened in the middle of the night with a no doubt highly coloured account of the invasion. He jumped out of bed to take command of the defence force. Meanwhile the "fiery cross" had been sent round to the local yeomanry and militia. There must have been many dramatic farewells and many heroic moments that night as squire and farmer said good-bye to their womenfolk, buckled on swords or grasped muskets and set off to fight the bloodless battle of Fishguard Bay.

Lord Cawdor arrived at noon on the following day with a mixed force of yeomanry and militia. His total force was about seven hundred and fifty, but his "army" was followed by a great rabble armed with mattocks, spades, scythes and reaping-hooks. A Captain Davies, who had seen active service, was entrusted with the responsibility of placing the British force in the most imposing formation. He wisely dotted it about the hills.

The French meantime were not happy. For some reason, which I think has never been explained, their fleet suddenly hoisted sail and deserted them! They were left on the rugged shore watching the mysterious preparations of the defenders. They saw gorgeously dressed and splendidly mounted men cantering about, and these—the Castle Martin Yeomanry—they mistook for the staff officers of a very imposing army. The wind that blew away the warships began to blow in the French camp! But—says legend—the Frenchmen's terror was increased when on the distant hills they saw the marching and counter-marching of redcoats. They did not know that cunning Captain Davies was using the Welsh women in their red cloaks and their tall beaver hats to impress them! It is even said that this Welsh Ulysses marched a file of women up and down a hill in the approved operatic manner in order to cause the enemy to believe that a huge army was marching to the support. For two hours the gallant "red cloaks" are said to have impersonated the British Grenadiers!

That night at ten o'clock two French officers came up under a flag of truce. They were summoned to a council of war held in the old Royal Oak Inn.

The end of it was, of course, the unconditional surrender of the French. They first opened the pans of their muskets and shed the powder, then, with drums playing, were marched without arms or colours to the junction of the Fishguard-Goodwick road.

[9]

The road takes you to a village with three streets. It is a hushed little village, and in the middle of it, looking as if it had been blown from a great church, is a grey tower. You discover, when you approach this tower, that it belongs to a splendid church that hides itself in a hollow. Whether its far-off builders placed it there to

94 *Lake Windermere, Westmorland*

95 *Rydal Water, Westmorland*

96 *The statue of Sir Walter Scott in George Square, Glasgow*

97 *Glasgow University
buildings from
Kelvingrove Park*

98 *Neidpath Castle and the River Tweed near Peebles, southern Scotland*

99 *The upper reaches of the Tweed near Drumelzier, Peebles*

safeguard it from the Atlantic winds or to hide it from pirates in war-boats we do not know, but no other great church hides itself so securely from the winds of God and the eyes of men. This is the Cathedral of St. David.

It is the most historic and the most significant building in Wales. I went down thirty-nine steps to it, and before I entered I sat for a time looking at it, thinking that from the outside there is nothing to admire. You must admire it with your imagination.

This is the oldest Cathedral in Great Britain. In its foundations Roman Britain and Wales meet. It was founded by St. David about the year 550—or forty-seven years before Pope Gregory sent St. Augustine to convert England! When the first Christian church was built on this site it is probable that the only other Christian churches in Britain were St. Ninian's white chapel at Whithorn and an anchorite's little cell at Glastonbury.

St. Columba had just planted his first monastery in the oak grove at Derry, but he had not yet deserted Ireland to found Iona. It is an astonishing experience to look at a church with a history that goes back beyond Iona, beyond Canterbury Cathedral, beyond Lindisfarne.

St. David is said to have been born in 530, just one hundred and forty years after Honorius withdrew the legions from Britain. He would be born into a Britain that was still Roman in thought and speech. All we know of him historically is that he was a notable theologian, an enemy of Pelagianism, and that he died at the age of seventy.

I entered the Cathedral and found myself in a building that impressed me at once, partly because of the tone of the purple and reddish stone of which it is built, partly because of the rich Transition-Norman arches, partly because of the magnificent but totally out-of-place oak roof and also because of the sharp contrast of the stern exterior.

Wales possesses more Norman castles in a small area than any country in Europe, but this was the first great Norman building I had seen which was dedicated to God. The small British churches on this site were burnt and pillaged by the Danes, and it was not until the time of the third Norman bishop, Peter de Leia, that the present St. David's sprang up in the hollow. Like all ancient churches, it has been rebuilt and restored from age to age.

The most perfect portion of St. David's is, in my opinion, the Sanctuary. Here is an exquisite and perfectly balanced exercise in stone, much as it was left by the builders in the time of Peter de Leia. Nearly every feature of St. David's can be surpassed by cathedrals in England, but this Sanctuary is, in its way, unique and perfect.

East of the choir is a plain, arcaded shrine known as the Shrine of St. David, although it is obviously merely the place on which rested the movable casket containing the relics of the Saint. A few yards away is a plain sarcophagus of Purbeck marble, the most interesting tomb in St. David's: the tomb of Edmund Tudor, Earl of Richmond, father of King Henry VII.

It is strange to stand in this church on the wild, western limits of the Principality above the father of the great Tudor and Elizabethan Age. This tomb stood originally in the Church of the Grey Friars in Carmarthen and was brought to St. David's during the Dissolution by the order of Edmund's grandson, Henry VIII.

Edmund was the eldest son of the handsome Anglesey squire Owen Tudor, whose secret love affair with Henry V's widow, Katherine de Valois, caused a deal of scandal at the time. Edmund's only claim to fame is that he married and became the father of a son called Henry. He was never to see the lad who was born to be king. Edmund's married life lasted barely a year, and the child was born after his death.

So rests the grandfather of Henry VIII and the great-grandfather of Elizabeth: a Welshman who never knew he had founded a new dynasty and reconciled his country to her ancient foe.

When the evening sun falls over St. David's Cathedral, gilding the old stone, shining on the gentle green hills, the white, twisting roads and the little farms, the smallest "city" in the kingdom lies lost in its mighty memories. The sea wind drops, the smoke rises upwards from the chimneys, and a man looking at the church in the hollow knows it to possess the longest memory in Britain.

[10]

Cardiff is a beautiful and dignified city. Upon seeing it for the first time one feels he is meeting some congenial and charming person of whom he has heard nothing but slander. For Cardiff is often said by those outside Wales to be a city of smoke, chimneys, Chinese laundries, mean streets, docks and an occasional race riot.

One reason for this is that the outside world gains its impressions of Cardiff from the newspapers, since writers about Wales, almost without exception, fight shy of Cardiff and Glamorganshire as if they were plague spots, or they slur over them in an apologetic way. This is wrong. Cardiff is the most important city in Wales, and no man can pretend to have seen Wales unless he visits Cardiff and the county whose minerals have drawn into it over one million two hundred thousand human beings, or about half the total population of the Principality.

Visitors from English industrial centres who go to North Wales in the summer in order to forget their own chimneys cannot, perhaps, be expected to feel any interest in Glamorganshire, but the real traveller in Wales must explore the coal valleys that stretch northward like the fingers of a hand, of which Cardiff is the palm.

Cardiff is surprising because it is one of the few beautiful cities to have grown out of the Industrial Revolution. This is because it grew up round Cardiff Castle, which is still its centre, and because the purchase of the adjoining Cathays Park from Lord Bute gave the Corporation the opportunity to group its civic buildings together in the heart of the city. Cardiff grew up as rapidly as any other industrial city of the last hundred and fifty years, but the presence of this untouched Park in the centre of her streets was her architectural salvation. All town-planning schemes of the last half-century have meant pulling down; Cardiff had merely to buy Cathays Park and build up.

No wonder the people of Cardiff are proud of Cathays Park. It contains some of the finest public buildings in Great Britain. They give to Cardiff a coherence and a definite centre such as few other great provincial cities possess. London is pulled together in much the same way by Whitehall in the west and the Bank to the east. And the first thing that happens to you when you enter Cardiff is a visit to Cathays Park. The Cardiff man who insists on taking you there looks proudly at the white buildings that stand back in a leisurely way behind grass and trees, and he points to a large and still unbuilt-on site.

"That," he says, "is reserved for the Welsh House of Commons."

And it looks it. Cathays Park with the Red Dragon over the City Hall has the appearance of a capital.

Cardiff is an ancient Roman fortress that has grown into one of the greatest commercial cities of our time. The buses run past a high wall. Behind the wall is a green park beside the River Taff, and in the grounds of this park is Cardiff Castle.

It is a strange meeting of ancient and modern. People on top of the Cardiff buses can look over this wall to lawns where peacocks walk, to a mound with its tall keep, to encircling ramparts that look like Roman walls. So a city that has grown up out of an age of steam and machinery preserves in its centre a vivid memory of an age of swords.

When Robert Fitz-Hamon, one of the Norman adventurers who was permitted to seize Welsh property, came to Cardiff in the year 1090, he saw the ruins of a Roman *castrum*. This was all that remained of Caer-Dyr, the stronghold on the Taff. It was in Roman times an outpost station of the legionary base at Caerleon. When the Norman Fitz-Hamon saw it, the walls were standing in a condition that made it possible to restore them. The gateways through which the II (Augusta) Legion marched out to police the district were still visible. The Norman dug a great moat, filled it with water from the Taff and on the cone-shaped mound of excavated earth built the first Cardiff Castle. When its time had come, it fell, like the Roman camp, into decay, and Cardiff Castle was built in a different part of the enclosure.

One of the most interesting features of the Castle is a modern reconstruction of a Roman gateway. It is, I think, the only one of its kind in the country. It is the north gate of the Roman camp, and it has been beautifully rebuilt, complete with its sentry walk where in the dim past the Eagles of Rome kept watch and ward over South Wales.

No industrial city in Great Britain lives on such intimate terms with its ancient Castle. Manchester, Birmingham and Liverpool have ages ago lost touch with their hereditary landowners, but men in livery can be seen at the gates of Cardiff Castle, the representatives of the custodians who have been on duty since Norman times!★

One feature of Cardiff that must impress every stranger is the University. You cannot dine out without meeting a professor; you cannot walk anywhere without meeting the youth of Wales. And this, I think, is partly responsible for the air of vitality about Cardiff. There are moments of the day when it seems a city inhabited by the young.

A splendid building in Cathays Park is that of the National Museum of Wales. It was founded "to teach the world about Wales and the Welsh people about their own fatherland". It is perfectly designed and arranged.

The collection that fascinated me is the "Bygones" Gallery. Here are assembled examples of Welsh handicrafts made before the era of mass production. There are sturdy Welsh "dressers"; Welsh country furniture, armchairs, basketwork, pottery, spinning-wheels, farm implements, pack-saddles and a hundred and one objects from a prettier and a more leisurely age.

★These functionaries were replaced in 1948 by those of the municipality when the third Marquess of Bute presented Cardiff Castle to the city.

The East and
North of England

[I]

Colchester is a busy town set on a hill and surrounded by a pinkish wall erected about eighteen hundred years ago by the ex-soldiers of Rome. Its ancient churches are built of Roman tiles; its Norman Castle is built of the debris of the Roman citadel; its streets are not winding and medieval, but run north and south after the plan of a Roman camp. And if you take a spade and dig in Colchester you find, below innocent-looking cabbage patches and beneath ordinary simple gardens, that Rome still sleeps only a few feet deep in a white powder of decayed oyster shells. Those oysters must have compensated many a miserable exile.

It was during the First World War, when stationed at Colchester for some time and moved by a mighty ennui, that I started digging at the end of a tennis lawn and came, at the close of a hot afternoon, to a beautiful Roman pavement of red and white tesserae. How the sun shone again on the bright cubes that had known the tread of sandals!

What a thrill exists in uncovering the everyday things of the past, of handling them fresh from the earth, of feeling the link that binds the present to the past, of saying: "When this was made Nero was Emperor and men still lived who had been present at the Crucifixion. . . ."

I arrived in Colchester as the sun was setting and decided to stay the night there. In the morning, after visiting the Castle and the Siege House, I took the field path to Lexden, which overlooks the Colne Valley. We used to flag-wag across this valley during the war. I suppose the Romans also signalled from these heights.

Weeks of rain followed by warm spring days had caused the soft earth in the hedge banks to crumble, with the result that large stones were pushed from the soil by their own weight and lay at the foot of the hedge. I always treat broken earth in Colchester with respect. I remembered the American who once said that you had "only to tickle Colchester with a spade and it coughs up bits of Rome". My comment is that you do not always need a spade: a walking-stick is often as effective.

As I walked along, prodding the earth here and there with my stick, I was delighted and not too surprised to see a touch of bright red in the brown soil. I placed my stick in the earth slightly above this red streak and flicked out upon the narrow path the base of a Samian bowl with the potter's name neatly inscribed in Roman capitals upon it. The letters I read when I had wiped the caked clay and soil from the potsherd were SEVERUS. F. The F. stands for *fecit*, so the inscription reads: "Severus made it."

The well-known Roman potters—and hundreds of them are known with the localities of their factories, the dates they exported their various specialities to the most remote corners of the Roman Empire—invariably signed their plates, bowls and vases in this way, or their names in the genitive preceded by OF. (*officina*, or "workshop"), or followed by the letter M. (for *manus*, or "by the hand of").

And so I stood polishing the little chip of ancient Rome with a handkerchief, marvelling that through the hazards of eighteen centuries it should yet exist to fall out of a hedge with its message: "Severus made it." What a message to receive from an English hedge on a windy April morning!

Severus was one of the famous East Gaulish potters of the time of Nero. Galley-loads of his bright red wares were shipped to Britain. The shops stocked it in Camulodunum, which is Colchester; in Londinium; in Verulamium, which is St. Albans; in Deva, which is Chester; in Eboracum, which is York. Traders carried it by pack-horse up to the great Wall of Hadrian where we may imagine it decorating the tables of the better sort. Most of this pottery was made in Gaul. Severus had his workshop on the Rhine at Neuss, which was then Novassium, one of the oldest towns in Germany.

When I held this relic in my hand I saw again so clearly the Britain with which it was linked, the misty island mentioned so casually by Suetonius, Dion Cassius and Tacitus, three writers whose businesslike sentences seem to blow aside the fog of history for a second to show us legions marching through Kent and Essex, heavy war galleys creeping like water beetles up wide river estuaries, cavalry scouts picking their way gingerly through marsh and forest, coming to hilltop villages fenced with wattle and desolate, for the tribes had fled to the forests, there to hide themselves from the Eagles and to bide their time.

In this fog the war horns of the legions low like bulls and grow fainter to the north, while behind them on hills beside rivers sound the carpenter's hammer, the woodcutter's axe, the stonemason's chisel, the song of galley slaves at the anchorages and, at last, the voice of a merchant praising his goods . . . London.

So England emerges from the mist.

[2]

I was lost in a Norfolk lane, so I stopped a man and said to him:

"Good morning!"

He looked at me.

"Good morning," I cried. "Can you tell me if I am right for Norwich?"

The ghost of a smile flitted over his rustic face, and he replied after some deep thought, rather reluctantly, and looking away from me:

"Well; you're right!"

I don't expect any one to believe this unless he knows Norfolk. Norfolk is the most suspicious county in England. In Devon and Somerset men clap you on the back cordially; in Norfolk they look as though they would like to hit you over the head—till they size you up. You see, for centuries the north folk of East Anglia were accustomed to meeting on lonely roads stray Vikings who had just waded ashore from the longboats.

"Good morning, 'bor!" said the Vikings. "Which is the way to the church?"

"What d'ye want to know for?" was the Norfolk retort.

"Well, we thought about setting fire to it!"

You will gather that Norfolk's suspicion of strangers, which is an ancient complex bitten into the East Anglian through centuries of bitter experience, is well grounded and should never annoy the traveller. They mean well. Once they bring themselves to call you "'bor" (which, I conclude, is short for "neighbour" or, perhaps, "boy"), you can consider yourself highly complimented. In East Anglia men are either neighbours or Vikings. If they promote you to 'bordom they will do any mortal thing for you except, perhaps, lend you money, for one Norfolk farmer could beat any three Yorkshiremen at driving a bargain.

The word "'bor" is the most popular one in the Norfolk dialect, except perhaps "mauther", which means girl. Norfolk is full of sturdy, good-looking mauthers with magnificent necks and arms. Some wear flaxen hair in plaits round their ears and look like young Brünnhildes, reminding you that sometimes the Vikings settled down in Norfolk.

The churches of Norfolk are unique. The art of using flint for building is here developed as I have seen it in no other county. Hundreds of thousands of flints a few inches square are embedded in the mortar, forming a polished grey wall hard as steel and indestructible. The effect is unusual, and if you have ever tried to chip flint—which is the most difficult, unreasonable, capricious stone in the world— you look at these churches with added reverence.

The most surprising thing about Norwich is that it contains the only Norman Cathedral in England unknown to Americans. Norwich is not on the pilgrimage map, and the reason is geographical. The tourist stream flows due south from Lincoln to Peterborough—Ely—Cambridge, leaving Norwich in the great eastward bulge of Norfolk fifty miles to the left. Someday, of course, the people who map tours will discover Norwich (and the fourteenth-century hotel that has hot and cold water laid on to the bedrooms); someday, maybe, Norwich may even discover itself.

It is a confusing, characteristic city. It was tied up into hasty knots centuries ago and has never been unwound. It is a monument to the north folk and it bears the marks of all their peculiarities—it has flint walls, and is difficult to know at a glance. Norwich in Somerset would be unthinkable; it is an expression of sturdy East Anglia. I came here knowing nothing about the city except that it has always made money, that it once was the third city in England, that when its weaving trade went north after the coalfields, Norwich just put on a flinty face and learned how to make women's shoes. Trust Norwich to survive!

I saw a red-roofed city dominated by two landmarks: a slim Cathedral spire second only to Salisbury and a great square Norman Castle on a hill in the heart of which—so George Borrow said confidently—sits an old heathen king "with his sword in his hand and his gold and silver treasures about him". I went through queer medieval streets, many paved with cobblestones, all distinguished by a picturesque dowdiness; some Flemish in appearance, full of houses with the big inverted V on the top storey where the handlooms were housed; and at night beside the river I might have been in the England or the Netherlands of the fourteenth century with the moon falling on huddled roofs, the lamplight moving in slow waters, the dark figures of men and women going through alleyways between the leaning eaves.

Norwich has been called the "city of churches". It struck me also as a city of public houses and canaries. In hundreds of little homes the shoemakers of Norwich breed prize canaries and discuss points as keenly as Newmarket discusses a horse. If you wanted to stop the traffic in Norwich the quickest way would be to walk through the city with a first-class Norwich Plain Head on your finger!

"Those are the boys that pay the rent!" said a shoemaker's wife to me, nodding to a cage full of little gold birds.

100 *The Eildon Hills from Scott's View, Berwickshire*

101 *Abbotsford House, Roxburghshire*

102 *Abbotsford, the home of Sir Walter Scott*

103 *The Castle, Scott Monument, and Princes Street, Edinburgh*

104 *The Edinburgh Tattoo*

105 *The Castle Mound, Edinburgh*

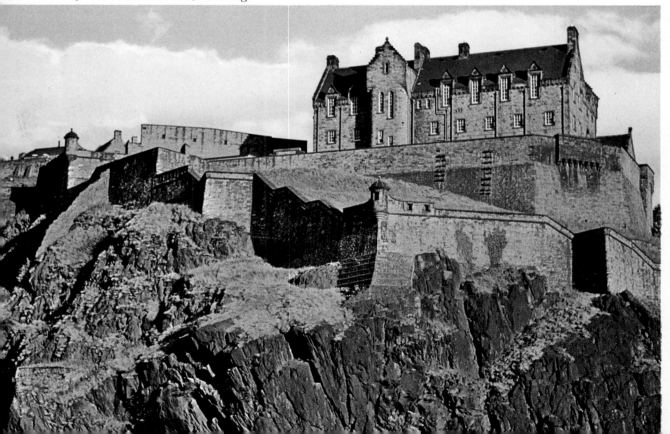

I met a man who keeps, in the season, more than five thousand canaries. He exports them to Australia, Canada, India, New Zealand.

There comes a time in the life of all old cities when the city fathers should decide whether their city is to preserve its ancient beauty or to become a second Leicester or a little Birmingham. Norwich, it seems to me, has reached this moment.

In fifty years' time Norwich will either not be worth looking at or it will be one of the most beautiful old cities in England. Few cities possess so many complete streets of half-timbered houses, some medieval, some Tudor—most are disguised by ugly Georgian plaster, which, if scraped off, would reveal the old red brick and oak. Under intelligent treatment Norwich would emerge like a restored oil-painting.

I descended into the nethermost dungeons of Norwich Castle, which are not open to the public. They are cut in the heart of the rock. The hole with a twelve-foot drop through which the miserable prisoners were flung into darkness is still in the roof. When the match went out the darkness was horrible. It seemed to close round me. I could feel blackness—the blackness of a living grave.

Strangers' Hall, which stands in a small courtyard in a busy street, is one of the most beautiful small medieval houses you will see anywhere. Norwich is packed with such unexpected sights.

The Cathedral is full of splendid Norman work, notably the nave. The clerestory, set back within a wall passage, has Norman lights; the aisles also are Norman. There is a curious opening in the roof through which the monks used to let down a swinging censer.

[3]

Well and truly was Chester called by the Britons Caer Lleon, the "City of the Legions". Chester is still the "City of the Legions", only they come from Louisville, and Oshkosh, New York and Washington.

For years I have heard people describe the wonder of a walk round the walls of Chester. Naturally the first thing I did when I arrived here was to find the wall, which is not difficult. Chester, as you must know, is the only city in England that retains its medieval wall complete: a high red sandstone walk with towers at various strategic points along its course; on one side a handrail to prevent you from falling into back gardens, on the other a waist-high barrier from which in old times the Cestrians were in the habit of defying their enemies with boiling oil —and anything else that came handy. "Blessed is he that expecteth little" is a wise

maxim that has been drummed into me since I first sat up and wanted the moon;
but I have never absorbed it. I realised this on the walls of Chester.

Any man might with justice, I think, expect that as he walked a medieval town
wall something at least heroic would meet his eye, but the walls of Chester gave
me only a much better idea of other people's washing, the gasworks and the
canal. You see, Chester within the wall remains medieval, but Chester outside
the wall is industrial. It has not been possible for Chester to retain a wide open
space outside the wall, and, consequently, the wall of Chester stands with its arms
round beautiful old Chester, while ugly new Chester peeps over the parapet from
the other side.

I had been walking for about ten minutes, admiring the small, reddy-brown
Cathedral through the trees, when I came to a turret approached by a flight of
ancient steps, and on the wall was this dramatic inscription:

KING CHARLES
STOOD ON THIS TOWER
SEPTEMBER 24TH, 1645, AND SAW
HIS ARMY DEFEATED
ON ROWTON MOOR

Inside the tower a man was presiding over a little Museum. He told me, just
as though he were present at the time, that when the Royalist army was riding
to reinforce the garrison at Chester, the Roundheads set upon them and routed
them, with poor King Charles standing on this tower watching every move of
the game. There are various battlefield relics in the Museum, also several Roman
antiquities that take the mind back to the days when that magnificent Legion,
the XX, known as the "Valeria Victrix", was the crack regiment of Deva.

I had been walking for miles, wondering if the wall of Chester ever completes
its circle, when I came to what any exhausted visitor must regard as a poor joke.
Here, near Bridge Gate, is a long flight of steps arranged in sets of three and known
as the "Wishing Steps".

"Why?" I asked a man who was standing on them, looking as though none
of his wishes had ever come true.

"Well," he said in the curiously blunt way they have here, "you have to run
up and down and up again without taking breath, and then they say you'll get
your wish."

I noticed a band of breathless Americans standing on the other side, utterly
vanquished. I decided to try no conclusions with the Wall of Chester and passed
on in a superior way, mentally deciding to have a wish—for I can never resist
these challenges of Fate—some morning when I could come fresh and vigorous

to the steps. That, however, I learn is not playing the game; you must walk the wall first and then "run up and down and up again", a feat I shall leave to the natives—and to the legions!

There is one feature of Chester that, to my mind, is worth ten walls. There is nothing like it in any English town—the Chester "Rows".

Like Verona, Chester is a town of balconies. The first impression I received was that of a town whose inhabitants spend a great portion of their lives leaning over old oak galleries, smoking and chatting and watching life go by below them in the streets.

"The Rows" are simply long, covered arcades formed by running a highway through the first storeys of a street of old buildings. You mount from the roadway to "the Rows" on frequent flights of stone steps and find yourself in the strangest shopping streets in England. Here are the best shops hidden away in the darkness of these ancient arcades, and it is possible to shop dry-shod in the worst weather. There is a peculiar charm about "the Rows". They are not typically medieval—there is no record of any other street of this kind in the Middle Ages—yet they impart a singular impression of medievalism: Through the oak beams supporting the galleries you see black-and-white half-timbered houses on the opposite side of the street, with another "Row" cut through their first floors, on whose balconies people are leaning and talking and regarding the flow of life.

The main streets of Chester give you the impression that a huge galleon has come to anchor there with easy, leisurely passengers leaning on the deck rails.

This peculiar feature of Chester has worried the antiquaries more than anything. Theories to explain how and why these peculiar streets grew up are numerous and none of them is definite.

"Who knows why they were built?" said a local antiquary. "One theory is that the ruins of the Roman buildings inspired the architects of later times. Another theory is that the arcades were formed during the Middle Ages to provide street defence against Welsh raiders; a third theory explains them on the ground that traders erected their buildings on the ruins of the Roman castrum, the most valuable ground, naturally, in the town, and, as other traders were attracted to the same profitable site, a further row of buildings rose up on the ruins behind the first, from which, of course, it is but a step to a covered arcade running the length of the street. But no one can say with certainty how they evolved. 'The Rows' are one of the architectural mysteries of England. . . ."

Chester is as "medieval" as Clovelly is "quaint". There is no getting away from it! At night a walk through "the Rows" is eerie. These long tunnels are almost pitch-dark. When the shops are closed they are deserted, for the Cestrians then take to the normal roadway, through colonnades upheld by vast oak beams, half-expecting to hear the scuffle of hired assassins and the gasp of a man with a dagger in his neck. I have yet to meet a more dramatic street.

Chester is so accustomed to ancient things that no one considered it strange to drink coffee in a twelfth-century crypt. There is a beautiful vaulted crypt that has been converted into a restaurant. I went there and sat utterly crushed by my surroundings. I looked round for the monks, but saw only young men and women, taking what seemed sacrilegious sips of tea and eating cream cakes!

One of the happiest memories of my search will be the recollection of the many times I have hung out of hotel and inn windows before going to bed listening to the night sounds of towns and cities and villages. I must write a story about them some day. At night, when the crowds have gone home, and the last American has drunk the last highball in the smoke-room, ancient cities like Chester come most vividly to life. So you must leave me in Chester, under a big round moon, leaning out in the soft coolness of the night, watching the Valeria Victrix stack spears in the main street and stand back waiting for orders to found one of the oldest cities in England.

And it was on the "holy Dee", the broad, slow river that winds itself round Chester, that King Edgar in 973 gave away his character to posterity by being rowed in his barge by tributary princes. And it was in Chester . . . I could go on through history picking out little pictures of Chester; but it is so late, and the moon is riding high above this silent city, where old houses dream across old streets with their roots among the little red tiles of Rome.

[4]

The change of country at the Cheshire–Lancashire border is as startling as the change between Cornwall and Devon or between the sweet lowland counties and the wild Marches of Wales. Here the traveller enters Industrial England.

I looked at the map. I was passing between Liverpool on the left and Manchester on the right, and about sixteen miles from both cities. Far off to the left I could see the Mersey Estuary, with red smokestacks rising. There was an ominous grey haze in the sky that meant Manchester. Here was a new England: an England of crowded towns, of tall chimneys, of great mill walls, of canals of slow black water; an England of grey, hard-looking little houses in interminable rows; the England of coal and chemicals; of cotton, glass and iron.

Yet how difficult it is to kill an English field, to stamp out the English grass or to deform an English lane! Even here, within sixteen miles of the two great giants of the north, men were raking hay in a field within gunshot of factory chimneys.

With the beautiful old England that I love so fresh in mind, I stood ready to be horrified by the Black Belt; yet, strangely, I stood impressed and thrilled by the grim power of these ugly chimneys rising in groups, by the black huddle of factories, the still, silent wheels at pit mouth and the drifting haze of smoke.

At Warrington I heard the clap-clop of clogs, since fallen into disuse; at Warrington I saw mill girls with shawls over their heads; at Warrington I smelt for the first time the characteristic aroma that permeates the industrial towns and villages of Lancashire—fried fish and chips.

Mill towns look grandly impressive from a hill, but when you dive into their streets, the stark ugliness of the long, barracky, prison-like houses, run up so quickly to serve the servants of the machines, gives you an ache. The only consolation is that these monster towns and cities of the north of England are a mere speck in the amazing greenness of England: their inhabitants can be lost in green fields and woodland within a few minutes. London is much more distant from a real wood than Warrington.

On Sundays, in all the grey villages of Lancashire, the miners sit on their haunches against the walls, their hands between their knees. They are the only Englishmen who squat like Arabs. In the centre of nearly every group is a white whippet on a lead. The men sit and smoke, regarding the highway with a certain bright expectation.

I saw with great interest a signpost marked "Wigan". Who could resist a glimpse of Wigan?

Wigan, were it not inhabited by a race of sturdy and rather tough Lancashire folk, would be the most self-conscious town in England. For years it has suffered from a joke. The words "Wigan Pier" spoken by a comedian on a music-hall stage were sufficient to make an audience howl with laughter.

Wigan, to millions of people who have never seen and never will see the town, represents the apex of the world's pyramid of gloom. So serious has the Wigan joke become that the go-ahead Corporation, who are full of local pride, take what steps they can to counteract it; but the silly old joke goes on! Certain Wigonians of high commercial standing believe that this joke delays the prosperity of Wigan, which not only affords rich sites for new factories, but also offers all the necessary conditions for manufacture, such as good transport, labour and coal, so to speak, laid on in normal times.

Now, I had been in Wigan just ten minutes when I saw that there is no joke! Wigan is a spa compared with towns like Wednesbury, in the Black Country, and with certain of the Staffordshire pottery towns. I admit that I, too, shared the common idea of Wigan. I admit that I came here prepared to write an impression of unrelieved gloom—of dreary streets and stagnant canals and white-faced Wigonians dragging their weary steps along dull streets haunted by the horror of the place in which they are condemned to live.

This is nonsense. I would not mind spending a holiday in Wigan—a short one.

"This town has been badly libelled," I said to a man who was standing in the main street.

"I'm reet glad to hear thee say that!" he cried warmly. "I've lived in Wigan all my life and wish for no better town."

He beamed on me. He offered to show me the chief glories of Wigan. I told him that I wanted to find them for myself. Still he beamed on me! They all do this in Wigan if you go up and say frankly that the town has a certain attraction.

When you enter Wigan expecting the worst, it is surprising to find a place that still bears some of the signs of an old-fashioned country town. Its wide main street meanders down a hill in a casual, leisurely way. Along this street are many modern half-timbered buildings. The Corporation of Wigan has made a rule that buildings on the main streets must be rebuilt in the Tudor style, so that in twenty years or so there will not be a more original or better-looking manufacturing town in the north of England.

During an hour's walk round Wigan I discovered many things. Wigan was made by the Romans. They called it Coccium, which I think is a much funnier name. Perhaps the legions went into fits of laughter when any one said "Coccium" in Roman Britain! All that remains of Coccium is a Roman altar, which I found built into the north window bay of the tower of the fine but much-restored fourteenth-century church.

King Arthur knew Wigan. It is famed as the scene of some of his most glorious exploits.

Beyond the Market Square I entered a park of about thirty acres. In it were Italian gardens and an ornamental lake. In slandered Wigan I found one of the few good war memorials I have seen in England, and also the largest open market-place outside Nottingham.

But no one could tell me the meaning of the word Wigan. So I went to the Town Clerk.

"The derivation is obscure," he said. "It is Saxon, of course, for we are very old. The Wigan motto is 'Ancient and Loyal', you know. I believe that the word Wigan means 'the rowan trees near the Church'."

"And this," I said, "is the name that rocks a thousand stalls!"

"Yes," he replied, "the Wigan joke has gone too far! It is surprising what a joke can do to a town. It can spread an entirely false idea. Now, just let me take you to the outskirts of Wigan, and you will agree that few manufacturing towns are surrounded by such rustic scenery. . . ."

We went round Wigan. Before we had left the town we smelt hay. Wigan is surrounded by fields that rise on the north towards Duxberry Hall, the only American pilgrimage in this part of the world, where the doughty Miles Standish was probably born. On the main road we came to the scene of Wigan's most cherished legend: a rough stone cross.

"That," explained the Town Clerk, "is Mabs Cross. It is mentioned in Walter Scott's *The Betrothed*. The story is that while Sir William Bradshaigh, a knight of Wigan, was away on the Crusades his wife Mabel, believing him to have been killed, married a Welsh knight. However, Sir William came home, discovered what had happened and killed the Welsh knight, for which he was outlawed for one year. His wife Mabel was publicly shamed. Her confessor imposed this penalty: that once every week she must walk, bare-legged and barefoot, to Mabs Cross. I believe it all ended happily and that husband and wife came together again!"

Within five minutes of notorious Wigan we were in the depth of the country. On either side were fields in which men were making hay; old bridges spanned streams; there were high hedges, delicious little woods and valleys.

"This is all Wigan!" said the Town Clerk with a smile.

This town is interesting as a perfect example of a busy industrial town with a fine record in pre-industrial England. Wigan is not a mushroom town that grew up overnight on a coalfield. It has history, and behind it is the tradition of centuries of loyalty to the Crown.

Henry I incorporated the town in 1100. A specimen of the twelfth-century seal may still be seen. During the Civil War, Cromwell pursued the retreating Royalist army through the streets of Wigan, and in 1651 the Earl of Derby suffered a defeat at the "Battle of Wigan Lane", which cost him his head. When the Mayor of Wigan goes out in state, before him is borne a sword that was given to the town in 1660 by Charles II in special token of his favour for the loyalty of Wigan at the Restoration.

That was the closing event in Wigan's pre-industrial history. Then came King Coal in the nineteenth century, and Wigan began a new life.

[5]

I am sitting in the great Abbey of Selby, recalling a story.

About the time when William the Conqueror was sharpening his sword, with an eye on the Channel ports, a young monk called Benedict was praying before the high altar of the Abbey of St. Germanus, at Auxerre, in France. The holiest object in the Abbey was the middle finger of the right hand of St. Germanus.

Now, as Benedict prayed, asking that God might deem him worthy to achieve some great deed, lo! St. Germanus came to him in a vision and said:

"Go to England, to a place called Salebeia [Selby], and there build a church to the glory of God and dedicate it to me."

Although Benedict revered his patron more truly than any other monk of Auxerre, he was too good a Frenchman not to view residence in England without a sinking heart. He even dared to procrastinate with the Saint; but Germanus appeared in a second vision and repeated his order. Benedict was still piously stubborn. Yet a third time the Saint appeared to the young man; this time he instructed him to take the sacred middle finger of the right hand from the high altar and to make a hole in his arm beneath the shoulder-blade and the elbow, assuring him freedom from pain or inflammation and, by virtue of the holy thing he bore, safety in England.

Benedict then obeyed.

Now, Benedict had misunderstood his instructions. We next hear of him not in Salebeia (which was Selby in Yorkshire) but in Salisberia (which was Salisbury in Wiltshire). He was preparing to settle down when St. Germanus, appearing patiently for the fourth time, corrected the young monk's geography.

He then found his way across wildest England to King's Lynn, in Norfolk, where, taking ship, he sailed up the Humber and planted his cross in Selby.

Now, while poor Benedict was working out his salvation, a Frenchman of a different type was rampaging through England with excellent cavalry. The arrow had fallen into the eye of Harold at Hastings, and the Tower of London was being built. At this time the Conqueror's baron at York happened to be sailing on the Ouse at Selby, where he saw a cross on a hill and a young man building a wooden church. He left his ship, heard his countryman's story and promised to enlist his lord's sympathy.

In a short time Selby Abbey was founded by royal charter from William I.

Selby is still royal. It shares with Westminster, York, the Chapels Royal, Windsor and Bristol, the right to robe its choir in red. It still remembers the King who built it so long ago. On 17 July 1928 all that is left of the great Abbey of Selby celebrated the nine-hundredth anniversary of the birthday of William the Conqueror.

All that is left? Its power and its grandeur have gone; its superlative beauty remains. It was once the third-richest abbey in the north. Its abbot was mitred.

106 *Stirling Castle*

107 *The new road bridge over the Firth of Forth at South Queensferry*

108 *The Forth Railway Bridge*

109 *The Palace of Holyroodhouse, Edinburgh*

He rode the way to Parliament. Kings came to Selby. Now its only endowment is £56 a year, and the hat is always going round to keep these lovely stones in repair.

"If only I were a younger man," said the vicar to me, "nothing on earth would keep me away from America. There I would get the money we need!"

He looked up eloquently towards the south windows of the choir, where George Washington's arms, the Stars (which are really spurs) and Stripes have been in position since 1584. Americans will go to any part of England to look at the Washington Arms.

There is another interesting piece of heraldry in the Selby windows. One shield shows a bend sinister, the sign of illegitimacy. Who on earth, people have wondered, wished to advertise this? The explanation is that when the window was repaired and re-leaded in 1866, this shield was placed inside out so that the "bend" became a "bend sinister".

The mystery of Selby Abbey is the dark room over the north porch. It is not open to the public, but I was taken up into it. Nothing has ever been written about this, and no expert who has seen it has been able to explain it.

The way up to it is by a series of dark, winding, spiral staircases on the south side of the west end of the church. Then, still climbing dark, dusty steps, you enter the triforium on the north side, go down some more steps and find yourself in a room that was never intended to receive one ray of light.

It is a pitch-black dungeon. It has never had any windows. The theory that it was a punishment cell for the monks seems disproved by the remains of an altar at the east end of the room. What service was held in the dark there?

[6]

It was early in the evening. The sun was going down over the Vale of York and the grey towers of the Cathedral Church of St. Peter rose over the flat lands. There was a wind blowing at my back or I might have heard the Minster bells, whose chimes, on a still evening, go over the fields for miles. As I went on between the hedges my spirits rose; York is the loveliest city in all England. She is England's last real anchor to the Middle Ages. Other cities have cathedrals, one has a wall, many have castles and ancient houses, but York is the supreme, unself-conscious queen of them all. She does not ask you to love her: She is like London in that. She is there—she is York.

As I saw the red roofs draw near, all the Catholic ancestors in me rose and shouted, and all the Protestants leapt up quickly and took them by the throat.

It was a marvellous feeling. I was not like one man going to York: I was like the arrival of an army.

York, let me tell you, is the last city left in England that a man should enter on horseback or on foot. Unfortunately, few people know this. When I came to the high, white machicolated wall that circles this city I looked up at the great bastions that guard its angles, at the cross-slits for the bowmen, at the gatehouses on whose topmost turrets little stone men, outlined against the sky, hug boulders to their stomachs and seem about to heave them down on you as you pass.

Men were driving cattle through the gates of York. There was a smell of smoke, the last sun lay warm over red roof tiles, and from within the walls came a marvellous feeling of men and women, of life, which, although present in all cities, lacks identity unless a city sits cosily behind its wall like a house full of friends.

I made a circle of the walls and walked round to Bootham Bar so that I might read this notice posted upon it:

"Entry from North through Forest of Galtres. *In old times armed men were stationed here to watch and to conduct travellers through the forest and protect them against wolves*"

I entered York and so up into High Petergate and Stonegate.

Above the busy noise of crowds and the sounds of shopkeepers closing their shops came the tolling of one insistent bell. I looked at my watch: It was eight o'clock. They were ringing the curfew from the belfry of St. Michael's, Spurrier-gate, not only to warn men to damp their fires, but also to guide wanderers through the long-vanished Forest of Galtres—which is still officially wolf-haunted every night at eight.

York is surely the loveliest fairy tale among the cities of the world.

The walls offer you a three-mile walk that I consider to be the best before-breakfast walk in England.

It was one of those hushed, sweet, washed-clean April mornings, the smell of grass in the air and the wind running round corners. An old man was shaking a religious mat on the south steps of the Minster, the sun was washing the east window and the great church lay in unexpected early morning shadows.

I climbed the steps into Bootham Bar and up a second flight to the wall an hour before the first smart little chocolate-maker had taken herself, her bicycle and her pink garters to work. (York, by the way, goes to work on bicycles, and every bicycle has its bell.)

The walls of York lift you above the chimney-pots. On one side is a six-foot fortification pierced every few yards with square, waist-high openings for boiling oil or for archers. Through these openings you look down over the green moat to the back gardens and the homes of York outside the wall where, in the early morning, people are awakening, pulling up blinds, making tea, dressing the babies or blowing up the inevitable bicycle tyre—a peaceful scene that would have astonished the fifteenth-century sentinels more than an army with banners!

On the other side of you the ground falls away from the wall to the Cathedral and the Deanery gardens. You see York Minster through a hedge of silver-white pear blossom. Everything is silver-white in the early sun. The wall itself is silver-white. Tadcaster stone is washed by every rain, so that the Wall of York has always looked new. And this white, enchanted ribbon twists on and around, never straight for more than twenty yards, losing itself in green bowers as the tops of the trees on either side arch themselves over the white bastions.

Rooks were cawing round the west towers. The Dean's gardener was bringing the lawnmower to a smooth lawn. A blackbird with the early worm in his saffron beak flew to an apple tree. A thrush was pouring out his heart from a high bough; the starlings, whistling, fighting, shining and beetle-backed, flew in truculent flocks, only becoming sober to rush to the help of some enormous and ravenous fledgeling whose shaking wings and open beak were the sole signs of infancy.

The Minster bell chimed a half-hour. Smoke began to curl from the chimneys above the red roofs. York was awakening. Beyond the wall the bicycles went by. There were bells, bells, bells! Did you ever hear of a medieval city without bells? (They even sell coal with a bell in York.)

So I went on to Monk Bar, where the stone men have been holding their missiles for centuries, on to Walmgate Bar, which has a great barbican, or outwork, lying before it and a wireless aerial attached to it. Here lives a member of the police force in the most romantic house in York. Then Victoria Bar and Micklegate, which bears on heraldic shields the lions of England quartered with the lilies of France; and so round the bend to Tanners Moat and right ahead that classic view of York Minster lifting its towers above the city and the white wall twisting on and on. . . .

What a walk, and what a city, for an April morning!

At night, after curfew, I like to walk in the streets as it grows dark. How York clings to the swinging shop sign. I like to walk up High Ousegate, past the Church of All Souls, mentioned in "Domesday Book", in whose open tower once hung a lamp to guide travellers through that awful Forest of Galtres. I wonder why York does not relight this lantern?

Then I go to Whipmawhopmagate just to smile at the way it looks on the street sign. Surely we have here the funniest street name in England. This was where they used to whip and whop the felons! Then—then I am delightfully lost.

I may find myself in Jubbergate or Goodramage or Swinegate or Stonebow-lane or Shambles, but it does not matter, because I like the names. If, however, I strike the Shambles, I discover the butchers—or fleshers—who have traded in this street for over five hundred years—in the act of washing down their shops after the day's work, so that the broadstone gutters run with water.

And the houses of the Shambles thrust out their upper storeys like paunchy aldermen and nod together over the narrow road, shutting out the sky and approaching so near that you could, I imagine, from the upper windows of at least one house, kiss the girl who lives opposite. The butchers joke together as they swill down their slabs, the little lamps throw just the right shadows, and I go on expecting to meet Pistol or Corporal Nym round the next corner. . . .

The Minster chimes strike ten. I go to bed conscious that I am sleeping within the Walls of York, loving her beauty, her peace, her dignity and the calm, unhurried way she has, anxious to be up early in the morning to white walls and apple blossom.

I suppose nine out of ten natives of York are unconscious of the most romantic sound in the city. I, a stranger, am acutely sensitive to it. I wait for it. If my watch is a bit fast and I do not hear it prompt to its time I get worried, restless, open windows and make a fuss until I assure myself that I have not missed it.

Sharp at 8 p.m. the curfew tolls from the white stone tower of St. Michael's, Spurriergate. The old tower seems to lean slightly, as well it might after so many centuries of curfewing. William the Conqueror started this bell ringing, William the Kaiser stopped it for a little while; but, with the exception of the war years (1914–1918 and 1939–1945), it has been ringing every night for over nine centuries.

It sounds when all the other bells of York are drowsy with their day's work. When the city falls into one of these chill, delicious April evenings, the sun setting, a stillness in the air, the chimney smoke going up straight, this bell, insistently tolling for two or three minutes, is like the ancient voice of York telling the children that it is time for bed.

"Oh, yes," says young York indulgently, "that's all very well, but you forget that we live in the twentieth century. Who's coming to the pictures?"

But the curfew rings on with the single-mindedness of the old.

[7]

I was sitting in the mighty nave of Durham Cathedral, wishing that someone with time and energy would write a popular history of English cathedrals. Every one of our great churches is built on a fine story. Take Durham. . . .

An Irish monk was writing by rushlight in the Monastery of Moville, in Ireland, in the year 559. Over four hundred years were to pass before a little church was to rise on a hill at Durham, but this church was nevertheless in the air when this young monk took pen and parchment at Moville so long ago.

Now, at this time Ireland was a Christian country, and the monasteries held the light of learning that had been extinguished in England when the Romans departed and the pirates came in. Irish monks, in coarse white gowns, with manuscripts hanging from their waist-belts in little leather pouches, wandered the world, and those who passed through England on their way home from the Continent told a story of a country without a Christian church, a country of slaughter and pillage, of Roman cities lying in ruins with the corpses rotting on the walls, a country given over to barbarism and the heathen.

The monk who was writing secretly and by night in the Monastery of Moville was known as Columcille—"Dove of the Church"—and was to become famous in later years as St. Columba. He was a guest at the Monastery, and the Monastery was famous for a beautiful Psalter which the Abbot Finnian kept in the church. The monk, who was a great writer, could not rest until he had made a copy of this rare manuscript. He told no one. He took it from the church and worked at it secretly, but one night the Abbot Finnian found him at his task. He was angry. He claimed the copy as his right. Columba refused to hand it over to him and appealed to the High King of Ireland, who decided against him.

"This is an unjust decision," cried the monk to the King, "and I will be avenged!"

That was not the threat of a singing man. Columba was of royal blood: He belonged to the powerful Clan O'Donnell.

It seems that fate was determined on trouble, because at this time the young Prince Curnam, a kinsman of Columba, sought refuge with the High King after killing a competitor by accident in the sports at Tara. The King slew him. Columba then roused the clans to a war of revenge. In 561 a battle was fought near Sligo at Culdreimhne and the High King was defeated with great slaughter.

But he was still the High King. Smarting under his defeat, he procured the excommunication of Columba, which was afterwards withdrawn on the intercession of St. Brendan of Birr. But Columba, no longer a soldier but a monk again, appears to have been filled with remorse. He went to a hermit, St. Laisren, who lived on a lonely island on Loch Erne, and asked his advice and help. The Saint imposed this penance on him: He must leave Ireland and never return until he had won as many souls for Christ as there were men slain in the Battle of Culdreimhne. And now events move towards England. . . .

Columba with twelve companions set sail from Ireland in 563 and, sailing towards the coast of Scotland, landed at Oronsay and climbed a hill from the summit of which he could still see, far off, the misty outline of the Irish coast. He went down to his ship again and continued his voyage, landing on 13 May 563, on the shore of Iona, from which, on looking south, he saw only waves.

Here thirteen Irish monks who were to become famous in the history of Christianity built themselves huts of wood and a little oratory. So was planted on Scottish soil the Church of Iona, from which missionaries went out to convert Scotland and the north of England.

We are still centuries from Durham Cathedral, but the great church seems to take shape in the clouds, when one day there comes to the little hermitage of Iona a young man called Aidan, who was an Irishman of royal birth. He joined the Monastery and remained there studying and teaching for forty years.

Long after Columba's death St. Aidan left Iona to found a monastery in imitation of it off the coast of Northumbria. He chose the barren little island of Lindisfarne, where in 635 the monastic ideals of Ireland took root in England— seventy-two years after the Irish Saint was driven from his own country for defying the High King.

Is there a more wonderful chapter in the history of Christianity than this time of ascetic saintliness in desolate places, of chants rising above the booming of the sea and the cries of sea birds, of men intoxicated with holiness moving through the wild country winning souls for Christ? Among the men drawn to Lindisfarne by the sanctity of St. Aidan was Cuthbert. He was Prior of Melrose and in direct spiritual descent from such men as Columba and Aidan. He was brought up under the influence of the mother church of Iona, a man wedded to poverty and holiness, a gentle saint who won his way into the wild hearts of a wild age by the beauty of his life and the force of his example. He retired from the Monastery from time to time to more desolate islands where he meditated in solitude, his reflections broken only by the cries of the gulls and the kittiwakes and the breaking of the waves against the rocky shores. When the See of Lindisfarne fell vacant all men cried out for Cuthbert, and the rough Saxon chiefs travelled over the sea to the remote island where the Saint had made a little cell in the rock; there they knelt on the sand holding towards him the crosier, the vestments and the ring of the vacant bishopric. The Saint became Bishop of Lindisfarne in the year of Our Lord 685. Two years later he died. On his deathbed he made the monks promise that if for any reason—for already the shadow of the Viking war galleys may have moved across his mind—they were driven forth from Lindisfarne, they would take his body with them on their travels and lay it in whatever church they made.

Little could he have dreamt how often and how far from his hermitage men in ages then unborn would disturb his bones and gaze upon them, century by century, as at a miracle. The legend grew that St. Cuthbert was incorruptible. It began about twelve years after his death, when he was canonised. In those days it was customary for the bodies of men elevated to the sainthood to be taken from their tombs and richly enshrined. The monks, with the abbot at their head, would pitch a tent over the grave, chanting the Psalms of David, while the oldest members of the brotherhood opened up the earth and gathered the bones of the holy man. These would be washed and then wrapped in silk or fine linen and deposited in a mortuary-chest.

Now Cuthbert had been buried in a stone sarcophagus in the little church at Lindisfarne. An ancient chronicler says:

"As soon as they opened the tomb they found, what is wonderful to relate, the whole body as entire as when they had first buried it eleven years before. The body was not fixed and stiff, with the skin shrunk and bearing the appearance of age and the sinews dried up, but the limbs were pliant with full vivacity in the joints. When they raised him out of the tomb they were able to bend his neck and his knees like those of a living person. All the vestments and the shoes that came in contact with his skin were undecayed. For when they took off the napkin that bound his head they found that it still contained the beauty of the original whiteness, and with the new shoes that he had worn, is to this day kept in witness thereof among the relics of our church."

For one hundred and seventy-seven years the body of the Saint rested in a wooden coffin in the church at Lindisfarne. But during this time the longboats of the Norse pirates were directed towards the English coast; the wild sea hordes came wading in through the sea mire, grasping their long swords, pillaging the little monasteries, stealing the jewels, putting the monks to the sword and sailing off again with their booty. It was in 875 that the monks of Lindisfarne decided to leave their island; and although there was no man alive at that time who had seen Cuthbert, the deathbed promise had been handed down faithfully through the years, and they took with them the wooden coffin containing the bones of the Saint. They crossed to the mainland, where they wandered, looking for a site for a new monastery.

What an amazing picture this is! How many fearful herdsmen must have told how at night they saw a body of monks crossing the heath or winding their way through the forest, bearing on their shoulders a great coffin.

"What do you carry with you?" they would ask, and the monks would reply:

"We carry the body of our saint, Cuthbert, to his new home."

So the monks with their holy burden spent eight years wandering the north of England. The many churches dedicated to St. Cuthbert in this part of the world constitute a kind of map of their journeys. They rested some time at Crayke, to settle down finally at Chester-le-Street. Here they remained for a little over a hundred years. Once more, however, they were forced to wander, and now a new body of monks took up the body of the Saint in 995 and, bearing it to Ripon, came at length after many adventures "with great joy and gladness" to Durham. They saw "a barbarus and rude place, replenished with nothinge but thornes and thick woods", and in this spot, on the crest of the great hill rising above the River Weir, they "first builded a little Church of wandes and branches wherein they did lay his body (and thence the church was afterward called bough church) till they did build a more sumptuous church wherein they might inshrine him . . ."

That was the beginning of Durham Cathedral. At first it was a little Saxon stone church completed by Bishop Aldhun in 999 (and that was the church the Normans saw when they rode through the north of England). But the Normans, full of big ideas and intoxicated with the wine of conquest, could not permit so great a saint to lie in so humble a tomb. In 1093 they pulled down the Saxon church and laid the foundations of the present Cathedral. In 1104 Durham Cathedral was so far completed that the body of St. Cuthbert was removed from a small building in the cloisters into its place behind the high altar, where you can see on a raised platform a stone slab that to this day bears the word: CUTHBERTVS.

[8]

Could I make a bargain with Time I would roll back sixteen centuries so that I might meet any Roman centurion who served on the Wall of Hadrian during the three hundred years of its military occupation. I would shake him warmly by the hand, stand him a drink and say:

"I'm sorry, Marcus! I sympathise with you! I crossed the Wall from Carlisle—which you called Luguvallium—to Newcastle-on-Tyne—which you knew as Pons Aelii—and it rained, Marcus—how it rained! Seventy-three miles of rain over the Wall, and, by Jupiter, such rain!"

110 *Ben Vair and Loch Leven, western Scotland*

111 *St Andrew's Harbour, Fife*

112 *The River Teith and Ben Ledi, near Callander, Perthshire*

113 *Tobermory on the Isle of Mull*

114 *Loch Lomond*

115 *Aberdeen Harbour*

He would, I am sure, look interested.

"It still comes down like Hades, does it?" he would ask. "Fancy that! We thought it was organised by the local gods against the Empire. It used to put out the cookhouse fires, get into the wine-skins, give the Spanish cavalry frog, and when you stood on the parapet it would beat up against your face, blinding you and, oozing behind your chin-strap, make your face smart like blazes! Jove's bolts! What a Wall!"

"I suppose you had duckboards; and did they send you mouth-organs and woollies from Rome? I can imagine you all sitting up there on wet nights singing, 'We are Fred Karno's Army; what ruddy good are we?'"★

"Yes, we had a song like that to the hymn of the Vestal Virgins. The Picts and Scots used to sit out on the other side of the Wall, too wet to raid us, and join in. We had another song in the Centurions' Mess about the troops on the Wall. There was only one Roman to every mile, you know! The rest were Dacians and Thracians and Moors and Scythians; a kind of recruiting office poster: Types of the Roman Army! The song went: 'Oh, the Tungrians, the Austurians, the Batavians, and the Greeks!' It had a good chorus, and was very popular with the regulars in Deva and Eboracum. . . ."

"We say Chester and York now."

"Do you really? We had another song on the Wall: 'Old soldiers never die, never die, never die; old soldiers never die, they only sneeze away-ee.' Which was true. The Picts used to say that as long as a regular Legion kept its nose there was no need to sound the war horn. We were a fine sight saluting the Governor of Britain or a visiting Caesar with the famous legionary sneeze—'the sneeze of the Faithful Thirtieth' we used to call it!"

"I suppose you got leave?"

"Leaf? Leaf? Not likely! The Wall was a life sentence. The first thing we did when we got up there was to marry and settle down. A British girl who couldn't marry on Hadrian's Wall . . . well, I can't imagine it! . . . I was Ballista Instructor to the Fourth Cohort of Gauls at Vindolana. You should have seen the raw recruits from every part of the world who wandered up and down that Wall with half the gods of the earth hidden away in their vests. We spoke about twenty-five different languages, from Luguvallium to Pons Aelii. I had an old-timer in my cohort who used to be batman to Vespasian. He was always changing his religion. If a Moorish or an Egyptian god answered a prayer he would buy an image of it at once and pray to be transferred to Londinium; but the gods of the Wall knew him too well. . . ."

★One of the most popular dirges of the British army, 1914-18.—H.V.M.

That rain from Carlisle to Newcastle! It swooped down from the north in great blown sheets, and it swept up from the south and met the northern sheets in midair above the Wall, where they fought in cross-currents and fell together, lashing the earth. Every few miles I left the car by the wayside and plodded off over soggy fields to spot the Wall, which you can trace almost without a break for seventy-three miles.

At Housesteads I stood thrilled to the marrow. I have seen Pompeii, and I have seen Timgad in Africa, but to see this great Roman monument in our own cold northern lands! That wall was the north boundary wall of the Roman Empire! At this place it runs six feet high for over twenty-five miles: you can walk on it! How it scorns the lie of the land! It marches on straight as a Roman road where possible, then wherever there is a hill the Wall climbs it; it commands all the high ground from Newcastle to Carlisle. To the north is a deep trench, to the south another trench and a military road.

The weather is rotting it slowly; miles of it have lately been cemented to stop decay. There are years of excavation along its course, for one can hardly dig anywhere without finding pottery or bones.

I stood wet through in Chesters and went over the ruins of one of the largest forts on the Wall: Cilurnum it was called when the Second Ala of Austurian cavalry was stationed there. The foundations of the gates are to be seen; in the north gates the socket-holes for the hinges are preserved; on either side are the guardhouses.

The prefect, or commanding officer, lived in superior quarters with a view of the Tyne. He had a bathroom and a heated sitting-room. In the centre of the fort stood a colonnaded forum. The stone gutter to take the rain drippings from the roof is still there; it was still full of rain! There are the ruts of chariot wheels in the stone pavements: three feet six inches from wheel to wheel, the same size as the chariot ruts at Pompeii. Underground is a vaulted chamber in which were found a rotted wooden chest and a pile of Roman coins: possibly the regimental pay-chest. Round the central buildings are the barrack quarters for about three hundred troopers. Near the river are the regimental baths.

The Wall links up with Cilurnum on the east and leaves the little fort on the west to run on over the hills. This fort has more gates than the other stations on the Wall; it has six, three of which open to the north of the Wall, or in enemy country. This has puzzled the antiquaries. Collingwood Bruce says that he supposes these extra gates opening into no-man's-land were there simply "because Cilurnum was larger than the other stations". I suggest another theory. This was a cavalry depot. Any man who has done any cavalry training will realise that when the Picts attacked the Wall the first thought of this garrison would be to mount, draw swords and get outside the Wall as quickly as possible. They could swing round through three gates upon the Picts, wheel into line and deliver a charge in about three minutes. This, I think, is why Cilurnum has more gates than the infantry forts and why they open to the north.

How little imagination it takes to see this Wall as it was: an eighteen-foot-high barrier from sea to sea, a tower or pillbox every mile and, dotted along the length, stone fortresses garrisoned by cohorts and *alas*. And behind each fort grew up villages where the married quarters were; villages with shops and workshops; and temples.

It is strange to think that for three hundred years the nations of Europe formed a defensive crust along the north of England. The regular army was at York and Chester, but the Wall was in the hands of the territorials, or auxiliary legions recruited wherever Rome had made conquests. Here, in the blinding rain and in the winter snows, were shivering Moors from Africa, men from Spain, from the forests of Germany, of France, of Belgium. All Europe and parts of Africa helped to defend England for three hundred years!

No doubt in time these foreign legions were alien in name only. When drafts did not come from distant lands I imagine the villages behind the forts gave many half-British recruits to the Eagles.

The crumbling wall of Cilurnum was covered with a pretty crimson-purple rock plant, whose name is, I think, *Erinus alrinus*. It is probably a South European plant. The legend, which I believe some learned man has contradicted, is that this tiny flower came over from Spain with the fodder for the chargers of the Second Ala of Austurians. . . .

I left the ruins of Chesters, and saw the Wall of Hadrian lying from sea to sea, firm and straight as a legion with linked shields. I lifted my voice and shouted, "Ave, Caesar!" There was no answer but the drip of the rain.

[9]

And now all the beauty of the day is gathered, as by the hand of God, in the west. The sun is setting behind the hills. Through my window I see a great sheet of water that within the last twenty minutes has lost all colour. The blue of Windermere has been drained away drop by drop as the blue has been drawn from the sky; it is now silver; the white swans are black against this glittering metallic sheet. The swallows fly high in wide circles; a jet-black boat moves on the placid surface of the lake, two silver lines widening from the stern. The sun, lost in a rich smouldering bank of cloud, drops minute by minute towards the crest of the hills. In the stillness sounds carry far . . . such sounds!

With shattering indifference to man, the black-and-silver nocturne of evening is played to the end. The sun goes. Darkness spreads between the trees. A deep grape-blue mist hangs over the woods; a fish jumps in the lake, making a black pool for a second in the still, silver water.

I will not dare to compare the soft beauty of Windermere with the majesty of Derwentwater or the grand solitude of Ullswater, or the high serenity of Thirlmere and Coniston. If I have any preference it is for the smallest of them all: little Rydal Water, which is three-quarters of a mile long, and, beside these watery giants, is just a spoonful of blue in a cup of green hills. Rydal Water is a magic, satisfying lakelet—a little looking-glass in which the woody heights, by which it is hemmed, lie as in a mirror.

I saw it first at night. It was a clear, moonlit night, with no breath of wind among the trees. In the middle of the little lake, round and golden as a guinea, lay the moon. Sights such as this, hiding round a corner, lurking behind trees and suddenly revealed, pull a man up sharply and fling him on his knees. Had Rydal Water been in Cornwall or in Wales, nothing could have disconnected it from the Excalibur legend; and most men would have believed it, for this is a mystic mere. . . .

As I looked, a waterfowl, surprised among the dark reeds, flew noiselessly over the lake in the night, its little feet just scoring a thin silver line in the water. The moon danced up and down once or twice; then the lake composed itself and went on dreaming.

Scotland

[1]

Flinging itself round the shoulders of hills, the road rises and falls, running on in bleak solitude. It narrows to a pass; it opens out into moorland wine-dark with heather; and there is no sound over it but the bleating of sheep and the whistle of the wind in the telegraph wires.

The clouds sail in close communion with the hill-crests. Crows like scraps of burnt paper, buffeting the upper air, cry harshly as they are blown downward to a distant valley. Here and there Man, exercising his amazing sense of property, has painfully built stone walls, breast-high and brown, to include a few steep acres of tough and soggy grass where black-faced sheep, perpetually optimistic, seek scattered nourishment as they wander, shaggy and unkempt, their long, limp tails swinging in the wind.

This is the Border.

Over it is the loneliness of the sea; the rise and fall of its hills are as the sweep of frozen billows, and the eye, like that of the sailor, searches the solitude for a sign of humanity: a shepherd with his flocks, a farmer in his field, or, best of all, a white house with a curl of smoke from its chimneys proclaiming the presence of the three vanguards of civilisation: a woman, a fire and children.

As I go on I feel that every bend of the road will bring me face to face with the promised land. A wilderness cannot continue forever. In the desert you can smell the oasis long before its palm trees break the skyline. So it seems to me as I mount hills and descend into valleys, cross streams and skirt the shoulders of hills, that I can feel Scotland round the next corner. But how wrong I am! The Border— that no-man's-land between England and Scotland—is a wide and persistent wilderness. It has a spirit of its own. These very rocks thrusting their sharp jaws from the brown moorland sheltered the Picts, who sat in the heather listening to the bees that made their honey wine as they gazed southward to the far smoke and the occasional heliograph of a brazen shield that marked the western limit of the Roman world. This side of the Wall was never tamed. It has known many play-mates but no masters. It has made many songs but no laws.

I stop my car. I take out a map. I climb a stone wall and strike off over a field to a high waste of heather, and there I discover my bearings. What names men have given to these hills! How snugly they fit! To my left are Corby Pike and Windy Crag, Dour Hill and Hungry Law; miles away are Bloodybush Edge and Beefstand Hill. Six names as right and racy as a ballad! On my right looms the bulk of Blackman's Law and beyond it the height of Oh Me Edge. It is almost too good to be true! What, I wonder, is the origin of the name of Oh Me Edge? Is it, like Weary-all Hill, near Glastonbury, a tribute to the effect of this ridge on the limbs of its victims?

The heather bends back before the wind until the smooth, smoke-grey stems shine like satinwood. Little pools of peat-brown water gather in my heel-marks, for the sun is shining after recent rains. Each footfall crushes from the wet moor-land the rich smell of autumn. From the wind, the heather, the peat water, the line of hill against hill, the bleating of sheep, the drone of insects in the heather, the trilling of larks and the utter solitude of earth and sky is distilled a powerful emotion that soothes while it excites me; for behind this visible world is an invisible but immortal host. I have not read my Border balladry in vain.

I seek a patch of dry heather and lie watching the smoke of my pipe going down the wind as I read my map. A name leaps out at me. What a fool I am! I passed this place without stopping, in ignorance, fifteen miles back along the road. Shall I go back and look at Otterburn? Here at the very gates of Scotland is the first milestone of romance:

> *It fell about the Lammas-tide,*
>   *When the muir-men win their hay,*
> *The doughty earl of Douglas rode*
>   *Into England to catch a prey.*
> *He chose the Gordons and the Graemes,*
>   *With them the Lindesays, light and gay,*
> *But the Jardines wald not with him ride,*
>   *And they rue it to this day.*

I remember the words of Sir Philip Sidney: "I never heard the old song of Percy and Douglas that I found not my heart more moved than with a trumpet." All the chivalry of ancient warfare flowered in that fight. To read Froissart's account of it—such a careful, authentic piece of description—is to feel the ache of having been born in an inferior age. I like, even better than the ballad-monger's story of the death of Douglas and the hiding of his body in the brier bush until the fight was won, the account by Froissart of the pursuit by the Scots knight, Sir James Lindsay, of the English Sir Matthew Redman, Governor of Berwick. I know of few incidents which illustrate more vividly the gallantry of that wild time.

After the battle Sir Matthew claps spurs to his horse and takes the road to safety —and Newcastle. The Scotsman, Sir James Lindsay, gallops after him crying: "Ah! Sir knight. Turn! It is a shame thus to fly! I am James of Lindsay!" But Sir Matthew has had enough! He declines the challenge and, spurring his horse again, tries to fling off his pursuer. The chase continues for three miles. Suddenly Sir Matthew's horse stumbles and the Englishman takes a toss. Lindsay, lance in hand, is on him. Sir Matthew draws his sword and prepares to put up a fight against the mounted man. Lindsay drives at him with his lance. Sir Matthew parries the thrust and in doing so severs the lance with one mighty sweep of his sword. First blood to the Englishman! Lindsay leaps from his horse and grasping the short battle-axe, which he carries slung at his back, sets about his adversary with great fury. So they pant and gasp, thrusting and cutting, until Sir Matthew, who had obviously seen quite enough fighting before the tenacious Scot came after him, puts down his sword and surrenders to Lindsay. Now what happens? After this bloodthirsty combat the two knights talk together like old friends! All their animosity vanishes. I will modernise Froissart:

"Well, what do you want me to do now?" asked the vanquished Redman. "I am your prisoner. You have beaten me."

Then he adds, in a matter-of-fact way for a man who has been so near to death's door:

"I badly want to go to Newcastle, but I will within fifteen days come to Scotland and surrender to you."

Lindsay is content to let him go on the word of one gentleman to another.

The enemies part on these friendly terms: Lindsay back to the Border; Sir Matthew to Newcastle. Now occurs what Froissart calls the "strange chance of a war" that gives piquancy to the story. Lindsay gallops into four hundred horsemen. He thinks he has come up with the Scots. But it is the English reserve led by the Bishop of Durham. They capture him, and in a few minutes he is following his recent captive along the road to Newcastle. They place him in the Bishop's lodgings. The first person he meets is his prisoner Sir Matthew, who finds him "in a studye lying in a windowe".

"What are you doing here?" asks the astonished English knight.

"I rather think," replies Lindsay, "that you will not now come to Edinburgh to surrender to me. We will exchange one for the other!"

"Well, sir," says Sir Matthew, in the words of Froissart, "we shall accord ryght well toguyder; ye shall dine this day with me."

(How perfectly English of him! He might almost have been to Eton!)

"I am contented to dyne with you," says Lindsay.

Thus the desperate encounter of the morning, the exchange of knightly trust, ends at evening over a dinner-table in Newcastle. How dearly would I like to have listened to their talk that night!

Is there a more perfect cameo of the Dark Ages or a more charming prophecy of the friendship, then so remote, between two nations?

So I look back to Oh Me Edge, remembering more than meets the eye. This is the spell of the Border. It grips you from Otterburn onwards: the spell of a country wild and untameable, whose every nook and corner is marked down on the map of romance. There can be no wild place in the world that men have embroidered more richly with daring deeds. It shares with all places in which generations of men have loved or hated an arresting importance, almost as if some part of their passion had soaked itself into the grass and into the hard surface of the rocks, making them different from other grass and other rocks.

And now I take to the road again, still feeling the nearness of Scotland, still expecting at every bend the wilderness to unfold, as unfold it must, towards the frontier of another country. Suddenly the road sweeps upward to a ridge. At last! They call this place Carter Bar. Below me lies Scotland. . . .

[2]

Certain views in all countries must quicken the heart of the man who sees them again after an absence. Such is the sight of Scotland from Carter Bar. It is a tender, lovely view. This is not "Caledonia stern and wild"; it is Scotland in a homely, gracious mood with a smile on her lips, a welcome in her eyes, a cake on the griddle, a kettle on the hob. It is a view of Scotland that burnt itself into the brain of that greatest of all Borderers—Walter Scott. It would be impossible, I think, for any Scotsman returning home by Carter Bar after years of foreign places to hold back a shout or perhaps a tear. It is so authentically Scotland and could be nowhere else. It seemed to me, as I stood there looking down into the valley, that here is something as definite and unmistakable to a Scotsman as the white cliffs of Dover to an Englishman.

116 *Craigievar Castle, Aberdeenshire*

117 *Loch Ness, Inverness-shire*

118 *Inverness Castle*

119 *Inveraray Castle in the Western Highlands*

120 *The 'Old Bridge of Dee' at Invercauld near Balmoral*

The heathery moors slope down to a distant valley. The sun is setting. The sky above the Lammermuirs is red and troubled. The wind drops. The autumn mists far below are creeping from wood to wood. The smoke from chimneys hangs motionless in the air. Thin veils of grey wrap themselves round the foothills. Faint white serpents of mist twist above the greenwood, outlining the course of stream and river. It is a study in blue. In the foreground, like a promise of the Highlands, and as notable as a ship at sea, rise the tall peaks of the Eildon Hills, blue as hothouse grapes, standing with their feet among the woodlands of the Tweed. To the far sky lie hills, always hills, fading in graduated subtleties of blue; ahead the long slopes of the Lammermuirs merge westward in the outline of the Moorfoot and the Pentlands. And it is so quiet and so still that I can hear a dog barking miles off in the valley.

I am all alone at the Border, one foot in England, the other in Scotland. There is a metal post with "Scotland" written on it. It is a superfluous post. You do not need to be told that you have come to the end of England. Carter Bar is indeed a gate: The historic barrier between Celt and Saxon, it is the gateway to Scotland.

I sit for a long time watching the light fade from the sky and the mist thickening and the blue deepening. In the hush of evening, with the first star burning above the Eildon Hills, the mystery of the Border winds itself round me like a spell. How can I describe the strange knowingness of the Border? Its uncanny watchfulness. Its queer trick of seeming still to listen and to wait. I feel that invisible things are watching. A blown tree against the sky looks like a crouching man. Out of the fern silently might ride the Queen of Elfland, just as she came to Thomas of Ercildoune in this very country with "fifty silver bells and nine" hanging from her horse's mane.

Likelier still it seems, as I look down over the moorland stained with heather like blood, that suddenly this land might leap violently to life in pinpoints of fire from tree-top to peel tower, from ridge to ridge, filling the dusk with the sound of swords and the mad gallop of horses and the wild clamour of a Border raid— "A Scott! A Scott!" "An Armstrong!" "An Elliot!"—as a dark horde sweeps on under the "lee licht o' the mune".

The Border is haunted still. It sleeps, but—with one eye open! And it is growing cold. I dip down into Scotland.

[3]

On these Border hills, or lying beside the troutful waters of these Border burns, or full length in the stubble of a Border harvest, a man will dream what dreams as a book falls from his hand! And the book? There is for me one book only in this land—Walter Scott's *Minstrelsy of the Scottish Border*. Had Scott done nothing but gather these deathless ballads he would have placed us forever in his debt. No one should explore this country without this book. The Border ballads come down to us with the wind and the rain in them, with some quiet, approving gleam of firelight over them, and between their lines the thin echo of a harp. We cannot fail to recognise in them the authentic gateway to another world. They are so naked. They are so unashamed. They are so sincere. They are as real as a sword dug up on a battlefield. I do not concern myself with the arguments of those meticulous ones who would tear a rainbow to pieces in the interests of analysis—the higher critics. They may take these ballads word by word and say "Scott put in this or that"; they may examine them line by line and turn them over just as furniture dealers go over every inch of a Queen Anne chair in search of false walnut; it is enough for me that these songs re-create the spirit of their time.

In the Border ballads the peel towers rise whole again from Berwick to Carlisle. The night is alive with riders. Through the gloom of green woods comes the knight in search of love or pain, or both. The Queen of Elfland rides silently out of the fern to claim a soul. There are wild hammerings on door and wild shoutings at casements; over the edge of the hill come the freebooters driving their startled kine. Many a host strikes its pallions on hilltop and moves down to battle; many a daring band slips over the boundary line to singe the beard of the March Wardens; many a fair maiden listens the long night through for the returning beat of hoofs. It is all sublimated journalism. Most of it happened. It is the history of a vanished age, refined in imagination and preserved by the approbation of generations who knew that it was true. To read these ballads once is to be haunted by them forever.

> *About the dead hour o' the night*
> *She heard the bridles ring,*

and

> *O there was horsing, horsing in haste,*
> *And cracking of whips out o'er the lee;*

and

> *The King sits in Dunfermline town*
> *Drinking the blude-red wine;*

and

> *They lighted high on Otterbourne*
> *And threw their pallions down;*

and

> *He belted on his gude braid sword,*
> *And to the field he ran;*
> *But he forgot the helmet good*
> *That should have kept his brain;*

and

> *They swakked their swords, till sair they swat,*
> *And the blood ran down like wine;*

and

> *It fell about the Martinmas tide,*
> *When our Border steeds get corn and hay,*

and

> *They shot him at the Nine-Stone Rig,*
> *   Beside the Headless Cross,*
> *And they left him lying in his blood*
> *   Upon the moor and moss.*

For sheer savage realism give me "The Fray of Support". I know nothing like it in English. It is a Red Indian war-dance! It is the cry of an enraged English Border-woman whose "gear", or goods, have been plundered in the night by a band of Scottish moss-troopers. Each wild verse ends:

> *Fy, lads! Shout a' a' a' a' a',*
> *My gear's a' gane!*

As she rouses the reivers to pursuit and vengeance she describes what happened to her. The Scots came and drove off twenty-four head of cattle and all her horses. She cries:

> *Weel mey ye ken,*
> *Last night I was right scarce o' men:*
> *But Toppet Hob o' the Mains had guestene'd in my*
> *   house by chance.*
> *I set him to wear the fore-door wi' the speir while I*
> *   kept the back-door wi' the lance,*
> *But they hae run him through the thick o' the thie and*
> *   broke his knee-pan,*
> *And the mergh [marrow] o' his shin-bane has run*
> *   down on his spur-leather whang:*
> *He's lame while he lives, and where'er he may gang.*
> *   Fy, lads! Shout a' a' a' a' a',*
> *   My gear's a' gane!*

If poor lame Toppet Hob o' the Mains came back to life he could tell to us no more of Border raids than we know from this. And the fearful things that happen in these ballads might have happened on any moonless night in the old days. Read "Jamie Telfer" and "The Lament of the Border Widow" and "Kinmont Willie", whose release from Carlisle Castle in April 1596 was one of the most daring deeds of the Scottish Border.

And as you go through this haunted country, now so peaceful, where the gaunt outline of the peel towers rises up from field or wood, you may see in imagination a solitary horseman, the presiding genius of this Borderland, reining in his horse to gaze round him with eyes that see more of Scotland than any man has ever seen —Walter Scott.

[4]

Every unresisting visitor to Scotland finds himself in Abbotsford, the home of Sir Walter Scott, and the scene of the most spectacular financial drama in the history of literature. Scott found himself at the age of fifty-five faced by a financial crisis that might have driven many a man to suicide. His co-partners failed for £117,000. There was no such thing in 1826 as a limited liability company. Scott was then at the height of his powers. He was making from his novels an income of £10,000 a year: this in the days before film rights and big American royalties. These figures seem paltry today. Probably an economist would know whether to multiply them by ten or twenty to reach an approximate modern value.

This middle-aged man decided to devote his life to paying off what he considered to be a debt of honour. It seems as though Fate was determined to test a brain whose fertility can be compared only with that of Shakespeare's. In six years Scott wrote himself into the grave; but in those six years his amazing effort resulted in the payment of £80,000.

The last six years of Walter Scott's life were as heroic as any of the knightly deeds in the pages of his novels.

Abbotsford is a many-turreted mansion standing among trees and built on rising ground that slopes gently to the Tweed. It looks as if it had been composed by the author of *Ivanhoe*. As you skirt the high walls that surround it and observe its towers, its air of having descended from Border keep and baronial castle, it would appear only proper that a herald should ride to the sound of a trumpet and inquire your status in Debrett. Unfortunately, such thoughts are not of long duration—visitors go in by the tradesmen's entrance.

A guide takes you up back stairs to the Hall. Here you find yourself in a museum. It is as Scott knew it: an incredibly Gothic apartment, almost as though the novelist had tried to pack the entire Middle Ages into one room. Crowds of Scottish and American visitors stand gazing doubtfully at the rich harvest of medievalism, thinking that it would be a difficult place to live in; as, of course, it would. It fitted Walter Scott's mind as his clothes fitted his body.

There are queer monastic carvings, suits of armour, grim relics of Border raids, bloodthirsty mementoes of Old Edinburgh—jail keys and executioners' swords—battle-axes and all the rough material of the romantic novel. It is like nothing so much as a studio; these were the lay figures from which Scott drew inspiration.

This also is an interesting side to Scott's character. When he began to make money he started with a more than feminine intensity to buy a beautiful frame for his personality. Abbotsford was to be his darling, the ideal background, the complete expression of himself.

He built it by instalments. When Washington Irving visited him in 1817 he found the novelist living in a small cottage on the estate, watching the lordly turrets of Abbotsford rise up under the hands of workmen. He wrote for ten years to make Abbotsford; and Abbotsford is, I am inclined to think, one of his greatest "historical novels". Each new success meant an addition to the house of his dreams, a new room, a new ceiling, a new area of panelling, a few stalls copied from Melrose Abbey or some other extravagant fancy which ministered to his atmosphere.

No man has ever worked with greater intensity to build the perfect home. When the crash came, he looked at the baronial mansion in which he had sunk capital and income and, with grim pathos, called it his "Delilah".

I am no Scott expert. I have not even read his *Journal*; it is many years since I read his biographer, John Lockhart; but it seemed to me as I explored Abbotsford that the only pleasure of his later years must have been the fact that he was permitted to live and work in the sanctuary he had made for his imagination.

The reality of Scott's race to make £117,000 before he died must appeal with force to every person who goes to Abbotsford. Every day visitors stand in his small, book-lined study with its gallery and its little monastic door leading to his bedroom.

His royalties were enormous. This age, which considers itself to be the age of colossal literary rewards, will perhaps be astonished to know that for his *Life of Napoleon*—a work better known in Edinburgh than in London—Scott received, in advance of future royalties, the sum of £19,000. Other advances were £6,075 for *Woodstock*, £11,400 for *Chronicles of the Canongate*, £4,200 for *Anne of Geierstein*, all of which can be multiplied many times to give modern values.

Facing the Eildon Hills on Bemersyde is "Sir Walter's View". It is perhaps the finest view on the Border. Here Scott loved to drive in his carriage and sit silently for half an hour gazing over the land whose legends were in his blood.

It was evening when I stood there. The sun was sinking above Melrose, and the smoke from the distant farms lay in the air and drifted in thin banks to lie over the waters of the Tweed. It was so still that I heard dogs barking far down in the valley; and as the sun sank, the grey mists grew denser between the hills, outlining the valleys and lying like grey veils in the hollow places.

[5]

Glasgow on a November evening. . . . The streets are full of light and life. Pavements are packed with men and women released from a day's work. And the Glasgow crowds in perpetual and puzzling flux go, some home to flats in Pollokshaws and—wonderful name!—Crossmyloof, where the Queen of Scots once sat a palfrey.

I go on through the crowds. George Square—Glasgow's Trafalgar Square—which looks like the centre of the city but is not, lies in graduated greyness, rather empty, a little removed from the main surge of life, the splendid municipal buildings wrapped in that same aloofness from the trivialities of a night that envelops Westminster when Piccadilly is gay.

This and Trafalgar Square in London are among the most impressive and well-balanced squares in Great Britain. Walter Scott as its Nelson is skied on a column with his plaid over the wrong shoulder and a lightning-conductor sticking like a dart from the back of his neck. Here, among stone horsemen, are some of Glasgow's few trees.

Glasgow is—Glasgow. She is self-centred. She is one of the most closely knit communities in Great Britain. She is the least suburban of large cities. She has become the most populous city outside London without dissipating her individuality in distant suburbs; and in no other city of this magnitude do more people know each other, at least by sight.

There is a transatlantic alertness about Glasgow that no city in England possesses. It might be true to say that she plays the part of Chicago to Edinburgh's Boston. She is a city of the glad hand and the smack on the back; Edinburgh is a city of silence until birth or brains open the social circle. In Glasgow a man is innocent until he is found guilty; in Edinburgh a man is guilty until he is found innocent. Glasgow is willing to believe the best of an unknown quantity; Edinburgh, like all aristocracies, the worst.

But the great difference between Scotland's two great cities is not a cultural versus a financial tradition. It is something deeper. Both these are poses. Edinburgh pretends to be more precious than she is; Glasgow pretends to be more material than she is. Hence the slight self-consciousness of the one and the slight roughness of the other. The real difference between these two cities is that Edinburgh is Scottish and Glasgow is cosmopolitan. That is why they will always secretly admire each other; also why Edinburgh is definitely the capital.

Glasgow is a mighty and an inspiring human story. She is Scotland's anchor to reality. Lacking her, Scotland would be a backward country lost in poetic memories and at enmity with an age in which she was playing no part. Glasgow, facing west to the new tradeways of the world, rose after the Union, calling to Highlands and Lowlands to forget old scores and to take a hand in the building of that new world destined to begin on a Sabbath afternoon in the spring of 1765 when James Watt walked over Glasgow Green occupied with sinful weekday thoughts. The new age began sinfully on that Sabbath, for James Watt had solved the problem of the separate condenser; as he walked over Glasgow Green a changed world lay pregnant in his brain: a world of steel and iron, tall chimneys and speed.

All over the world the last candles of the eighteenth century guttered and died. Glasgow rose: a Liverpool and a Manchester in one; a monument to the genius and the vigour of the Scot.

[6]

Dusk falls over a rock that wears a castle like a crown. This rock, which carries something of Glencoe into the very heart of Edinburgh, slopes gently towards Holyrood, bearing on its ridge black spires and pinnacles that in certain lights resemble the spears and banners of an army.

Down on the level plain is modern Edinburgh, planned in straight lines. Tramcars run through the town, and crowds fill the north side of Princes Street. But beyond the emptiness of a deep valley the wall of rock rises, dark and brooding, lifted against the sky in a passionate concentration like sleep.

Once, when I lived in a room overlooking a harbour, a great liner was tied up to the dockside. I would find myself going to the window to assure myself that it was still there. It was something improbable and, in a way, fantastic that belonged, yet did not belong, to the land. And, like many a stranger in this aristocratic city, I am always going to the window to make sure that the Castle and its embattled ridge have not sailed away into the region of those "old unhappy far-off things" to which they so clearly belong.

I find myself looking with the eyes of an artist at the rock on which old Edinburgh crouches. I would like to paint it in all its disconcerting moods: in the chill freshness of an autumn morning, in the calm sunlight of an afternoon, but most of all in that time that is not day and not night when the shadows gathering on the rock steal down like a band of cloaked men.

I climbed the Rock to visit again the Scottish National War Shrine. I have put into words elsewhere the emotion this Shrine creates in the mind of one who sees it for the first time; a second visit deepens the conviction that it is the most beautiful memorial in the world.

Genius, it would seem, haunts this rock. It might have been thought that nothing more could have been done to add to its overwhelming significance. But not far from the shrine I found the recently opened Scottish Naval and Military Museum, another labour of love that tells the story of "an old and haughty nation proud in arms".

They have assembled a wonderful and colourful collection of naval and military relics, a harvest from the countless fields on which the Highlands and the Lowlands have drawn the sword. Most museums of this kind are pathetic and dusty. They speak not of the glory of causes and the splendour of conviction, but of death and decay. It must be very difficult to keep the chill atmosphere of the tomb from a museum of this character. But the organisers have succeeded brilliantly and unforgettably. They have brought together mementoes of old wars and they have shown them in the heroic manner, so that one is conscious, not only of the gallantry of Scotland's long war record, but also of the ideals for which Scotsmen have so often surrendered their lives. It is not the funeral march that one seems to hear wailing through this Museum, but the blood-stirring tap of a drum and a jingle and creak of cavalry on the march.

I cannot find words to praise the oak statuettes made by Pilkington Jackson. They show men of the Scottish regiments at various periods in history. He has given to each figure, whether it wears the long wig of the Marlborough period, the cropped hair of Covenanting times, or the bag-wig of the Georgians, a good Scottish face. If ever I meet Mr. Jackson I shall ask him how many of these splendid little figures are portraits. If the Naval and Military Museum contained only this series of statuettes it would have justified itself. It is a gallery in which Scotsmen may see their forefathers to the very life, dressed in the varied splendour of old uniforms, grasping pike, musket and sword.

There are relics in plenty; bonnets and helmets and tunics, also the fine Colville collections of ancient weapons.

I suppose the most interesting of all the relics is the uniform Prince Charlie

121 *Cawdor Castle, Nairn*

122 *The Caledonian Canal, Inverness-shire*

123 *The Valley of the Spey, Morayshire*

124 *Balmoral Castle, Aberdeenshire*

125 *Ballater, Aberdeenshire*

126 *The Four Courts, Dublin*

127 *O'Connell Bridge, Dublin*

wore at Culloden. He must have presented a variegated sight, for tunic, trews and jacket are all of different tartans. Even with the knowledge that such garments would be treasured and handed down with veneration from father to son, one marvels at the freshness of the colours.

What a magnificent war record Scotland possesses! As I went round this Museum it occurred to me how much history can be hidden in a button, and how much courage may be summed up in a plume.

[7]

Stirling is the best centre from which to explore one of the most fascinating parts of Scotland. Bruce, Wallace and Mary Queen of Scots have left their names to the countryside: Bannockburn is nearby; Stirling Bridge is only a few yards out of the town, and the Lake of Menteith is not far off. The ancient capital of Dunfermline is a few miles to the east and the Trossachs about the same distance to the west. But, in addition to this, you have Stirling Castle, which, with Edinburgh, is the most romantic castle in Scotland. . . .

Early in the morning I decided to climb the Wallace Memorial. It was the right day for it: a clear, windy day with plenty of high cloud. This great tower, which reminds me of a castle on the Rhine, rises on the height of Abbey Craig and stands sentinel above the "Links of Forth". It was built about sixty years ago as a national memorial to William Wallace.

I plunged into a stone corkscrew. I climbed up and up; the wind grew bitterly cold as it whistled through the Victorian arrow-slits.

A half-way house is called the Hall of Heroes. You are faced by the marble stares of sixteen notable Scotsmen. It is dangerous to quarrel with heroes, but the temptation is sometimes too great to be avoided. Walter Scott is, naturally, first on the list; then comes James Watt, Allan Ramsay, Robert Tannahill, Adam Smith, Sir David Brewster, Hugh Miller, Carlyle, William Murdoch, John Knox, David Livingstone, Robert Burns, Thomas Chalmers, George Buchanan, Bruce and—William Gladstone!

The little guide book says, after naming the heroes: "The object which will claim the most devoted attention of the visitor will undoubtedly be the shrine containing the Wallace Sword."

I have no idea how many swords Wallace possessed, but if only a percentage of those said to be his are genuine he must have had some difficulty in selecting one when he wished to kill an Englishman. This sword is, of course, the genuine one from Dumbarton. It was lying by his side when he was betrayed as he lay asleep in a barn at Robroyston in 1305.

Up I went again through the stone corkscrew. The top of the tower is a windy place that offers you one of the most wonderful sights in the world. It was a clear and perfect day.

Stirling, in a blue haze, lay below with the "Links of Forth" twisting round her like a serpent. But what a barrier is that stupendous mass of the Grampians lying to the northwest! I saw Ben Lomond, Ben Venue, Ben Ledi, Ben More and, far to the east, Ben Vorlich, without a cloud on their old heads, standing up blue in the sun, magnificent, far off and in some way ominous.

I saw five battlefields; Bannockburn and, just beyond it, Sauchieburn, Falkirk below the ridge of the Pentlands; Sheriffmuir on the high land by the Black Hill and, right below me on the fringe of Stirling, that place where Wallace swept down from the site of his memorial and smote the stupid Surrey and the fat and foolish Cressingham.

There is probably no other view in Great Britain that tells so much of a country's history.

[8]

I wish some one would find the treasure-chest of the Tobermory galleon. Then at least we might know the truth about this mystery.

If they found gold even in small quantities—say £5 worth—it would be encouraging. But no: Nearly every year the same eager treasure-hunters arrive in Tobermory with their innocent, hopeful faces and their divers and dredgers. And Tobermory, which has seen this display of hope since 1640 when, in fact, Tobermory was nothing but a few scattered huts, smiles in its beard. The Spanish galleon is Tobermory's typically long Scottish joke!

The latest treasure-hunters have fished up the usual bits of hardwood and a few odds and ends, but the mighty treasure-chest of the Spanish Armada, which has been thought to contain gold valued at anything (and everything) from £500,000 to £30,000,000, has eluded their enthusiasm.

The wreck lies in deep water and beneath silted sand only a few yards from Tobermory Pier. While the treasure-hunters are at home finding shareholders, the Tobermory River at the back pours itself into the harbour and covers the ancient timbers with new mud and sand.

When the Spanish Armada was defeated in 1588, many of the great galleons were blown by storm to various parts of our coast, thus complicating an ethnological problem that has given much fun to the learned in Galway and Cornwall. Several of these ships were wrecked off the Scottish coast.

There is one lying today all ready for treasure-hunters in Loch Don, opposite Oban. Another lies close to the entrance to the Sound of Mull at a spot called Rhu-na-Rhidire.

But no one troubles about these two galleons, because it is believed that the pay-chest of the Spanish Armada went down in a big galleon called the *Florida*, which was blown up by the wild and terrible MacLeans in Tobermory Bay. The reason why they blew it up shall be told in a moment.

Now is this ship the *Florida*, and, if so, was the pay-chest aboard her when she sank? It is hardly credible that any self-respecting Highlanders would permit a ship to sink with a treasure-chest in her!

The *Florida* was an Italian ship fitted out by Tuscany. She appears in Spanish records sometimes as *Galeon del Duque de Florencia* (the galleon of the Duke of Florence), or *Almiranta de Florencia* (the flagship of Florence) and sometimes as the *San Francisco* (the St. Francis).

The Armada was a saintly navy. There were three ships named *San Francisco*, eight *La Concepcion*, eleven named *Nuestra Senora*, and at least eight *San Juan*.

Which *San Francisco* is supposed to lie in Tobermory Bay?

If it is a *San Francisco* that lies in the Bay, what proof is there that she carried the pay-chest? If it is not the *San Francisco*, but a ship called *San Juan*, as some people have suggested, what proof is there that she carried the pay-chest?

Possibly the treasure-hunters will settle this problem someday.

That millions in gold lie still in the strong-room of this wreck seems supported by the story that when Charles II, who had a nose for ready money, heard that the Duke of Argyll had got a diving bell from Sweden and intended to seek the treasure, he sent a man-of-war to Tobermory to stop the operations.

Then followed a long lawsuit, in which the Duke defeated the Crown and established his sole right to carry on the campaign of hope, a right still maintained by the present Duke.

The best thing that has come from the wreck is in the gardens of the Duke of Argyll's seat, Inveraray Castle. This is a beautiful bronze cannon about ten feet long that the second Duke dredged up in 1740. It bears the monogram of Benvenuto Cellini and the arms of Francis I of France.

Spanish records state that several such guns were on board a ship provided by the State of Tuscany, hence the belief that this ship is the *Florencia* or the *Florida*.

Another piece of evidence was collected in later years.

A piece of plate was found bearing a coat of arms, evidently a silver dish used by the Commander. The then Duke of Argyll approached the Spanish and Portuguese authorities and discovered that the arms were those of the Fareiga or Pereira family, which is the name local legend attributes to the foreign soldier in command of the Spanish ship.

That is about all the positive evidence that every year lures the optimists to Tobermory. But I cannot feel sorry for them. It is a wonderful place for a holiday.

[9]

A feeling of excitement spreads through St. Andrews when the time arrives for the new Captain of the Royal and Ancient Golf Club to play himself into a year of office.

Golf is really a royal and ancient game. The enemies of Mary Queen of Scots charged her with heartlessness because she played "goif" soon after Darnley was murdered. She was seen at Seton one day "right oppinlie in the feildis with the palmall and goif". Charles I was playing golf at Leith when the news of the Irish Rebellion was brought to him. James, Duke of York—afterwards James II and VII —was a great golfer and played what was probably the first Scots-English international at Leith Links. The title of the "Royal and Ancient" was approved by King William IV in 1834, and this monarch, although not a golfer, presented a gold medal to the Club on which the word golf is spelt "golph", probably the error of some London goldsmith.

The royal connection with golf was continued by King Edward VII who, when Prince of Wales, became Captain of the "Royal and Ancient", allowing himself to be played in by proxy. Edward, Prince of Wales, and his brother, George VI, then Duke of York, both played themselves into office, the Prince in 1922 and the Duke in 1930.

I rose at 7 a.m. to watch the Captain take office. It was a magnificent morning. The North Sea was breaking against the sandhills and the Old Course looked as if it had been pressed by its valet during the night. An old man was sweeping the first green with a long switch of hickory, obliterating the evidence of any worm that had had the impertinence to intrude. An official of the Royal and Ancient was dragging out a little old-fashioned cannon of the kind seen sometimes in the gardens of retired sea captains. And so, with the dew still on the grass, the stage was set for the most solemn ceremony of the golfer's year.

I am, as I have already admitted, not a golfer, and in St. Andrews I feel much as a Christian must feel in Mecca or as an infidel ought to feel in Jerusalem. I am an outsider, one who does not know what Tom Morris did long ago or what Harry Vardon or Bobby Jones have done in our own time. I can only look with reverence at the Royal and Ancient Club, which stands beside the sea like a strip of Pall Mall on holiday, and marvel at the atmosphere of solemnity that precedes the new Captain's ceremonial whack.

The citizens of St. Andrews appear on the course and surround the Clubhouse. It is the greatest day of the year in a town dedicated to golf. Few would be absent from the ceremony. No one in St. Andrews would care to say that he, or she, had not seen the new Captain drive off from the first tee. The caddies, who are as distinct from other men as stable-boys or fisher lads, gather in great numbers. When the new Captain plays himself in every year, they scramble for the ball and the caddy who retrieves it receives a golden sovereign. They stand about in the cold morning air, terribly alert and cynical, as if they know all the jokes about golfers.

The terrace fills with people. Men and women stand about gazing out lovingly over the greens and the bunkers. At last the new Captain appears. He is an elderly man in a noisy suit of plus-fours. The retiring Captain walks with him to the green. Someone sees to the priming of the cannon.

The professional of the "Royal and Ancient", whose name is known all over the world, bends down and tees up the ball. As soon as he does this, the caddies spread out over the course and wait ready to race for it. The crowd gazes at the new Captain as worshippers in ancient times might have watched a high priest in the act of performing a sacrifice.

The new Captain takes a practice swing. Then he takes another one and looks out over the course.

I think how dreadful it would be if he missed the ball altogether! I have a vision of baronets dying by the score, of old county families losing their heirs and of the grey stones of the Royal and Ancient crashing down as if an earthquake had struck St. Andrews.

"Has a captain ever missed a ball?" I whisper to a friend in the crowd.

"No," I am told sternly, "but many a one has foozled or sliced his drive."

This sounds terrible, and I stand inwardly praying that the new Captain will neither slice nor foozle.

Up go his arms, bang goes the sea captain's little cannon, and a white pill soars swiftly over the links in the direction of the waiting caddies. As its arc declines, the caddies begin to run. The ceremony, which began like a game of golf, now develops into a Rugby scrum. The caddies fight for the ball as gulls fight for fish. I see a mass of waving arms and kicking legs. Men retire from the battle nursing their fingers. At last a rather startled young man comes running towards us holding a golf ball. Reporters dash at him.

"How did you get it?" they ask him.

"I was underneath," he says with stark simplicity, "and some one kicked it my way, so I just lay on it."

They lead him to the Captain who shakes hands with him and gives him a golden sovereign. So the ceremony ends. St. Andrews has a new Captain. The Parliament that draws up the laws of golf has welcomed its annual Prime Minister. All over the world golfers may drive and foozle secure in the knowledge that somewhere in the sacred city of golf is enthroned the authority that extends itself to every green and bunker throughout the world.

And the Captain, well pleased with his drive, after receiving the congratulations of his fellow golfers, goes off to—slice his morning egg.

[10]

It is early morning. The sun is rising. The sound of Aberdeen at this time is a bright jingle as dray-horses plod steadily over the stone roads. I go through the half-light to one of Aberdeen's most fascinating sights—the morning auction in the Fish Market.

At the bottom of Market Street I am pulled up by an unexpected beauty. The rising sun, struggling through a veil of clouds in thin streamers of lemon-yellow and flamingo-pink, flings a bridgehead in dark silhouette against the sky. I have no doubt that in ordinary lights this is a very ordinary bridge, merely a path of steel girders linking quay to quay. But in the early morning its round turrets, like a Border keep, stand mirrored in the still water of a dock looking for all the world like some ancient fortress of romance dreaming above its moat.

The Fish Market is something no visitor to Aberdeen should miss. Every fish market is fascinating. That man is not normal who will not linger beside a fisherman in the hope of prying into his basket. How much more exciting, then, are these markets on whose floors are laid out the stranger mysteries of deeper waters?

It is the largest fish market in the country. It is a broad, covered way built right round the Albert Basin. The trawler fleet lies—"berthed" is, I suppose, the right word, but "parked" is much more expressive—at the quayside, thick as motorcars at the Derby. They steam gently with the effort of their incoming. Their decks are foul with fish scales and slippery with crushed ice. Salt is on their smokestacks, and their high fo'c'sles are wet still with North Sea spray. The grimy faces of engineers peer up from hatchways; down companionways clatter the crews in enormous thigh boots. Vivid, arresting and even, as are all things connected with the sea, exciting as this fleet is, it simply fades before the spectacle of its cargo.

Imagine a million bare babies being soundly smacked and you have the sound of Aberdeen Fish Market as a million fish are slapped down on the concrete! The sound of this slapping continues perhaps for an hour until each ship has landed her catch. Then come men who sort out the fish according to their kind, and other men who take each limp pyramid and dress it by the right in neat, fearfully defunct, rows.

I walk with a faint feeling of generalship. It is like inspecting several army corps. The poor fish lie in rows with a N.C.O. at regular intervals set at a slightly different angle to indicate the count. There are gigantic skate with tails like sting-ray, there are colossal halibut taken from deep waters, there are cod like young sharks. Some of the catch has come from the Faroe Islands.

When the fish is paraded, there occurs the most mysterious commercial transaction I have ever witnessed. The auctioneers appear with little books. They walk up to each battalion. A crowd of buyers follows. There is no shouting, no gesticulation; they might, in fact, be performing a burial service in some unknown tongue. I defy a stranger to discover unaided what passes between auctioneer and buyer in Aberdeen Fish Market. A man may be able to buy a Rembrandt at Christie's for £100,000, but I am willing to bet him that he would find it impossible to buy one haddock by auction in Aberdeen! It is not an auction: It is a secret society.

The formula, whatever it is, could not be more effective. In less time than it takes to perform a leisurely walk round the victims, each dump has been sold. Fish begins to melt as swiftly as snow in sun. Large areas of asphalt become visible. Soon there is not a fish to be seen.

"Where does it all go?"

"London mostly."

"When does it arrive?"

"Tons of it will be eaten for breakfast tomorrow morning."

That is Aberdeen's most spectacular hour.

[11]

If you would see a perfect picture postcard stretch of Scotland, take the road from Braemar to Ballater any afternoon when the sun is shining. Every yard of this road is a coloured postcard. All the graciousness, all the gentleness, all the sweetness and the prettiness that is denied the majestic mountain pass from Perth has taken root in the Valley of the Dee. Here on fine days the Highlands wear a perpetual smile. It is true that there are wild places, but you are never quite deceived by them: You know that every pine tree near Balmoral has a valet, and that no matter how cold the wind, how cruel the mountainside, how bleak the rolling moor, there is a hot bath at the end of every day.

These are the Highlands that have been so often pushed through your letterbox in London with the inscription: "Birds terribly scarce this year", or "Want rain badly" (this, of course, from a fisherman); and in spite of the fact that they do not thrill as the hard, naked hills can thrill, there is a charm about Deeside like the charm of an armchair after a storm.

I went on beside the Dee, for this road is like a promenade beside the river, and I saw that characteristic sight, a fisherman up to his thighs in the stream wielding a great salmon-rod, in the background an experienced and slightly cynical gillie holding an as yet unnecessary gaff. Over the trees on the right of the road fluttered the Royal Standard from a turret of Balmoral. This baronial castle of white Crathie granite lies at the foot of Craig Gowan beside a bend of the Dee, and it is haunted by the ghost of an elderly lady in black who admires the scenery from a little trap drawn by a shaggy Highland pony. The Highlands will never forget Queen Victoria. I talked to an old man in Braemar who referred to her always with a spiritual genuflexion as "her late gracious Majesty".

And among the delights of this road from Braemar are the little pine woods beyond the boundary wall. They are dappled with sunlight and carpeted with the softest fern. I explored more than one, and found myself in a green heaven of bird song through which trickled a thin tinkle of invisible water. In little clearings among the pungent pine trees were blue harebells and yellow buttercups; in the darkest part of the wood were alluring toadstools painted pink and scarlet. Through the tall stems of the pines I could see the great mountains on the opposite bank of the river towering to the clouds in a haze of mauve and purple. There is in a Scottish landscape, even in lyrical woodlands, something most dramatic and definite. A wood is much the same the world over. I know woods in Italy that might be in Sussex. But the Scottishness of these little brakes beside the road along Deeside is such that I feel the pine trees rule them. It's when they sigh. If a man were taken up blindfolded and shot from the other end of the world to open his eyes on Deeside, he would say at once: "I am in Scotland!"

Ballater. . . .

The railway gives up at Ballater, with a sigh of relief. This is the railhead station for Balmoral. All the notabilities of the Victorian era, and a good many of the

128 *The Library of Trinity College, Dublin*

129 *Glendalough, Co. Wicklow*

130 *The Avonmore River near Rathdrum,*
Co. Wicklow

131 *The Plain of Tipperary*

132 *Lismore Castle, Co. Waterford*

133 *Cahir Castle, Co. Tipperary*

Edwardian and the Georgian, have stepped down on its platform. The station officials have developed such an eye for personalities that nothing so recommends itself on this station as a statesmanlike bearing. A Gladstone collar would create a panic! Guards of honour have often been posted outside the ticket office. Distinguished parcels are, throughout the autumn, carried tenderly from luggage vans.

Worship for members of the royal family is probably carried to greater lengths at Ballater than anywhere else in a loyal kingdom. Even the Prince Consort is still revered in Ballater, and no one in this town has ever been heard to utter a word against the Albert Memorial. To do so would be disloyal.

It is a glorious spot. The fishing hotel, complete with loyal lithographs and the slightly indignant heads of dead stags, is built beside the Dee, so that you could fish from the bedroom windows if you were a lazy millionaire. They look out over the old bridge to wooded hills, and night and day there is the sound in Ballater of the shallow Dee moving gently over its amber stones.

[12]

The road dips down from Nairn to Moray Firth and Inverness.

I have tried to describe views whose beauty has appealed to me from the Border onward, but this view on a day of brilliant sun is one of the most perfect things I know. There are glimpses through pine woods of distant blue waters. The hills round Moray Firth are that incredible Atlantic blue that almost breaks the heart —the blue of Aran and Achill Island off the west coast of Ireland—a blue so blue, and yet so soft, that to look at it is to think of the islands of the Hesperides or the land of the Lotus Eaters. It is a colour not of this world: It is a paint they use only in heaven. Beyond the Firth lie piled the distant hills of Cromarty and Dornoch, etched in the same even, tender magic; and, more remote still, lying in a haze of heat, are the clustered highlands of Sutherlandshire and the coastline that swings up to Caithness.

I dipped down into this with a queer feeling of unreality. A railway poster had come true! This was not the Scotland of popular fancy, it was not the Scotland framed in so many hearts all over the world. What is the Scotland that rises before the eyes of the exile? It is the Scotland of slow clouds steaming down a little way into the gullies of gaunt hills, the Scotland of blown mist and drizzle. Notice how in three of the best songs of exile outside Ireland emphasis is placed on the mist and the storm. Neil Munro has written:

Are you not weary in your distant places,
Far, far from Scotland of the mist and storm,
In drowsy airs, the sun-smite on your faces,
The days so long and warm?
When all around you lie the strange fields sleeping,
The dreary woods where no fond memories roam,
Do not your sad hearts over seas come leaping
To the highlands and the lowlands of your home?

Let torrents pour then, let the great winds rally,
Snow-silence fall, or lightning blast the pine;
That light of Home shines brightly in the valley,
And, exiled son of Scotland, it is thine.
For you have wandered over seas of longing,
And now you drowse, and now you well may weep,
When all the recollections come a-thronging
Of this old country where your fathers sleep.

The same note sings through Stevenson's "In Exile":

Blows the wind today, and the sun and the rain are flying,
Blows the rain wind on the moors today and now,
Where about the graves of the martyrs the whaups are
crying,
My heart remembers how!

Then, too, in that magnificent "Canadian Boat Song" whose author is unknown:

From the lone shieling of the misty island
Mountains divide us and a waste of seas—
Yet still the blood is strong, the heart is Highland,
And we in dreams behold the Hebrides.

There is no sunlight in the poetry of exile. There is only mist, wind, rain, the cry of whaups and the slow clouds above damp moorland. That is the real Scotland; that is the Scotland whose memory wrings the withers of the far from home; and, in some way that is mysterious, that is the Scotland that even a stranger learns to love.

[13]

I entered Inverness. Moray Firth was as blue as the sea at Capri, and the light in the streets was as glaring as in Tangier. It was very pleasant, but it was all slightly incredible!

Inverness is as unique among the cities of Scotland as York among those of England. It has none of York's visible age, yet, strangely enough, here is a city that has swept away its antiquities without losing an air of antiquity. It is almost as though centuries of history steam upward through the soil of Inverness. Like Edinburgh, Stirling, Dundee and Perth, it has the appearance of having been founded by a member of the Royal Academy in a landscape mood. Few human communities are so fortunate as the cities and towns of Scotland in their sur-roundings. That is the virtue of a turbulent youth. Peaceful and law-abiding countries build their towns in sheltered places; wild countries fly to the protection of hills. Now that the savage seas have ebbed, these cities of Scotland are left like great arks stranded magnificently on their Ararats.

Inverness annoys and disturbs me. I thought until I saw it that Edinburgh was the most romantic city in Scotland. Now I am uncertain. It is not right that one country should have two such candidates. Edinburgh is more magnificent, enthroned as it is in authentic regality; but Inverness is more—romantic. It has the distinction that only a river can give to a city, a broad, lovely river that flows through the heart of it. Is there to be seen from any other city in Scotland a lovelier coastline than that of Moray Firth curving north to Tarbat Ness and eastward to Burghead? Blue water reflects blue hills. There are the landlocked firths of Beauly and Inverness, which lie peacefully at the very doors of this city. From high ground you look southwest down the valley where the broad brown Ness flows seaward from its loch; and around you the Highlands lie piled hill against hill, wood against wood, mountain against mountain, in every shade of blue. Inverness is the watch-tower of the Highlands. The Castle on its high mound —not, I believe, the site of Macbeth's castle—is a window that looks out over all northwest Scotland, and wherever you turn is something perfect and unforget-table—mountain, sea or firth. Go at sunset to the turret of the Castle and watch the sun sink below the western hills. Of all the sunsets to be seen in Scotland, this is, I think, the most memorable.

[14]

I set out on a clear morning towards Blairgowrie with a mind as eager as that of any tourist.

In days before the Highland clans migrated to the London Telephone Directory —and this point in their "tragedy" must not be overlooked!—they constituted the last colony of uncontaminated Celts. They were the only Celts in the British Isles who had never known the proud foot of a conqueror. No Roman satrap attempted to line them up with the Empire, no Norman count tried to bring them into the feudal system. They were isolated in a prehistoric atmosphere that they retained until modern times when Bonnie Prince Charlie's defeat broke down the barrier between the new world and the last stronghold of the old.

In Ireland the Celt suffered a different fate. True, he escaped the Romans in order to enjoy a brief era of culture devoted to the export of saints; but the time came when he went down before the chain mail of the Norman. Not so the Highlander. His bare knees flash through history at frequent intervals, the skirl of his pipes is heard in the front of various battles, but no matter how far he may stray he is always observed returning to the fastness of his mountains and the birthplace of his clan. It is truly astonishing that a tribal system as old as man existed and flourished in the Highlands into modern times. The political events that caused the Borders to sheathe a sword that had been flashing for centuries had no effect on the Highlands. These men remained wild and warlike when the rest of Scotland had been tamed.

Most Englishmen, who know little about the history of Scotland and nothing at all about that of Ireland, do not realise that, with the exception of the North and South Poles, the Highlands of Scotland were the last portion of the earth's surface to be explored. This sounds inconceivable, but it is true! America was already an old country when the Highlands were discovered. Until the Rebellion of 1745 opened them to travellers they were a land of mystery.

How amazing to think that as recently as two hundred years ago there existed within five hundred miles of London an enormous tract of country inhabited by tribes whose way of life was that of Brian Boru! Here in the Highlands were until modern times many "miniature courts"—to use Macaulay's words—"in each of which a petty prince attended by guards, by armour bearers, by musicians, by a hereditary orator, by a hereditary poet laureate, kept a rude state, dispensed a rude justice, waged wars and concluded treaties".

The Highland clans are a genuine link with the Golden Age. There is a primitive splendour about them. Looking back at them from the safety of our own time and with a critical faculty unbiased by a lifted herd of cattle or the working out of a blood feud, we seem to see the Highlanders as the lineal descendants of the Homeric heroes. What could be more Homeric than the Macneill who, as Kenneth Macleod states in his notes to the *Songs of the Hebrides*, used to send a trumpeter to his castle tower every evening after dinner to make the following proclamation: "Ye kings, princes and potentates of all the earth, be it known unto you that Macneill of Barra has dined—the rest of the world may dine now!"

How absurdly—magnificently—Highland that is! How many times have you heard a Highlander at the height of a heated discussion—and perhaps heated a little with his native wine—suddenly lose patience with words, call on his clan and invoke his regality with the cry: "My name's Campbell and I don't care who knows it and—ye can go to hell!"

There is something in the environment of the Highlands and also of Ireland that saps the initiative and fosters the natural laziness of the Celt, so that if you want to see the Highlander and the Irishman at their best you must seek them in London or New York.

The Highlander is a born aristocrat. The enormous gulf between baron and serf, which existed in England for centuries, was unknown in the Highlands, where the meanest clansman bore the name of his chief. The Highlander goes through life with a fine superiority complex: His name is itself a crest for all men to see.

It was Sir Walter Scott who introduced him to polite society. Before that time the courteous Highland gentleman, filled to overflowing with the sturdy virtues of the Golden Age, was by his contemporaries regarded as a lowdown cattle-lifter and assassin. All Lowlanders regard all mountaineers as thieves and bandits. But when Walter Scott turned the light of romance upon him, all the meanness left him, and he stood before the world in the grandeur of his rugged virtue. Here, it was discovered, stood Nature's last perfect gentleman. Even the death of the clan system against the bayonets at Culloden became a noble and heroic thing. The clans were dead. Long live the clans! The tartan, driven from the hills by cruel Acts of Parliaments, began to return again, not to the hills, but to the drawing-rooms. And then a shape rears itself in the mists of Deeside. Balmoral is ready to be born.

Ireland

[1]

The Customs Officer handed me a list and asked if I had anything to declare. There was something apologetic about him. He asked me to open a bag. He went through it with an air suggesting that to do so was a deplorable breach of good manners. The man next to me had among his bags a leather silk-hat box.

"And what might that be?" asked the Customs official, pointing to the box.

"A silk hat. I'm going to a funeral," replied the passenger.

"Och—God help ye!" replied the official, and at once marked every piece of this man's luggage with chalk.

That was my first impression of Ireland; one that I was to recall time and again.

Dublin in the early morning, with the sun shining, is a city the colour of claret. The red-brick Georgian mansions, with fine doors, fanlights and little iron balconies at the first-floor windows, stand back in well-bred reticence against wide roads, quiet and dignified, as if the family has just left by stagecoach. Dublin shares with Edinburgh the air of having been a great capital.

This city is as completely a creation of the eighteenth century as Bath. It is a superb, indolent aristocrat among cities, with an easy manner and a fine air of unstudied elegance. The Liffey, crossed by eight bridges, some of them good-looking, cuts the city into a north and south division, and there is pervading Dublin that subtle something as vivid and distinctive as the feel of ships and docks, due to the nearness of great mountains. Just behind Dublin the long, smooth Wicklow Hills lie piled clear-cut against the sky, brown-green in colour, and from them on clear days, I am told, a man can see across the Irish Sea to the mountains of Wales.

One of the first things that charmed me, as it must delight all visitors, is the Irish voice. The Irish do not like the "Dublin accent", but it is not so much a matter of accent as of intonation. I found myself listening to people in the street. The cadence of the Irish voice is catching. The habit of giving a little upward kick to the end of a sentence is a charming habit; in women it is adorable.

Why has Dublin been called "dear, dirty Dublin"? This surely is an ancient libel.

In the streets stand among the taxicabs many of the oldest horse cabs on earth, objects of remarkable antiquity that surely, by some virtue of the Irish temperament, continue to function, and there is also that strange but famous vehicle, known to the English as a "jaunting car", but called in Ireland an "outside car". When you hire one of them and sit sideways to the world, Dublin smiles indulgently at you from the pavement. I went round behind a spanking bay pony while the jarvey pointed out the sights with his whip.

The crowds in the Dublin streets are vastly different from English crowds. You do not see the haggard money look that is becoming characteristic of all large English cities. There is more laughter. There is no painful rushing about. There is a cheerful ease about Dublin, a casual good temper, which makes it difficult to realise the dark times through which this city has passed. There are certain apparent superficialities, however, that possess a certain significance. The English red has vanished from the streets; the mailboxes are green. So are the envelopes in which telegrams are delivered. So are the mail vans. And the names of the streets are written in Gaelic, which not one in a thousand Dubliners can read! Still, this proves a change in ownership and a striving to be Irish.

When we came to the end of the journey the jarvey said, when I asked how much he wanted:

"I'll leave it to yourself."

A Frenchman would have taken my enormous bribe with a surly doubtfulness, but he was quite frankly overpaid and showed it with Irish candour. "God bless ye," he said. "And now what about a bit of a drive tomorrow?"

In the hotels of Dublin at teatime enter men in riding breeches and girls in habits with mud on their boots and wind in their cheeks. In the season they hunt and get back to Dublin in time for tea. This nearness to the country and to that abiding passion of the Irish, a horse, is another of Dublin's Georgianisms. A Dublin man can shoot grouse on the hills within six miles of the General Post Office. He can grass trout within the same distance. He can take a day from business, ride to hounds and be home in time to look through the evening post.

This gives Dublin a balanced sanity. She is an ancient capital with the health of a county town. She is Georgian not only in her architecture but in her attitude to life.

In London, and in other large capitals, social life is formal and meetings are premeditated. This is not so in Dublin. There is, of course, a fair proportion of stately dinners, but more important, and more socially interesting, are the unorganised parties that just happen night after night. It is difficult to be alone in Dublin.

[2]

The stranger passing through the gates of Trinity College beneath the gaze of Burke and Goldsmith finds himself on a wide expanse of cobblestones planted by some ancient humourist to torture the bunions of learned men. Most cities possess a sanctuary that offers, or appears to offer, an escape from everyday things, and, like the Temple in London and Cheetham's Hospital in Manchester, such places become more impressive when they lie in the very heart of the city. This is so with Trinity College. You pass through its gates into a rather thoughtful world.

Trinity College is the only monument to the Elizabethan Age in Dublin.

"Its foundation is the first real landmark in the Dublin that we know—the metropolis of Ireland; and it expresses the positive or constructive side of Elizabethan rule," writes Stephen Gwynn in *The Famous Cities of Ireland*. "English statesmen had now fully determined to make Ireland into a Protestant nation, and men of English race in Ireland saw that such a nation needed the machinery of instruction both to educate Protestants and also to convert the Catholics. At the entreaty of several distinguished clerics, among whom were Adam Loftus, the Archbishop, and Henry Ussher, the Archdeacon of Dublin, a charter was obtained from Elizabeth for the foundation of a University. Its site was placed on the lands of the Augustinian Monastery of All Hallows. In the confiscation under Henry VIII the Mayor and Corporation had become possessed of its buildings, and they now granted both to the new institution. But funds were slow of coming in, and the best proof that the settlers felt a real need for knowledge is the manner in which provision was made. When the Spanish forces in Kinsale and the Irish army under Hugh O'Neill and Red Hugh O'Donnell were defeated in 1601 by Mountjoy and Carew, the victorious soldiers offered their booty as an endowment to the new college. They had conquered with the sword the forces of Popery; the conquest had to be extended with the arm of science.

134 *The Rock of Cashel, Co. Tipperary*

135 *Blarney Castle, Co. Cork*

136 *View from Brow Head, Co. Cork*

137 *St Patrick's Bridge, Cork*

138 *Near Muckross,
Killarney, Co.
Kerry*

139 *Lady's View,
Killarney, Co. Kerry*

140 *Lough Mask, Co. Galway*

141 *The Spanish Archway, Galway*

142 *Carrickfergus Castle, Ulster*

145 *Donegall Place and Royal Avenue, Belfast*

144 *The Botanic Gardens, Belfast*

146 *The Mourne Mountains, Co. Down*

147 *Another view of the Mountains of Mourne*

148 *Lough Neagh, Co. Armagh*

149 *Armagh City, Co. Armagh*

150 *Camlough, Co. Armagh*

"From the beginning of the seventeenth century onwards the University has been there, not cloistered and apart like those of Oxford and Cambridge, on whose model it was planned, but making part of the metropolitan life: closely in touch with the governing powers of Ireland, sharing officially their point of view, repressing, indeed, so far as in it lay, any turbulent tendencies among its students, but, when all is said, providing there a kind of vat in which the life of Ireland's Protestant youth worked out its fermentation."

Every visitor to Dublin should go to Trinity to see one of the most precious books in existence—the famous Book of Kells. It is taken from its case every evening and locked in a safe in the vaults; every morning it is carried reverently to its glass case again, and one leaf is turned each day.

What is the value of the Book of Kells? Many men have wondered. Professors have been known to speculate in the sanctity of the family circle how much it would mean a year if Trinity sold the beastly book and devoted the proceeds to the staff. (This, of course, is an Irish joke!)

The value of the Book of Kells is the sum that one millionaire, bidding against another millionaire, would pay at Sotheby's for it. This depends, in its turn, on the depth of hatred and rivalry between them. Both of them might think they had won, for instance, if the price was £500,000! And the Book of Kells is not insured! There can be no other book of its character in the world that is not insured. The College authorities, no doubt wisely, say that money could not produce another such book, so that the best insurance is to spend a fraction of the premium that would be necessary on extra fire hoses and watchmen.

I was permitted by the courtesy of the Librarian to examine the book. He even allowed me to turn one of its thick vellum pages.

What is the Book of Kells?

It is an illustrated copy of the Gospels dating from the eighth century, written by an unknown Irish monk in the Abbey at Kells in Meath. He was one of the world's great illuminators.

He enriched his book with a thousand fantasies and a thousand beauties of intricate design. He poured into this book all the power of his imagination. Men looking at it today wonder not only at the fertility of his brain but also at the keenness of his eyes. How is it possible that a man, unless he employed a type of magnifying glass unknown in his day, could pen such microscopic designs, so perfect that sections of them no larger than a postage stamp, when photographed and enlarged, show no flaw in the intricate interlocking of lines and spirals?

This great relic of Irish art was placed in a costly gold shrine. Later in history it was stolen from the sacristy of the Abbey of Kells. It was found two months afterwards hidden in the earth. The thief had taken it for the shrine; and so the book, flung carelessly away, was recovered and remains the most perfect expression of Christian art to have survived from the Golden Age of Ireland.

Near the Book of Kells they show you the "Harp of Ireland", supposed to be the famous harp that sounded "once through Tara's halls", but no one believes this. It is, however, the national emblem of the Free State.

"The story is," the guide will tell you, "that after Brian Boru was killed at the Battle of Clontarf, this harp was given to the Pope Alexander II. It remained in the Vatican for nearly five hundred years, and was given, in 1521, to Henry VIII in recognition of his defence of the Seven Sacraments. Twenty years later Henry VIII gave the harp to the Earl of Clanricarde, and it was handed down until it came into the possession of a Limerick antiquary. . . . I myself remember when there were strings on the harp, but they've gone now. . . ."

It is a pretty story, but the archaeologists say that the harp dates back no further than the fourteenth century.

It is in the Book of Kells that Ireland's remote past lives gloriously in subtle line and perfect colour. When a man turns the pages of that great book he turns back the centuries to a world of Irish saints, of Irish poems, of Irish legends, of Irish boats sailing over the sea taking with them the light of the Christian Church.

[3]

The road that runs due south from Cashel, through Cahir and Clogheen over the mountains to Lismore is one of the most beautiful I have ever travelled. You have the wide Plain of Tipperary round you for miles, and facing you are the Knockmealdown Mountains. Just beyond Clogheen the road rises and you mount quickly into the wild hills. You come to a hairpin bend, the Devil's Elbow (his other elbow is in Scotland on the Blairgowrie road to Braemar!) and, when you can safely do so, stop and look back.

This is one of the grandest views in the British Isles. Below lies the great Plain of Tipperary with white roads intersecting the greenness of fields and the darker green of woods. West of Cahir are the Galtee Mountains and on the east is Slieveamon. On a good day you can see the Rock of Cashel rising from the green plain twenty miles to the north.

It is difficult to tear yourself away from such a sight. But the road goes up into mountains, bare and barren and brown; then it falls to one of the sweetest glens in the world where a laughing stream runs all the way to Lismore.

Here on the banks of the broad, slow Blackwater—a mighty salmon stream—rises the magnificent Castle of Lismore, owned by the Duke of Devonshire—the Warwick Castle of Ireland. It is not perhaps as fine as Warwick but the mind immediately connects them, both majestic, both throned on wooded rocks, both reflected in water.

The courtyard of this Castle is one of its chief beauties. The view downward from the drawing-room is terrifying. No wonder the timid James II, who spent a night at Lismore during his flight from the Battle of the Boyne, started back in horror from it when he looked from one of the windows.

Lismore is delightful, a clean, reserved and dignified country town. I was pleased to find two kilted pipers wearing Black Watch tartan playing in the streets. When I hailed them as Scotsmen they answered me in the accents of Cork!

"It's Irish we are entirely," they said. "Would ye care to subscribe some little thing, now, to the pipe band of Cark?"

[4]

Cork was the most foreign city I had seen in Ireland—foreign not in appearance but in atmosphere. One was surprised to hear the crowds talking a high-pitched English. I felt that on a summer's day Cork should be full of vivid striped umbrellas, beneath which the visitor might sit in the shade and sip grenadine.

It was in 1920 that at the height of the madness of the "Trouble" half of Cork was burnt down. I felt sorry that the city has not taken advantage of this disaster to rebuild its streets in a fashion more in keeping with the distinctive character of its people.

Cork is the capital of Munster: If anything should happen to Dublin it would be, obviously, the capital of the Free State. It is built on an island in the centre of the River Lee. A man, who should have known better, told me that it gets its name because it floats like a cork on the water. Cork, however, is derived from an Irish word meaning marsh.

There is a legend in Ireland to the effect that a Cork man can make a fortune where any other man would be applying for outdoor relief. It is certainly true that the people of Cork are different from the people in other parts of Ireland. They have a tradition as aristocratic as that of Dublin. They are clannish. For centuries they intermarried within their own walls, so that a family feeling exists between all men of Cork, which explains why when a Cork man takes over a business, say in Dublin, other men of Cork appear as if by magic in the firm.

Brilliant conversation began in Cork during the eighteenth century, and it is still going on. It is carried on in a quick, high-pitched, musical Welsh accent. (Or have the Welsh a Cork accent?)

They stay up so late in Cork making epigrams that the shops do not open until 9.30 to 10 a.m.

Cork owes the most modern shopping street in Ireland to a tragedy of the "Trouble". St. Patrick's Street, burned down in 1920, is now rebuilt. Grafton Street, Dublin, is the Bond Street of Ireland; St. Patrick's Street, Cork, is the Regent Street.

There are certain things in all historic cities that are done by tourists and no other people. They are generally of a nature to confirm local inhabitants in the belief that all tourists are half-witted. In Cork you are supposed to kiss the Blarney Stone and to hear the bells of Shandon.

The bells of Shandon do, indeed, in the famous words of Father Prout, "sound so grand on the pleasant waters of the River Lee". And Cork must know them by heart! Every time a curious visitor enters the belfry the bell-ringer treats the city to a concert. He will tell you that in the summer when Americans dash through Cork on their way to Killarney (which is all they see of Ireland!), the bells of Shandon are never silent all day long.

Kissing the Blarney Stone is a difficult and not too pleasant act. It is hard to discover why generations of travellers have endured it and still more difficult to know why that particular stone, one hundred and fifty feet above ground-level, achieved its world-wide fame.

The dictionary says that "blarney" is "to talk over, or beguile by wheedling speech; flatter; humbug with agreeable talk".

The village of Blarney lies five miles to the northwest of Cork. In the middle of a pretty wood rise the ruins of Blarney Castle. It is the third castle built on that site. The present tattered shell was constructed in the reign of Queen Elizabeth, the strongest castle in that part of Ireland.

The word "blarney" entered the language, so they say, when the Baron of Blarney was required to surrender the fortress to Elizabeth as a proof of his loyalty. He said that he would be delighted to do so, but—something always happened at the last moment to prevent the surrender! His excuses became so frequent and so plausible that the Lord President, who was demanding the Castle in the name of the Queen, became a joke at Court.

Queen Elizabeth (probably) said, when these excuses were repeated to her: "Odds bodikins, more Blarney talk!"

The first question you ask when you enter Blarney Castle is, "Where's the Blarney Stone?"

A caretaker points skyward to the turret of the donjon. You see, one hundred and fifty feet from the earth, and on the outside of the wall, a large brown stone. Your enthusiasm begins to wane! You go round and round a spiral staircase and emerge on the turret.

You sit down with your back to a sheer drop. Your guide then sits on your legs, holds your feet and tells you to lie back over the drop and grasp two iron handrails. By wriggling down (your eyes closed to shut out the distant inverted landscape), you bring yourself to kiss the base of the stone. You then lever yourself up and say, "Well, I did it!"

How did this custom originate? No one knows.

"And what," you say to your guide as you wind earthwards, "will the Blarney Stone do for me?"

He then recites these lines by Father Prout:

There is a stone there,
That whoever kisses,
Oh! he never misses
*   To grow eloquent.*
'Tis he may clamber
To a lady's chamber,
Or become a member
*   Of Parliament.*

You go thoughtfully away, comforted by the thought that it is all blarney!

The solitude is deathlike. There is no sound but the cries of wild birds and the bleating of black-faced sheep. There is no movement but the clouds that steam gently over the crests of the mountains. The road to Killarney winds round and up through a gorge as destitute of life as the Valley of the Dead in Egypt.

When I turned a corner I saw approaching slowly over the mountain path a coffin lying in a motor car. Behind were three cars full of women with white, tear-stained faces. A mourner ran beside the coffin tightening the ropes that held it in position. This funeral might have been a vision called up by the grim spirit of the hills.

So I went on for twenty miles into a wilder solitude. This pass is drenched in the uncanny mystery of all high places; over it lies the watchful hush of hills and sky. Then—Windy Gap!

Is there a greater surprise in the British Isles? With a suddenness that takes the breath away you are faced by one of the grandest views in Europe! There is no warning. You can hardly believe it! Behind you the abomination of desolation; below you an earthly paradise—the three blue lakes of Killarney.

Every graciousness and softness that Nature has denied the mountains have been poured out into the rich Valley of Killarney. It is almost too good to be true; almost too opulent to be quite credible. You feel that it might at any moment dissolve into mist, leaving you in the stern reality of the hills. . . .

When the sun is strong the hills become blue and purple and mauve. You can spend days in the woods and thickets marvelling at the incredible richness of the soil. There is a touch of jungle vegetation about it. Tall palm trees lift their spiky heads against the blue sky. Kerry is warmer in winter than any other part of the British Isles. In the month of February, I am told, spring is already in Killarney, the gorse is in full bloom, the chestnut buds are unfolding.

In summer Killarney is a botanist's paradise. Here grow cedars of Lebanon, arbutus, wild fuchsia, the Mediterranean strawberry tree, which is unknown elsewhere in the British Isles, the scented orchid, which grows along the Mediterranean coast and in Asia Minor, the great butterwort, which is a native of Spain, the "blue-eyed grass", which you will see only in Canada.

There was once a Frenchman, I am told, who said that Ireland was the jewel of the West, that Kerry was the jewel of Ireland, that Killarney was the jewel of Kerry, and that the little uninhabited Isle of Innisfallen was the jewel of Killarney. I have nothing to add to this.

[5]

I came over the mountains of Clare into the grey town of Galway as men were lighting lamps in the harbour. An unearthly afterglow lingered in the sky, a dull red haze hung over the hills and the edges of the Atlantic were washed in a colour so strange and so vivid, almost a pale green, that melted marvellously into the blue of the dusk. And as the light was drawn out of the sky, a few stars hung over the grape-blue heights of Connemara.

Such a velvet softness pervaded Galway, and in those first moments I felt, as one feels sometimes on meeting a stranger, that a new loyalty had come into life. Galway did not seem to belong to any part of Ireland that I had seen; it seemed to belong only to itself.

I know now that strange beauty that flies like dust through Galway to the spirit of Gaelic Ireland, something that is a defiance to time, something that is like a declaration of faith. Galway must be almost too beautiful to an Irishman.

He must feel about it as an Englishman would feel if, in an England conquered for centuries, and speaking a foreign tongue, he came one night to a little town in Somerset and heard men talking in English.

When the hotel porter was unloading my luggage he drove away a determined old woman shrouded in a black shawl who was trying to tell me something. I went after her and asked her what she wanted. Her husband was out of work and her sons were out of work. She was a gentle old creature, and when I placed a shilling in her hand she said:

"May the Virgin bless you and bring you safe home."

I encountered her twice during my first walk round Galway, and each time she repeated her blessing with a gratitude out of all proportion to the miserable gift, so that I felt that my first steps in the west were taken in sanctity. . . .

I went through many a narrow street, past a ruined Spanish house, for Galway reflects Spain in the eyes of its people, and, here and there, in a square house with a central courtyard and a gate flush with the street.

But what a town of yesterday! The curse of Cromwell lies heavier on Galway than on any other Irish town. It is a town of dead factories and great houses brought to decay. In the Middle Ages, Galway was the Bristol of Ireland. Its very name has the ring of a great city in it—London, York, Bristol, Dublin, Galway; there is something high and authoritative about such names.

The fourteen Anglo-Norman families of Galway, who gained for their town the title of "Galway of the Tribes", were the most exclusive families in Ireland. I believe that they intermarried for so long that special dispensation had more than once to be obtained to establish canonical legality. They founded the fortunes of the town. The quays were stacked with the wine-casks of Spain. The galleons of Galway were as accustomed to the ports of Spain as they were to Irish waters. During the Civil War, Galway remained loyal to Charles, but Cromwell had his way with it in the end, and Galway has never recovered.

Its inhabitants a hundred years ago numbered forty thousand; today the population of this once crowded seaport is reduced to that of a small country town.

The parapet of Galway Bridge is worn smooth as glass by the arms of those who lean over it when the salmon come up from salt water. This is one of the sights of Ireland.

At first when I looked down into Galway River I could see nothing. Then something I took to be weeds moved strangely; and I realised that I was looking down on the backs of hundreds of salmon. I have never seen anything like this great crowd of fresh-run fish with the sea lice still on them lying still, fanning themselves with their noses towards the sweet lakes. Could I have dropped a brick into the river I must have hit at least ten eighteen-pounders; for they lay side by side, apparently touching, edged together in one incredible queue.

Now and then some monster would seem to become impatient, and he would, with a muscular movement, urge himself forward; but so tight were his companions pressed about him that he would make no progress and be forced to fall back into his place.

There were three earnest salmon fishermen on the bank below me. I watched them casting for at least an hour and—not a rise did they get! One man constantly hit the water immediately above at least thirty mighty fish, but not one of them took the slightest interest in the fly!

Yet men must catch fish in this place or they would not pay a great amount of money on the condition that they keep only one in three.

Stephen Gwynn, a great fisherman, has said that one man killed a ton of salmon in about three months' fishing. So thick are the salmon in Galway River that I find it difficult to understand how it is that if you do not hook a fish in the orthodox manner you do not hook him in a fin or in his tail!

In the early morning you will lean over the bridge and see that the salmon have moved up in the night. Only two or perhaps three are left. One morning I saw for the first time the fish that killed an English king—the lamprey. He was a curious fellow, half fish and half eel, lying low down against the stones of the riverbed and swaying with the stream.

[6]

I have heard people say that Belfast has no history.

In the eighteenth century the town—it had then a population of about fifteen thousand—became the centre of nationalist aspirations and won for Ireland a political independence similar to that of the Free State today.

It was the time when the American War of Independence let loose on the British coasts a number of privateers, chief among whom was the Scottish gardener's son, the famous John Paul Jones. There was also the fear of a French invasion. Ulster's sympathies were wholeheartedly with the American colonists. Were they not suffering similar injustices?

On 20 April 1778, a ship disguised as a merchantman appeared off Carrickfergus. She was the notorious *Ranger*, commanded by John Paul Jones. The crew of a fishing smack boarded her, and Jones, on learning that they were pilots, detained them. They told him that the ship he could see lying in Belfast Lough was the *Drake*, a British sloop-of-war of twenty guns. John Paul Jones then planned an attack that was to reverberate all over Britain and, incidentally, lead to the temporary independence of Ireland.

Jones, who loved to write long-winded narratives, has left a detailed description of the fight. His idea was to lumber up to the warship looking like a harmless merchantman, overlie her cable and fall upon her bow, thus exposing all her decks to his fire. But things went wrong. A storm blew up, and Jones made off to carry out his daring and historic raid on Whitehaven. He burnt the shipping in this port and a few hours later landed on St. Mary's Isle, Kircudbright, with the strange idea of capturing the harmless Earl of Selkirk. On the morning of the 24th he was again off Carrickfergus, where he saw the *Drake* moving out of Belfast Lough. News of his wild escapade at Whitehaven had, as he guessed, reached Belfast, and the *Drake* was under orders to find him.

The *Drake's* boat was sent to reconnoitre the *Ranger*. When the officer boarded the privateer he was at once made prisoner. The British ship was accompanied by five small vessels full of Belfast folk who wanted to see a naval fight. As the *Drake* approached and the *Ranger* manœuvred for position, alarm smokes appeared on both sides of the channel, and, as Jones says, the sightseers "wisely put back".

The *Drake* came within hail and hoisted the Union Jack. The *Ranger* ran up the American stars. (Surely this was the first occasion on which the American flag was hoisted in British waters!) In a few moments the first broadside broke from the side of the *Ranger* and swept the *Drake*. The two ships then engaged hotly and obstinately for over an hour. The *Drake* then called for quarter. Her fore and main top-yards were cut away. Her top-gallant yard and mizzen gaff were both hanging up and down along the mast. Her ensign was riddled with shot and hanging in the water. Her hull was galled with shot.

Such was America's first naval victory won in open fight and in view of thousands of Belfast people. No matter what may be said of the morals and manners of John Paul Jones, none can deny that he had the Nelson touch.

The alarm created throughout Great Britain by this incident, and the raids on Scotland, was something like that caused thirty years later by the fear of a Napoleonic invasion. The alarm was based, of course, on the French treaty with America, so that John Paul Jones appeared to be the vanguard of invasion. Militia camps sprang up all over England. "Camps everywhere," wrote Horace Walpole, "and the ladies in the uniforms of their husbands. All the world are politicians or soldiers or both, servants are learning to fire all day long."

The Irish, Protestants and Catholics, demanded that as England could not defend them in the event of war, they should be allowed to organise a volunteer force similar to the militia that was training all over England. It was the old story of England's difficulty and Ireland's opportunity. Belfast led the way. She enlisted forty thousand men within a year, put them in uniform and armed them. This force was officered by the public men of the time. Henry Grattan and Henry Flood were colonels. Grattan, who had represented Charlemont in the British Parliament at the age of twenty-nine, was the leader of the Patriot Party. The Volunteer movement spread all over Ireland. Grattan, with the immense influence of an armed country behind him, pressed for the lifting of the restrictions on Irish trade and the repeal of the harsh laws against Catholics. (Grattan was, of course, a Protestant.) He won freedom for Irish exports, and in 1782 certain of the penal laws were lifted. Grattan then fought for Parliamentary independence under the British Crown. On 16 May 1782, Ireland went wild with happiness. She had received legislative independence. She had achieved Home Rule. An Irish Parliament sat in Dublin.

In the years that followed, another great Irishman trod the streets of Belfast. He was Wolfe Tone, the founder of the United Irishmen. This society sought only the welfare of Ireland. It was joined by Catholics and Protestants. Then, denied a constitutional outlet, it became a great secret society and a means for hatching rebellion.

In a few years Ireland was once more at war with England. The terrible years dragged on in bloodshed. Gallant men, mistaken men and evil men added their story to that of Ireland's sorrows. In 1800 the Irish Parliament listened to the impassioned voice of Grattan, then an invalid of fifty, as he sat in his seat too weak to stand, wearing the faded blue-and-red coat of the old Volunteers. He pleaded with his fellow Irishmen not to fling away their political independence by supporting the Act of Union. The inspired voice fell on deaf ears. The Act of Union became law. Over a century was to pass before England's extremity was again Ireland's opportunity. History has never repeated itself with more unfailing and consistent regularity than in Ireland. The Act of Union went down and the Free State Flag went up.

But Belfast was no longer the Belfast that Grattan knew.

[7]

Near Belfast is the ancient capital of Ulster, Carrickfergus, which remembers the time when her great neighbour was a humble fishing village. There is a magnificent Castle on a rock—a square Norman keep and a great wall—and the guns of this Castle could, if they were not muzzle-loaders, command Belfast Lough.

The Castle has been created an "ancient monument". The admirable government department that controls abbeys, castles and other historic relics has begun the necessary task of restoration. Experts are stripping the walls of ancient plaster, pulling down partitions and generally restoring Carrick Castle to its original condition. When they have done their work they will have given Northern Ireland one of the finest Norman strongholds in the country.

Carrick Castle takes us into the wildest days of Ireland's history when the Anglo-Welsh adventurers were riding over the country staking out their claims. It is said to have been built by one of the most tempestuous of these, a knight called John de Courcy. He was, like so many of the men let loose on Ireland in the reign of Henry II, a penniless adventurer. De Courcy was a discontented giant who had heard a legend—one of the spurious prophecies of Columcille—that Ulster would be conquered by a pauper knight from a foreign country, a white knight on a white horse bearing birds upon his shield. So great would be the slaughter that men would wade up to their knees in blood. This prophecy suited De Courcy down to the ground. It obsessed him. He even kept a little book of Columcille's with him although he could not understand one word of the Gaelic.

He made himself as much as possible like the knight of legend. He was a fair-haired man. He rode a white horse, and he bore heraldic birds upon his shield. With a small, well-armed band of three hundred and twenty knights and Welsh archers he set out to conquer Ulster; and the terror of the prophecy preceded him. He advanced on Downpatrick so swiftly that the town was surprised by the sound of bugles and the clatter of his cavalry. The half-starved troops sacked the town. They ate and drank everything. They slaughtered. They pillaged.

The Pope's legate, Cardinal Vivian, who happened to be in Downpatrick, witnessed the scene and attempted to persuade De Courcy to go back to Dublin. When he refused, the indignant Cardinal exhorted the Irish to defend themselves and drive back the invaders. They fought a tremendous battle, but they broke themselves against the steel mail of the trained soldiery. What hopes had the Irish with their Danish axes and their javelins against the finest cavalry of the time in Europe and the best archers in the world? In this battle part of Columcille's prophecy was said to have been fulfilled, for De Courcy's men, when chasing the Irish along the shore, sank to their knees in the blood-stained sand.

De Courcy fought for years to conquer Ulster, consolidating any victory with a castle like Carrick, a policy in Ireland, as in England, that was the basis of Norman rule. The end of this adventurer was ruin and disgrace. His enemies, the De Lacys, intrigued against him with the King and procured his arrest as a traitor. His own servants betrayed him at Downpatrick. They came upon him on a Good Friday when, unarmed and in sackcloth, he was kneeling in penance for his many sins in the Cathedral. When he saw De Lacy's men advancing to slay him he sprang up, in rags and barefoot, rushed into the churchyard and, grasping the nearest weapon, a huge wooden cross on a grave, dashed out the brains of thirteen men before he was overpowered.

But for some strange reason he was not killed. His end is a mystery. There are entries in the Irish Annals that suggest that he, like many another ruffian, went on a Crusade in the Holy Land. Then this wild character is lost to history.

In the harbour at Carrickfergus is a stone low down in the wall on which King William landed. Probably few people could tell you much about De Courcy, but there is not a man, woman or child in Carrickfergus who could not describe to you how on 14 June 1690, King William III stepped ashore on this stone on his way to fight the Battle of the Boyne.

This and the Treaty Stone at Limerick are, for opposite reasons, Ireland's most venerated boulders.

[8]

No matter which road you take from Belfast, north, south, east or west, you arrive in some beautiful place. I know few capitals that lie amid such varied splendour. To the north are the exquisite Antrim glens; to the west is the great inland sea, Lough Neagh, the largest lake in the British Isles; to the south are the Mourne Mountains; to the east is the ravishing beauty of Strangford Lough with its salt water and its white gulls.

I left Belfast by the eastern road through Dundonald, where I branched off and came to Comber. I went south into County Down along the west bank of Strangford Lough. County Down is a place of little friendly green hills. I took the west bank of Strangford Lough, a name given to it by the Vikings—Strang Fiord, the "violent inlet"—a tribute to the force of the tides that thrust themselves through a narrow opening about a mile in width.

I shall never forget the sight of this lough from a high hill near Killinchy. The salt water was stirred by a sea wind. The edges of the lough were fringed with that glorious golden weed called by Western Islesmen in Scotland *femin feàrnaich* (I cannot guarantee the spelling), a weed full of iodine, from which, I imagine, the ancient Irish obtained the saffron dye for the kilt. The near bank of the loch was dotted with small green islands that looked as though the children of the hills of Down were playing in the water. These miniature hills lifted their green domes out of the green sea water, and some of them were sown in vertical strips with different root crops, strips of bright mustard-yellow would alternate with squares of golden wheat or the dark green of beet. The gulls circled over the water and stood in white companies in the yellow weeds on the shores of these fairy islands. Strangford Lough is Ulster's Killarney.

In nine miles or so I came to the town of Downpatrick, and I went straight up to the top of the hill where, it is said, the bones of St. Patrick lie in the shadow of the Cathedral. There was no need to ask anybody the way to his tomb. A much-trodden path led through a graveyard overgrown with trees. There is a big slab of rough granite with a Celtic cross on it and the word "Patric".

Several places have claimed to be the burial place of St. Patrick, among them Armagh. There is a legend in Downpatrick that St. Brigid and the great Columcille lie also buried with St. Patrick in this little graveyard. The truth of this will perhaps never be known.

St. Patrick died about the year 465, probably in the little village of Saul in County Down. The whole of Ireland went into mourning. From every monastery monks with heads shaven from ear to ear set out to attend his obsequies. Great saints and scholars of the Celtic Church converged on Saul from every part of Ireland. For twelve days and nights the sound of chanting rose round the body of St. Patrick. The night was as bright as day with the fire of torches. The Chiefs of Oriel demanded that the Saint should be buried in Armagh; those of Ulidia demanded that he should lie in their capital of Dun-da-leth-glas, which became Downpatrick. The tradition up to Norman times was that:

> In Down three saints one grave do fill,
> Brigid, Patrick and Columcille.

Strangely enough this couplet is attributed to that bad man, John De Courcy, who, it is said, took the remains of St. Brigid, who died at Kildare in 523, and Columcille, who died in Iona in 597, and placed the three great saints of Ireland in one grave.

It is certain that Columcille was buried first in Iona and that, when centuries later the Danes ravaged the Western Isles, his followers took up his relics and translated them to another place, just as the followers of St. Cuthbert fled with their Saint's bones from Lindisfarne and wandered all over the north of England with them until they built over them the church that became Durham Cathedral.

Whether or not Columcille or St. Brigid lies in Downpatrick, it is certain that St. Patrick was believed to lie there in the time of De Courcy. There are letters in existence from the abbot of a Norman monastery founded in Downpatrick offering the bones of St. Patrick in exchange for a summer, or holiday, establishment in England.

[9]

I went on all that afternoon through gentle country where the broad fields rose and fell on either side of me. Fields were full of millions of the minute blue flowers of the flax plant. In mid-August these crops are taken up and placed in bog holes and ponds to rot. They are then spread lightly over the fields to dry. This simple process removes the woody portions of the plant and makes it a stem of dry, hair-thin fibres. Before it can be called "flax", as it is known to the spinning-mills, it goes through a further refining process in a "scutch" mill.

But no lovelier sight is to be seen in an Ulster field than flax in bloom. They call it "lint" and have a charming phrase to describe it in midsummer—"when lint is in the bell".

It was growing dusk as I entered Armagh, a city of red marble. Romance will always linger in the quiet streets of Ireland's Canterbury, for although there is little about it today to remind one of ancient times, its fame is not written in stone but in the history of faith and learning. The two cathedrals, the Catholic and the Protestant, rise on their hills. The Protestant Cathedral is a small, modest building of red sandstone; the Catholic Cathedral is an imposing but unattractive and un-Irish building that lifts twin towers on the highest hill. But the story of this Cathedral is remarkable. It was erected "to the Glory of God and the Honour of Ireland" by Catholics in every part of the world. One looks at its stones knowing that they have been bought by a nation at home and at the ends of the earth. "I wonder how many thousands of day-labourers gave their mite to its building in the thirty years since the work began," wrote Stephen Gwynn.

The peace that enfolds all cathedral cities lies over Armagh. It has known peace and storm and peace again. St. Patrick founded his church there in 432, and a beautiful legend says that when the Saint was solemnly consecrating the site with bell, book and holy water a timid doe followed by her fawn broke from a thicket, startled by the crowds that had gathered to witness the strange rites. Some bystanders would have slain her, but the Saint, rebuking them and offering them a first object-lesson in Christian tenderness, picked up the trembling fawn and carried it down the hill where he set it at liberty, the doe following. Then he returned to the place where the doe had lain and said that on the spot should God's altar stand.

The Book of Armagh was written in the Monastery in 807. It is a copy of the New Testament in Latin, and bound up with it is the *Confessio* of St. Patrick. At the end of the Confession the scribe Ferdomnach wrote: "Thus far the volume which Patrick wrote with his own hand." This was written three centuries after the Saint's death and suggests that Ferdomnach was copying a manuscript—now, alas, lost—in St. Patrick's writing. Those who look at the book, now in Trinity College, Dublin, will see with interest a much-thumbed page at the end with an entry dated A.D. 1004, stating that the great King Brian Boru on his triumphal journey through Ireland visited Armagh, made an offering of gold on the altar of St. Patrick and confirmed the city in its ancient religious supremacy.

For centuries the Book of Armagh was the most venerated of all Irish manuscripts.

The school of Armagh that grew up beside the Monastery was one of the most celebrated in the Ireland of the sixth century. It opened its doors to scholars from every part of Europe. One part of the city was called Trian-Saxon, the "Saxon's Third", from the numbers of Saxon students who lived there. When the Norman invaders wrecked the ancient Gaelic civilisation, there were three thousand scholars in residence at Armagh receiving knowledge that Ireland alone among nations had saved from the wreck of the Western World.

Index

The numbers in italics indicate the illustrations

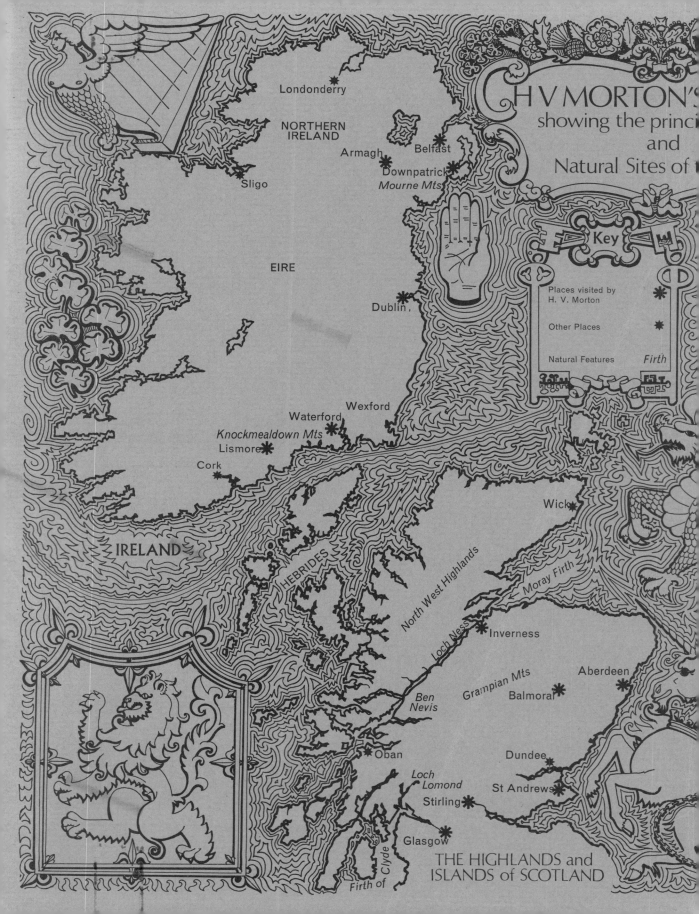

C H V MORTON'S
showing the princi
and
Natural Sites of

Key

Places visited by H. V. Morton	
Other Places	
Natural Features	*Firth*

Londonderry

NORTHERN IRELAND

Armagh Belfast
Downpatrick
Mourne Mts

Sligo

EIRE

Dublin

Wexford
Waterford
Knockmealdown Mts
Lismore
Cork

IRELAND

Wick

HEBRIDES

North West Highlands

Moray Firth

Loch Ness Inverness

Grampian Mts Aberdeen
Balmoral

Ben
Nevis

Oban

Dundee

Loch Lomond
Stirling St Andrews

Glasgow

Firth of Clyde

THE HIGHLANDS and ISLANDS of SCOTLAND